Dear Amy,

Thank you for all of your encouragement and feedback while I was writing my dissertation. This is a clearer and more interesting book than it would have been otherwise.

Best,
Alex

Locke

and the Legislative Point of View

Toleration, Contested Principles, and the Law

ALEX TUCKNESS

PRINCETON UNIVERSITY PRESS   PRINCETON AND OXFORD

Published by Princeton University Press, 41 William Street, Princeton, New Jersey 08540

In the United Kingdom: Princeton University Press, 3 Market Place, Woodstock, Oxfordshire OX20 1SY

Library of Congress Cataloging-in-Publication Data
Tuckness, Alex Scott, 1971–
Locke and the legislative point of view : toleration, contested
principles, and the law / Alex Tuckness.
    p.   cm.
Includes bibliographical references and index.

ISBN 0-691-09503-5 (alk. paper)—ISBN 0-691-09504-3 (pbk. : alk. paper)

1. Locke, John, 1632–1704—Contributions in political science. 2. Locke, John,
1632–1704—Contributions in natural law. 3. Political ethics. 4. Legislative ethics.
5. Legislative power. I. Title.

JC153.L87 T83 2002
172′.2—dc21   2001058004

British Library Cataloging-in-Publication Data is available

This book has been composed in Sabon

Printed on acid-free paper. ∞

www.pup.princeton.edu

Printed in the United States of America.

10   9   8   7   6   5   4   3   2   1

For Jack and Winnie Tuckness

Do not be wise in your own eyes.
—PROVERBS 3:7a (NRSV)

In everything, do to others as
you would have them do to you.
—MATTHEW 7:12a (NRSV)

CONTENTS

ACKNOWLEDGMENTS

Many people and institutions have helped me bring this book to publication. The University of Chicago's Donnelley Exchange Scholarship allowed me to spend a year studying Locke at Cambridge University the year after I graduated. Cambridge was the best possible place for me to pursue my interest in Locke. The M. Phil. Program in Political Thought and Intellectual History provided enormous flexibility and allowed me to research and write my thesis on Locke's theory of natural law, a theme that figures prominently in the present work. Although the present work is less historical in its focus, it is still shaped by the work that I did at Cambridge. Richard Tuck served as my primary advisor that year, and John Dunn provided considerable help as well. Even after I left Cambridge both have been willing to take the time to discuss my current research and provide helpful suggestions. It was also at Cambridge that I met John Michael Parrish, another student in the same program, who has been an invaluable friend and colleague ever since. He has read and commented on several drafts of the present work.

This book is a substantially revised version of the Ph.D. dissertation I wrote at Princeton University. Both in the people who were there and in the resources that were available, Princeton was an ideal location for my project. Support from the Politics Department, the University Center for Human Values, and a University Honorific Fellowship allowed me to devote most of my time to research and to finish much more quickly than would otherwise have been possible. While I was a student there I also received a generous grant from the Harvey Fellows Program that allowed me to go to Oxford for one month to read in the Locke archives at the Bodleian Library. I owe a debt of thanks as well to the faculty and to my fellow graduate students at Princeton who made it a vibrant political theory community: Oliver Avens, Paul Bou-Habib, Aurelian Craitu, Patrick Deneen, Suzanne Dovi, Denise Dutton, Stephen Holmes, George Kateb, David Korfhage, Jacob Levy, Brenda Lyshaug, Paul Safier, Jason Scorza, Roy Tsao, and Maurizio Viroli. Posthumous thanks go to Moshe Levy, whose untimely death was a cause of great sadness for us all.

Special thanks go to the members of my dissertation committee. Robert George and Paul Sigmund gave trenchant criticisms and helpful suggestions for revisions. I owe a special debt to Jeremy Waldron, who was actively involved in advising me on the dissertation from its inception. His comments on my work, together with his own insights into Locke, law, and legislation, have left a definite imprint on my own thought that will be apparent to those who read the present work. My greatest academic debt is to Amy Gutmann, who served as my primary dissertation advisor. Despite a demanding schedule, she was generous with her time. She read multiple drafts of each chapter, giving comments that were simultaneously critical and encouraging. The present work is much clearer, better argued, and more accessible than it would have been without her help.

The Iowa State University Council on the Humanities assisted with the revision of the present manuscript by providing summer support. The Political Science Department provided funds for a research assistant, John Chiodo. Richard Mansbach and Mary Ann Teterault both read and commented on chapter drafts. Matthew Robinson read and commented on the entire manuscript. The referees for Princeton University Press provided suggestions that have improved the manuscript. Richard Vernon provided helpful comments on multiple drafts of the manuscript. Ian Malcolm has been an exemplary editor. The responsibility for the mistakes that remain, despite all of this help, is mine.

Portions of chapter 2 are reprinted by permission from "Legislation and Non-neutral Principles: A Lockean Approach," *Journal of Political Philosophy* 8 (2000): 263–278.

In addition to these academic debts, there are two other groups to whom I owe special thanks. At every step along this journey there has been a community of faith to encourage and support me. I have also benefited from a family that is as supportive and encouraging as any I could imagine. My parents have been the most important members of both groups. I am very thankful for their love and friendship. This book is dedicated to them.

ABBREVIATED REFERENCES

References to the following of Locke's primary works are given parenthetically as follows:

Sample Reference	Full Reference
Essay, 4.10.1	*Essay Concerning Human Understanding*, ed. Peter Nidditch (Oxford: Clarendon Press, 1979), book 4, chap. 10, sec. 1.
Letter, 37	*A Letter Concerning Toleration*, ed. James H. Tully (Indianapolis: Hackett Publishing Company, 1983), p. 37.
Political Essays, 195	*Political Essays*, ed. Mark Goldie (Cambridge: Cambridge University Press, 1997), p. 195.
Reasonableness, 8	*The Reasonableness of Christianity as Delivered in Scripture*, ed. George W. Ewing (Washington, DC: Regnery Gateway, 1965), p. 8.
Treatises, 2.6	*Two Treatises of Government*, ed. Peter Laslett (Cambridge: Cambridge University Press, 1988), *Second Treatise*, sec. 6.
Works, 6:224	*Works of John Locke* (London, 1823; repr. Germany: Scientia Verlag Aalen, 1963), vol. 6, p. 224.

Where possible I use widely available modern editions. In particular, I use Goldie's invaluable edition of Locke's minor works, *Political Essays*. Many of these are out of print and thus difficult to obtain. References to Locke's *Essays on the Law of Nature* are from Von Leyden's translation reprinted in *Political Essays*. References to Locke's *Second Letter Concerning Toleration*, *Third Letter Concerning Toleration*, and *Fourth Letter Concerning Toleration* are taken from *Works*, vol. 6, listed above.

LOCKE AND THE LEGISLATIVE POINT OF VIEW

Introduction

Political argument in liberal democracies is characterized by both agreement and disagreement. The disagreement is obvious. Citizens profess a wide variety of conflicting beliefs about politics, morality, and religion. Competitive elections, by their structure, encourage the expression and clarification of disagreement. Among the causes of this pervasive disagreement are self-interest, human fallibility, and the complexity of difficult moral questions. The agreement in political argument is less obvious but very important. Just as we must agree on certain linguistic conventions in order to communicate at all, so also we must agree on at least some moral ideas if we are to have moral debates that are intelligible. Even persons who are moral relativists can acknowledge that within particular communities there are particular ideas and claims that are understood to have moral weight.[1] In liberal democracies, most people will acknowledge in principle that their fellow citizens are moral agents, that they are equals in at least the sense that we should treat them according to some moral standard of reciprocity rather than as objects we can manipulate according to our desires, that the same moral rules should apply to all of us, and that we should all be able to know what those rules are. I refer to these four ideas as moral agency, moral equality, generality, and publicity. Many people give only lip service to these ideas, and our practice, both individually and collectively, often fails to respect them. Nonetheless they provide ideas that most persons recognize as carrying moral weight and provide a framework in which moral debate about politics can begin.

This broad description of the problem of political disagreement, some of its causes, and some of the relevant moral intuitions is one that a wide variety of citizens and political theorists could accept. Nothing in the above description of the modern predicament is inconsistent with theoretical approaches as diverse as Michael Walzer's communitarianism, John Rawls's political liberalism, Robert Nozick's libertarianism, or

---

[1] See, for example, Michael Walzer, *Spheres of Justice* (New York: Basic Books, 1983), chap. 1.

rule-utilitarianism.[2] A vast range of conclusions could flow from this common starting point. Libertarians, for example, would considerably reduce the reach of government, while Rawls would expand it drastically in the service of the least well off. There are two obvious reasons why all these theories could endorse the set of assumptions with which I began. The first is that I have not defined what is meant by key terms like reciprocity. Second, and even more importantly, none of these theories asserts only the above premises; they make other claims as well, and many of these genuinely conflict.

One method of doing political theory is to proceed directly to those places of substantive disagreement between the various theories. In the end we must do so, since they do make conflicting claims about how states should use political power. Although we must do so, it does not follow that we must only do so. We should also think about the perspective from which we view both ur agreement and our disagreement. I argue in this book that if we accept the common assumptions and moral intuitions above, they suggest a perspective from which we should assess political claims that I will call a "legislative point of view." Adopting the legislative point of view will not eliminate substantive disagreements, but it can meaningfully guide how we think about the relationship between our substantive views about morality and the legitimate use of political power.

The legislative point of view uses a legislative metaphor as a heuristic to guide political deliberation. One imagines oneself in the position of a legislator when deciding what moral principles should guide the use of political power. I will argue for one version of the legislative point of view, one derived from the writings of John Locke, that flows from the moral intuitions described above. A theory that rejects one or more of the four assumptions will ask persons to make political decisions from a nonlegislative point of view. Someone who rejected the notion of moral equality adopts what we might call a "tyrannical point of view." A tyrant will not feel the need to justify his actions to others and will see others as mere means to his own ends. Someone who rejects the belief that others are moral agents adopts what we might call a "guardian's point of view." A guardian makes decisions, perhaps on grounds that take morality very seriously, for others who are not capable of acting as moral agents them-

---

[2] John Stuart Mill, on one interpretation, is an example. While act-utilitarians might object to the principle of publicity, rule-utilitarians use the idea of publicly known rules to avoid some of the counterintuitive conclusions of act-utilitarianism. For example, an act-utilitarian would favor framing an innocent person for a crime if doing so would increase the total happiness of all the persons affected. A rule-utilitarian would not do so because if there were a general rule, known to the public to that effect, persons would fear that they would be framed and wonder if those punished were really guilty. See John Rawls, "Two Concepts of Rules," in *Philosophical Review*, 64 (1955), pp. 3–32.

selves. Someone who rejects the principle of generality takes on what we might call a "radically situated point of view." All points of view are situated to the extent that they are held by particular people with particular histories, and so on. None of us actually has a view from nowhere. Someone thinking from a "radically situated point of view" would deny that the moral principles that apply to her[3] apply to others, and vice versa. Someone taking on a "vanguard's point of view" would reject publicity and work to further moral ends, even ends that serve the interests of others as equal moral agents, on the basis of moral principles that he would not want others to follow.

There is more than one version of the legislative point of view. Before giving an overview of the Lockean legislative point of view, I briefly describe two other versions that are more commonly discussed: the utilitarian, and the Kantian. One utilitarian conception is associated with Jeremy Bentham. On that view, the legislative point of view is simply the set of moral considerations that are binding on those who make the law. In its simplest form, utilitarianism teaches that the right action is the one that produces the most happiness and the least unhappiness. Utilitarianism, in this form, would hold that a legislator should adopt the law that would produce the greatest amount of happiness. It is worth remembering that Jeremy Bentham's seminal articulation of utilitarianism was in a book entitled *An Introduction to the Principles of Morals and Legislation*. Bentham offered up the principle of utility as a moral constraint on legislative deliberation. Legislators should enact those laws that will generate the most total pleasure and the least total pain. Utilitarians since Bentham have altered and refined his theory, but the basic idea that we should enact those laws that will produce the best consequences measured in terms of pleasure, happiness, or satisfied preferences plays an important role in legislative deliberation, especially insofar as the discipline of economics informs legislative choices.

There is, however, a second way utilitarians use a legislative point of view that is more important for the purposes of this book. Rule-utilitarian theories come closer to a true legislative point of view because they imagine us deciding between rules that are generally binding and judging them based on their consequences, just as utilitarian legislators would judge a law. Unlike an act-utilitarian, who judges individual acts separately, a rule-utilitarian uses a legislative metaphor to adopt *moral* principles, as well as laws. The principles of morality are those principles that a wise utilitarian legislator would adopt.

---

[3] I use masculine pronouns when articulating Locke's original theory and his argument with Proast for reasons of historical accuracy. Elsewhere, I use either masculine or feminine pronouns.

The idea of a legislative point of view is understood differently in the Kantian tradition. John Rawls is the most famous contemporary proponent of that tradition. Rather than directly prescribing moral principles for legislators as Bentham did, Rawls and others in the Kantian tradition ask citizens and legislators to imagine an *ideal* legislative situation and determine what would be done from that ideal perspective. Moral principles that should guide real legislators emerge from this idealized legislative point of view. Perhaps the most important difference between this view and the rule-utilitarian one has to do with the moral principles that guide the ideal legislator. Kantian legislators do not attempt to maximize happiness. Rather, they look for laws and principles that they believe *all* persons could accept as free and equal citizens. The details of Kantian theory need not detain us here. The point is that this is a different way of utilizing the legislative point of view.

In contrast to the Kantian and utilitarian traditions that have dominated modern thinking about the legislative point of view, I explore a third conception derived from John Locke. There are aspects of Locke's thought that resemble each of these traditions. It is not that in any historical sense Locke anticipates the later authors, but rather that there are moral insights present in each of these traditions that are combined and expressed in Locke's unique conception of the legislative point of view. Locke's conception of the legislative point of view has lain essentially dormant since he formulated it. This may seem a surprising claim. Few past works compare to Locke's *Two Treatises* in the extent to which they defend such modern themes as government by consent and respect for individual rights. There has been significant and sustained scholarly debate over the theory of legislation that Locke articulated in the *Two Treatises*.[4] The legislative point of view that I will describe and defend, however, is not one that Locke developed in the *Two Treatises*. Instead, it is a view expressed primarily in his lesser-known writings on toleration. In the seldom read *Third Letter Concerning Toleration*, Locke developed an important argument while confronting the question of toleration. Specifically, he was forced to ask why a person should refrain from using political power to bring about a real good or to enforce a true moral principle. In his last published writing on toleration (as well as his uncompleted *Fourth Letter*), Locke finally articulated a line of thought that had been implicit in his earlier writings on toleration and, to a lesser extent, in the *Two Treatises*. The argument is not a substantive one for toleration like his more famous argument that true belief cannot be forced. It is an argument describing the formal conditions that any argument for tolerance or

---

[4] See, most recently, Jeremy Waldron, *The Dignity of Legislation* (Cambridge: Cambridge University Press, 1999), chaps. 4, 6.

intolerance must meet. It is possible to reread Locke's substantive discussions in both the original *Letter Concerning Toleration*[5] and the *Two Treatises* in light of these formal criteria and find a deeper coherence in his thought than has been previously supposed.

Locke argued that natural law places moral restrictions on the way force may be used, both by individuals and by governments. When there is disagreement about the content of this law, we remind ourselves that God is the legislator of natural law and that, therefore, it must be reasonable from His perspective. God has created us as moral agents under a set of public and universal moral rules. As moral agents we must interpret and apply natural law. Because we are fallible, we sometimes do so incorrectly. God takes into account the way controversial terms will be misinterpreted and misapplied. God, as a reasonable legislator, does not enact laws that will be self-defeating when applied by fallible human beings.

This argument has received almost no attention in the Locke literature. Locke's *Third Letter* is long and often repetitive and, for that reason, has not received the kind of scholarly attention that his first *Letter* has, much less the *Two Treatises*. In particular, those interested in applying Lockean arguments to contemporary political discourse have almost completely ignored it.[6] This is again not surprising in that the argument is explicitly theological in character. The general assumption has been that if Locke is relevant at all, it is in the secular-sounding portions of his theory like his doctrine of consent and not in the more explicitly theological portions of his thought such as his theory of natural law.

In this book I will use what might be called an "analogical" approach to Locke's argument.[7] This approach requires first explicating an argument in its original context and then developing an analogous version of the argument to apply to a new context. The first step is to try to reconstruct Locke's argument according to his original assumptions, even if many modern readers reject those assumptions. While we can reflect on whether modern assumptions are really better, we can also bracket the

---

[5] More properly, *Epistola de Tolerantia*. I will refer to Locke's *Epistola* by its English name and quote the translation of Locke's contemporary, William Popple. Although Popple's translation is a bit exuberant at times, Locke stood by it. In fact it was Popple's translation, rather than the original Latin, that Locke bequeathed to the Bodleian Library in Oxford. See James Tully's introduction to John Locke's *A Letter Concerning Toleration* (Indianapolis: Hackett Publishing Company, 1983). For a critical discussion of Popple's translation, see the introduction to *Epistola de Tolerantia: A Letter on Toleration*, ed. Raymond Kliblansky and J. W. Gough (Oxford: Clarendon Press, 1968).

[6] An important exception is Richard Vernon, *The Career of Toleration: John Locke, Jonas Proast, and After* (Montreal and Kingston: McGill-Queen's University Press, 1997). See note 8 below.

[7] I am indebted to John Michael Parrish for suggesting this term as a description of my project.

question of which set of assumptions is right and ask whether modern readers who reject Locke's fundamental grounds could affirm his intermediate principles on different grounds. If so, then we may find important arguments in unexpected parts of Locke's thought that draw out the implications of beliefs that are common, or at least viable, in the world today. This method will work best if we are still confronting a question that Locke himself confronted, such as the question of toleration.[8] I refer to this approach as analogical because someone who accepts Locke's intermediate principles on different grounds and who applies it to different problems takes a position that is, as a whole, analogous to rather than identical to Locke's original position. The term "analogical" also reminds us that taking an intermediate principle out of its original context may change it in subtle ways. It is always logically possible that the historical Locke might have altered the intermediate principle if he saw it being applied in an unexpected way. The argument is analogical because it tries to remain true to the core idea Locke held but freely presents the argument in a very different way than Locke did.

Specifically, I argue that even people who do not believe in God or universal moral principles can still accept an analogous version of the argument, one that uses the same intermediate principles and rests them on alternative foundations. In general, persons who accept the four moral claims with which we began (moral agency, moral equality, generality, and publicity) should be able to adopt a version of Locke's argument. Such persons will take on a legislative point of view when considering whether the state should use force on behalf of a moral principle that they believe true or valid. I follow Rawls in thinking that it is a strength of a theory if people who do not share a particular set of religious or philosophical beliefs can endorse it.[9] I set to the side the question of whether the aspiration toward principles that all can accept is of such overriding importance that persons are morally required to appeal only to such principles, a question that will be discussed in more detail in chapter 4. Even

---

[8] My approach is similar in methodology to that of A. John Simmons in *The Lockean Theory of Rights* (Princeton: Princeton University Press, 1992) and in subject matter to Richard Vernon in *The Career of Toleration*. Simmons recognizes the theological structure of Locke's theory of natural law and then tries to show how an analogous version of the Lockean argument could appeal to persons who reject Locke's theology. Simmons, however, focuses on the *Two Treatises* rather than the writings on toleration and so passes over the argument that I develop below. Vernon's book is the most sustained contemporary attempt to apply the arguments from Locke's later writings on toleration to contemporary political theory, and so there will of course be points of similarity in our arguments since we are reading the same texts. Vernon, however, tends to neglect the theological dimensions of Locke's thought in favor of the more easily translatable idea of consent.

[9] Rawls, *Political Liberalism,* Rev. paperback ed. (New York: Columbia University Press, 1995), p. 38.

without endorsing such a view, one may still hold that, all else being equal, a theory is better and more useful if people who hold a wide range of foundational views can endorse it. Moreover, in situations where there is deep disagreement at the foundational level, discussion of intermediate principles will likely be a more fruitful approach. Although I share Rawls's aspiration in this sense, my approach will be different. Whereas Rawls begins with a secular formulation that he hopes people with comprehensive religious and moral beliefs will be able to adopt, I begin with a Lockean theory that assumes the existence of both God and universal moral truths and argue that even persons who reject the argument in this form can still adopt an analogous version of the argument that can meaningfully guide deliberation about the principles that direct political force. Even atheists who believe that there are no universal moral principles could accept the intermediate principles I propose and apply them in important instances. I choose this approach not in order to disparage theological arguments; I am personally sympathetic to some of them. Rather, I choose this approach because the main point is one that people from a variety of moral and religious backgrounds can possibly accept.

This analogical approach avoids three common objections to Lockean theory. The first, already mentioned, is that Locke's theory is too dependent on Christian assumptions to persuade persons of different religious beliefs. Although there will certainly be resonances with Christian thought in what follows, given its origin, the intermediate principles and conclusions are ones that could be affirmed by persons of very different religious beliefs, including atheists. In fact, Locke's Christian context provides an important benefit for his theory. Because Locke was trying to convince other Christians, he did not try to ground toleration in moral skepticism. Given the persistence of religious beliefs at the beginning of the twenty-first century, it is a strength of a theory if persons of faith can affirm it. However unpopular religious belief is in some academic circles, its persistence in the population at large makes a theory that begins with skeptical assumptions unlikely to attain widespread appeal. More than that, a theory based on skepticism will likely be ignored by precisely the person the religious skeptic would most like to persuade to adopt a tolerant attitude, the religious fundamentalist.

Second, by focusing on the formal criteria that guide deliberation rather than a specific list of rights, we can set aside objections to Locke's substantive theory of natural law. In the same way that one could accept Kant's categorical imperative and disagree with Kant about whether a prohibition on suicide flows from it, one can accept Lockean formal criteria while rejecting Locke's specific conclusions about what should be tolerated. Criticisms of Locke's views on property, suicide, and the like are thus beside the point. The formal criteria are still controversial because they rest on substantive claims about the moral relations between persons, but they should be less controversial than a full-blown theory of natural law.

Third, Lockean theory is often criticized for resting on a factually suspect theory of the state of nature. It is a matter of considerable dispute among Locke scholars whether Locke intended us to believe in a historical state of nature.[10] Even if Locke did think that there was such a state, an analogical approach allows us to set aside both Locke's claim and the objections to it. Instead we can ask whether political actors find themselves in contemporary situations sufficiently analogous to the state of nature to allow deliberative guidelines developed for the state of nature to apply to the contemporary situation as well. Locke believed that in the state of nature one would have to ask oneself what the law of nature directed one to do and to act on one's best interpretation of natural law. Persons in the state of nature have no higher instituted authority to which they can appeal that can instruct them as to how they should act. I will argue below that political actors are quite often in a situation analogous to the state of nature.

The above comments make it clear that not only is my application of Locke's ideas to the present analogical, it is also not comprehensive. I do not attempt to defend every argument Locke made. I do not even discuss every argument he made for religious toleration. I do not claim that Locke thought of the argument I emphasize as his most important one for toleration. But I do claim that it is Lockean in a meaningful sense. It is Lockean in that the intermediate principles I will articulate are principles that Locke himself supported and defended. It is also Lockean in the sense that it is inconsistent with Locke's theory only to the extent that Locke himself was inconsistent. Generally speaking, although some of Locke's specific conclusions seem hard to reconcile with his principles (for example, his seeming indifference to slavery in the American colonies is hard to reconcile with his views on slavery in the *Two Treatises*), his general political theory is consistent with the position developed here. Because my presentation is not comprehensive it is also underdetermined; it is compatible with other theories with which Locke would have disagreed. This is intentional since my goal is to discuss a general point of view from which we can debate the substantive differences between theories rather than to settle those differences.

Rather than defending Locke's entire theory, I will defend a portion of it. The most important part has to do with what I have termed "the

---

[10] Compare Dunn, *The Political Thought of John Locke* (Cambridge: Cambridge University Press, 1969), pp. 96–119, with Ashcraft, *Locke's Two Treatises of Government* (London: Allen and Unwin, 1987), pp. 97–122.

legislative point of view." I will, however, make use of other aspects of Locke's thought where they are helpful for drawing out the implications of the legislative point of view for more complicated political problems. Chapter 3 will explore the relationship between the legislative point of view and Locke's theory of consent. Chapter 4 will discuss Locke's understandings of political justification and freedom. Chapter 5 will discuss his understanding of political roles and the separation of powers. By tying in the legislative point of view with other prominent themes in Locke's work, we can see that the legislative view reflects more than a few isolated passages in his later writings. It provides a means to understand these larger themes in a new way.

This is not, therefore, a comprehensive treatment of all aspects of Locke's theory of toleration or of legislation. Rather, it is an exploration of some very important but neglected themes in his work that are of contemporary relevance but can only be understood when first described in their original historical context. Holding these together, I write with two audiences in mind: those persons interested in questions of liberalism, toleration, and contemporary political theory, and those persons interested in Locke's political thought.[11] For a discussion of the implications of the Lockean argument I develop in this book for the interpretation of Locke's theory of toleration, readers should also consult my previous work.[12] Readers primarily interested in the interpretation of Locke will find chapters 2, 3, and 5 of the present work most relevant.

Part I focuses on the question of which moral principles may serve as a justification for coercive action, particularly the laws of the state. In chapter 1, I introduce the idea of a legislative point of view as a possible solution to the "paradox of toleration" by comparing contested laws and contested principles. Liberals are often accused of skepticism when they claim that persons should not act for political purposes on some principles they believe to be true. This accusation is prevalent because a liberal theory must include a theory of toleration if it is to count as liberal. Toleration, in turn, seems to be paradoxical. Why should one refrain from putting a stop to something if one really believes it to be wrong and one has the power to do so? A similar paradox arises when there is disagreement about how a recognized principle should be interpreted and applied. Why should one refrain from acting on what one believes is the

---

[11] In deference to the first group, much of my dialogue with the secondary literature on Locke and many quotations from Locke are placed in the footnotes. Footnotes rather than endnotes are used to minimize the inconvenience for those interested in the textual derivation. In deference to the second group, I also include two appendixes that provide textual arguments in support of some of my more controversial interpretive claims.

[12] See especially "Rethinking the Intolerant Locke," *American Journal of Political Science* 46 (April 2002), pp. 288–298.

correct interpretation of the principle? By drawing on an analogy to contested laws, I argue that *if* contested principles were thought of as principles chosen from a legislative point of view, it would provide a solution to the paradox.

In chapter 2 I turn to Locke's dispute with Jonas Proast to derive his argument for why persons should adopt a legislative point of view. I focus on deliberation about whether a state (or a person in a state of nature) may punish persons who have violated a valid moral rule or should tolerate the wrong. As I develop the Lockean position I clarify it by contrasting it with another liberal position that gives similar reasons for toleration, rule-utilitarianism. I then present Locke's argument in such a way that persons who reject its original theological grounds might accept it and apply it to two concrete political problems: hate speech and civil disobedience.

In the remaining chapters I take the idea of a legislative point of view and apply it to progressively more complicated problems. Chapter 3 deals with the additional complexities that arise on a Lockean view when the state seeks to promote some conception of the public good rather than simply enforce rights. While Locke held that individuals in the state of nature may punish a rights violation, only a legitimate state may use coercive power to promote the public good. In a legitimate state, the idea of consent surfaces as an intervening idea. I distinguish between two different ways that Locke used the idea of consent: contractual consent, which grounded his theory of political obligation, and legislative consent, which grounded his theory of the proper ends of government. I argue that if we understand consent in the legislative sense, Locke's view allows us to see how we should decide between competing conceptions of the public good from a legislative point of view. This view also provides a more satisfactory account of why we should be tolerant than one that determines the ends of government by asking what agreement instrumentally rational persons would reach.

Chapters 2 and 3 develop the central theory for those cases where the legislative power is clearly defined and the relevant persons occupy fairly traditional legislative roles (they are members of a legislative body, citizens deciding which legislators to elect, or citizens attempting to pressure legislators to change the law). Before proceeding to more complex problems of contested institutional roles in chapters 5 and 6, I compare in chapter 4 the general Lockean approach with other prominent liberal approaches to the problem of disagreement. Since chapter 2 examines utilitarianism, chapter 4 focuses on two other approaches: the liberal neutrality of Rawls and the liberal perfectionism of Joseph Raz. Since it is in the liberal tradition that the issues of toleration and disagreement figure most prominently, I situate my argument there. Some of the arguments will apply to illiberal versions of perfectionism as well.

Part II examines how particular political actors should decide the moral principles upon which to act given the particular roles they occupy within government. Whereas in part I the government is thought of as a unified entity considering various moral principles, part II acknowledges the reality that persons are often asked to bracket principles they believe true because of the role that they occupy, and the reality that the meaning of the roles themselves is often disputed. These chapters argue that the legislative point of view is both compatible with recognizing roles as a reason to refrain from acting on otherwise valid moral considerations and useful for specifying roles when they are contested.

Chapter 5 looks at how the legislative point of view applies in cases where persons exercise some measure of legislative power, broadly understood, but do not occupy a traditional legislative office. It addresses the problem of how the legislative point of view changes depending on an actor's institutional context. I argue that the legislative point of view can in some cases provide a nonconsequentialist reason for not acting on one's own view of morality because of one's institutional role. As I develop this position I supplement Locke's argument for a legislative point of view with his theory of the separation of powers. It is of course true that one could accept Locke's general argument for the legislative point of view and its compatibility with institutional roles without accepting his specific understanding of legislative and executive roles. Nonetheless, by exploring these roles we understand how Locke thought that in some cases one should not act on what one thought was the best interpretation of natural law because of one's roles. But more than that, Locke has a more sophisticated understanding of institutional roles and separation of powers than most readers might suppose. His way of understanding legislative, judicial, and executive roles makes the legislative point of view applicable to all of them, albeit in different ways, rather than only to legislators in the traditional sense.

Chapter 6 combines the analysis of the legislative point of view and of institutional roles and applies it to situations where the institutional roles themselves are in dispute. Of particular interest are constitutional disputes in which part of what is contested is how legislative power is to be allocated among the different branches of government. It is not only substantive moral principles that are contested. Those principles and rules that determine *who* will make political decisions are often contested as well. When they are, a variant of the legislative point of view can instruct deliberation about how a given officeholder should try to define her role. To make this problem more concrete, I focus on a particular contested role: United States Supreme Court justice. I argue that the ongoing debates about the proper interpretive theory and the relative roles of Congress, president, and Supreme Court illustrate what can happen when the rules delegating legislative power are vague and contested. There is already a history of worrying about how to arrive at "neutral principles" in constitutional interpretation in American jurisprudence.[13] My argument will suggest how the contestation of the rules that allocate power is related to the contestation of the actual principles judges pronounce when handing down judgments. I argue that our understanding of the justice's role is closely connected with our understanding of constitutional interpretation.

Finally, a note on methodology. Since in chapter 6 I will apply Lockean ideas to United States constitutional interpretation, one might object that it is anachronistic to apply Locke's theory to the interpretation of a constitution written almost one hundred years after his death and significantly modified over the last two centuries; Locke's jurisprudence was based on natural law, and he did not grasp the uniqueness of the institutional role of the judge. Although it is true that Locke did not contemplate institutions like the U.S. Supreme Court, he was quite familiar with the idea of a constitution. The first constitutional act of any Lockean society is establishing a legislature. Still, it is worth considering the objection briefly. There are two senses of the general charge of anachronism. The first sense is valid but does not apply to my argument. Whenever we take a theory and apply it to a new situation that the author did not contemplate, we must be tentative in claiming that the author supports our conclusion. It is always possible that, confronted with new implications of his theory, Locke would have revised the theory to avoid them. The more remote the application, the less we can be sure of what the historical author would have thought. It is for this reason that throughout the book I speak of a "Lockean theory" rather than Locke's views when discussing the application of his theory to contemporary problems. As long as one is clear about the distinction, the theory is not anachronistic. We can apply the logic of Locke's theory, whether the historical Locke would have liked it or not, to new situations.

There is a second sense of the objection, however, that makes a more serious accusation. It claims that the original theory is deficient in that it ignores conceptual categories or rests on false assumptions that make it inapplicable to the modern context. It is not that Locke might have changed the theory, it is that the theory itself must be seriously distorted

---

[13] Herbert Wechsler in his classic article "Toward Neutral Principles of Constitutional Law" worried about the difficulties of finding principles that were neutral between the disputants. See *Harvard Law Review* 73 (1959), pp. 1–35.

to apply in a modern context. For example, someone who attempts to develop a theory of rights from a thinker who did not even have access to the concept of a right in the modern sense would be vulnerable to this objection. I do not mean to suggest that where such conceptual gaps exist the earlier thinker becomes irrelevant. There still may be parts of the original theory that spark the imagination of the modern theorist. In such cases, however, it is better for the modern theorist to argue in his or her own voice and note the debt of inspiration than to claim that he or she is applying the original theory. This should, however, be a last resort. Before assuming that the situation is hopeless, the interpreter should carefully weigh whether the current conceptual framework really *is* superior. Part of the reason for studying past authors is precisely because we reject the belief in inevitable progress. The conceptual framework of the earlier author might actually be superior. My goal is to combine a recognition of the original context in which Locke wrote, which was theological, with a belief that we still have important things to learn from him.

PART I

The Legislative Point of View and the Ends of Government

CHAPTER 1

Contested Laws and Principles

Toleration is a defining aspect of liberal thought. Although it is quite difficult to give a definition of what set of characteristics is necessary and sufficient to describe a view as liberal, one can say that any view that completely rejects the idea of toleration is not liberal. A doctrine of toleration holds that there are times when it is morally right to refrain from attempting to put a stop to some action or state of affairs that one thinks is morally wrong. It holds that there are moral reasons not to do so even when discouraging the action is feasible. Liberalism thus requires a certain kind of "bracketing" where individuals decide not to act politically on certain principles and values that they believe to be true.

It is precisely this core aspect of liberal thought that has drawn criticism because it is clear that in many cases "bracketing" is the wrong response. Michael Sandel, for example, argues that we often cannot bracket controversial moral beliefs without begging the question against those who disagree with us. Sandel gives two stark examples: debates over slavery and abortion. Before the United States Civil War, Stephen Douglas claimed that we should bracket the question of whether slavery is right or wrong and, as a nation, be neutral on the question. Each state should decide for itself and tolerate other states that come to different conclusions. Lincoln replied that it was reasonable to bracket the question of slavery's morality only if one had already decided it was not abominable. In the case of abortion, prochoice advocates claim the government should tolerate abortion, allowing each person to choose for herself just as the government allows each person to choose what religion she will follow. "But if the Catholic church is right about the moral status of the fetus, if abortion is morally tantamount to murder, then it is not clear why the political values of toleration and women's equality, important though they are, should prevail."[1] Sandel's point is not to argue against abortion but to suggest that we cannot give a coherent answer to a difficult question like this without invoking controversial beliefs.

The problem Sandel identifies is not a new one. In fact, liberalism from its earliest formulations has drawn the criticism that it begs the crucial questions.[2] The problem lies in the very idea of toleration itself, as

---

[1] Michael J. Sandel, *Democracy's Discontent* (Cambridge: Belknap Press of Harvard University, 1996), p. 21.

[2] As we will see in chapter 2, this was Proast's objection against Locke.

toleration seems paradoxical. To use Sandel's examples, if one really believes abortion or slavery is wrong, why would one think it morally right for the government to tolerate such practices? We can see this more clearly if we state the definition of toleration more precisely.[3] The most important part of the definition is that, strictly speaking, the question of toleration arises only when one confronts something of which one disapproves.[4] Thus, strictly speaking, a person who does not think there is anything wrong with homosexuality does not tolerate it. Such a person is either indifferent to it or approves of it. The latter case does not present a paradox. If one is indifferent to or approves of homosexuality, then it is relatively obvious why one is under no obligation to try to put a stop to it.[5] But for someone who truly does think it is wrong, the paradox seems quite real. It is a paradox because we not only agree that the action is wrong, we also agree that tolerating it is right. Were tolerating the action wrong, the paradox would again disappear.[6] The paradox is heightened when we note that genuine cases of toleration arise when we actually have

[3] For a helpful overview of the different uses of the concept, see Susan Mendus, *Toleration and the Limits of Liberalism* (London: Macmillan Education, 1989), chap. 1. See also John Horton, "Three (Apparent) Paradoxes of Toleration," *Synthesis Philosophica* 9 (1994), pp. 7–20, and Glen Newey, *Virtue, Reason, and Toleration: The Place of Toleration in Ethical and Political Philosophy* (Edinburgh: Edinburgh University Press, 1999), chap. 1. Much of what follows in this section reflects a growing consensus about the conceptual description of toleration in the literature.

[4] I leave it open for the moment whether the disapproval must be specifically moral or whether it is enough that one substantially dislikes something. However one defines the outer limits of toleration, it is moral disapproval that presents the hardest case, and it is on this case that I will focus. For a discussion of whether only moral disapproval is an occasion for toleration, see Peter P. Nicholson, "Toleration as a Moral Ideal," in *Aspects of Toleration: Philosophical Studies,* ed. John Horton and Susan Mendus (London: Methuen, 1985), pp. 160–163; Mary Warnock, "The Limits of Toleration," in *On Toleration,* ed. Susan Mendus and David Edwards (Oxford: Clarendon Press, 1987), pp. 125–127; and Mendus, *Toleration and the Limits of Liberalism,* pp. 9–15.

[5] Nicholson, in "Toleration as a Moral Ideal," prefers the term "nonrejection" to the phrase "refrain from putting a stop to." It is possible to qualify the former so that the two amount to the same thing. I use the latter in order to focus the discussion more squarely on external actions rather than on internal cognitive states.

[6] A semantic question arises as to whether calling someone "tolerant" necessarily implies praise. In practice people are sometimes described as "tolerant" in this sense, and thus to call someone "intolerant" is to make a negative moral judgment about them. But at the same time we can intelligibly say that persons are "too tolerant," meaning that they tolerate things that they should not. If one adopts the former convention, one will conclude that those who are "too tolerant" are not really tolerant at all. See, for example, J. Budziszewski, *True Tolerance: Liberalism and the Necessity of Judgment* (New Brunswick: Transaction Publishers, 1992). The alternative is to take tolerance simply as a description of an actor's subjective intention and claim that in some instances toleration is good and in other instances toleration is bad. Context should make it clear which sense of the term I employ.

the power to put a stop to, or at least discourage, the action or state of affairs in question. Toleration is thus very different from acquiescence.[7] Many people accept a state of affairs simply because they feel powerless to do anything about it. Again, in such a situation, there is no deep paradox. If ought implies can, cannot implies a permission in most cases to refrain from trying. Genuine cases of toleration arise precisely when there is some action you might take that would be instrumentally effective in combating what you think is wrong.

One common solution to this apparent paradox is to claim that toleration rests on a kind of skepticism. Bernard Williams, noting the above paradox, sees toleration as a skeptical virtue because a tentativeness regarding our own beliefs will make us less likely to oppress those who disagree with us.[8] Indeed, this fits with a particular view of toleration in which the battle is between dogmatists who attempt to impose their views on others and more tolerant and reflective sorts who are less sure that their own views are right. Interestingly, the very justification Williams gives is precisely the one early liberals tried hard to avoid. Locke tried hard to rebut the accusation that he was a religious skeptic. His critics claimed that someone who sincerely believed his own religion was true and the only way to heaven would not be so callous toward others as to propose toleration but would instead use every means possible to bring them to the true religion. Locke insisted that although he believed that humans are fallible, even on matters of religion, this did not make him a skeptic because he did not believe all positions were equally reasonable.

On this point Locke was correct. Leaving aside the historical question of whether Locke was a skeptic (I believe he was not), there is an important conceptual difference between a belief in human fallibility and skepticism. Human fallibility simply means that as a matter of principle no human being is exempt from the possibility of being in error. Skepticism, on the other hand, is the more radical claim that general statements about right and wrong in such cases are impossible or nonsensical. Neither position, by itself, constitutes an argument for toleration. The belief in fallibility does not because it does not provide any particular person with a decisive reason not to act on whatever principle she *thinks* most likely to be right. For example, it does not follow that because I might be incorrect in believing that forced child labor is wrong that I should not try to put a stop to it. After all, if I am right and do not act, evil consequences may follow. If I think that I am more likely to be right than wrong, I have a prima facie reason to act. Human fallibility may be coupled with other

[7] Preston King, *Toleration* (London: George Allen & Unwin, 1976), pp. 22–24.

[8] "Toleration: An Impossible Virtue?" in *Toleration: An Elusive Virtue*, ed. David Heyd (Princeton: Princeton University Press 1996), pp. 18–27.

substantive moral principles as part of a larger argument for toleration, but it is not an argument by itself.[9]

Skepticism also fails, by itself, to provide a persuasive argument for toleration. But unlike human fallibility, skepticism undermines the other moral principles it might be combined with as part of a larger argument for toleration. Since skepticism is so often associated with theories of toleration, I should make it clear why I reject the skeptical alternative by comparing it to two other ways that a theory of toleration might relate to foundational moral beliefs. A foundational belief is a religious and/or philosophical position on which the justification for our actions ultimately rests. It functions as a moral first premise from which we may derive other moral premises. Some foundational theories claim that there is a uniquely correct comprehensive view that requires toleration. So, for example, one might think that Christianity is the one true religion and that it commands toleration, or one might think that Kantianism or utilitarianism is the one true philosophy and that the one true philosophy commands toleration. "Political liberalism," associated with John Rawls, is a second approach. Political liberalism is agnostic about whether there are foundations for toleration and instead asserts a doctrine of toleration as a freestanding political principle that may be endorsed from a variety of different foundational positions. Thus, to use Rawls's example, there might be a political principle of toleration that Kantians, utilitarians, and Christians could affirm even though they would disagree about what considerations ground the principle.[10] A more detailed discussion of this approach must wait until chapter 4.

Skepticism represents a different approach. Skeptical positions deny that any foundations exist and claim this as a reason for toleration. Historically, many people have tried to claim skepticism as a ground for toleration. After all, so the argument goes, a person who is unsure whether his beliefs are true will be less likely to harm those who disagree with him. The often noted problem with this argument is that one could just as easily draw the conclusion that since there are no right answers to moral questions, one is free to do whatever one wants, including persecute others. Richard Tuck has pointed out that there have been many instances in history where the skeptics were supporters of authoritarianism rather than liberal toleration.[11] In sum, the true skeptic has no grounds upon which to criticize the persecutor since the persecutor's

[9] Steven Wall makes a similar point in *Liberalism, Perfectionism, and Restraint* (Cambridge: Cambridge University Press, 1998), p. 96.

[10] *Political Liberalism,* p. 145.

[11] Richard Tuck, "Scepticism and Toleration in the Seventeenth Century," in *Justifying Toleration: Conceptual and Historical Perspectives,* ed. Susan Mendus (Cambridge: Cambridge University Press, 1988), pp. 21–36.

worldview is just as valid. The skeptic is not claiming that all views are equally right since that would imply there was some common scale on which they could all be measured. The claim is instead that the different views are incommensurable, and the fact that two goods are incommensurable does justify treating them as if they were equal. This approach is problematic from a practical standpoint because so many people are not skeptics. While it might be possible to formulate a theory that claims that all people ought to be skeptics and that skeptics need not be constrained in their political actions by the fact that there are many nonskeptics around, this is not a move open to many current liberal writers, certainly not Rawls.[12] To *require* skepticism, in Rawls's view, would be to require people to accept a metaphysical principle about which there is reasonable disagreement. The clinching point for our present purposes is that skepticism gives us no guidance when the question is "what laws should we adopt." In the same way that rejecting free will in favor of determinism provides no help in deciding which of two actions to perform, so relativism provides no help when we must decide which of two moral outlooks to endorse.[13]

The first and second ways, by contrast, do affirm substantive political principles and therefore can be of use in practical deliberation about toleration. I draw upon the approach of political liberalism in that I will put forward political principles that persons from a variety of religious and philosophical traditions could adopt. When I examine Locke's arguments, I will try to find versions of them that could be endorsed both by those who share Locke's Christian beliefs and by those who reject them. Still, it is important to note that the success of my argument does not in the final analysis depend on the success of political liberalism. Although every theory of political liberalism will include a theory of toleration, the converse is not true. A theory of toleration could be based on a particular comprehensive doctrine that is true rather than posited as a freestanding doctrine, as political liberalism requires. Thus I leave open the possibility that the position I develop below might need to be grounded in a particular comprehensive doctrine, although I do not do so here. Persons are of course politically free to believe that their worldview provides the best justification for the political principles I will develop below.

The above considerations show why it would be desirable to find moral reasons for toleration that do not rest on skepticism. Actually providing such reasons is the more difficult task. In the remainder of this

---

[12] *Political Liberalism*, 62–63. Rawls says explicitly that political liberalism cannot endorse skepticism and still hope to achieve a reasonable overlapping consensus.

[13] Gordon Graham, "Tolerance, Pluralism, and Relativism" in *Toleration: An Elusive Virtue,* ed. Heyd, pp. 44–59. On the problems with skeptical justifications of toleration, see also Newey, *Virtue, Reason, and Toleration,* chap. 4.

chapter I claim that, under certain conditions, the paradox of toleration is only an apparent paradox. The paradox depends in large part on framing the problem of toleration in very broad terms. Historically, however, theories of toleration were developed with more specific problems in mind and framed in much narrower terms. Specifically, early toleration theorists like Locke were particularly concerned with political toleration and the use of force.

There is often more than one way to try to stop an action. For example, if person X has the power to restrain someone through physical force but refrains, it is an example of toleration; X has rejected one possible method for trying to put a stop to the action. But persuasion is also a way in which an individual tries to alter the beliefs or actions of others.[14] One could thus distinguish between civil and political toleration. The former would articulate moral principles that should govern noncoercive interactions between persons; the latter, coercive actions, either between persons or between persons and the state. Is a religious fundamentalist who tries to persuade others to join her religion, while renouncing the use of physical force and intimidation, tolerant? As a matter of political tolerance, the answer is yes. Given the power differences that often exist between private citizens, acts of persuasion can certainly generate interesting moral questions. But the focal case of toleration, especially a political theory of toleration, must be political toleration. Positive laws are generally characterized by the presence of physical sanctions for noncompliance. Because positive laws are physically coercive, political toleration concerns the relationship between moral principles and the use of force.

If we focus on political toleration and the use of coercion and threats of coercion, toleration becomes, at least potentially, less paradoxical. If the use of a particular *means* carries moral weight, then there is a non-skeptical reason for toleration. If a person's moral beliefs contain insights about means as well as ends, then *political* toleration is possible without paradox or skepticism. Much of the literature on "dirty hands," for example, rests on the moral intuition that some means, such as violence, are problematic simply as means. The claim that violence is a problematic means is not uncontroversial. An act-utilitarian would, for example, say that the use of violence is wrong only insofar as it produces particular undesirable outcomes. The very logic of consequentialism requires that all means, taken simply as means, are morally equivalent since only consequences count. But although the claim that violence is suspect is not

[14] William Walker, "Force, Metaphor, and Persuasion in Locke's *A Letter Concerning Toleration*," in *Difference and Dissent: Theories of Toleration in Medieval and Early Modern Europe*, ed. Cary J. Nederman and John C. Laursen (Lanhan, MD: Rowman & Littlefield, 1996), pp. 205–229.

uncontroversial, it is nonetheless widely held. Persons have moral beliefs about how one ought to act, and this includes beliefs about when to use force. One's belief that an action is wrong creates a reason to try to stop it, while one's beliefs about the appropriate uses of force restrict how one goes about stopping it.[15] When persons conceived of religious toleration in the seventeenth century, it was as a doctrine of political, not civil, tolerance. Many of the paradoxes fall away when it is seen in this light.

Although the belief that violence is a problematic means is widely shared, it is not enough by itself. Although it points to a way of thinking about the problem of toleration such that it is not logically incoherent, it does not dispense with the need actually to develop arguments that specify *when* refraining from the use of force is the correct response. Pacifism, like act-utilitarianism, is a minority view. Most people believe that there are some times when states should use force to prevent morally wrong actions. Most, for example, would support the use of police power to stop murder or rape. We need a more specific, and more controversial, argument in order to set the appropriate line between things we should tolerate and things we should not.

Normally when theorists reach this point in the argument they appeal to particular substantive values, such as autonomy or equal concern and respect, both to justify toleration and to define its scope. In this book I take a more indirect approach. Rather than fully specifying a theory of toleration, I instead want to note a pervasive feature of debates about toleration and propose a moral perspective from which we can assess competing moral arguments. The pervasive feature in question is the fact that moral principles are almost always contested both as to their facial validity and as to how they should be interpreted.

Take, for example, Ronald Dworkin's famous claim that all persons should be treated with equal concern and respect. Dworkin claims that this principle implies that government "must not constrain liberty on the ground that one person's conception of the good life of one group is nobler or superior to another's."[16] If true it would certainly justify toleration in some instances. But Dworkin himself admits that the phrase "equal concern and respect" is a general concept and that there are a variety of more specific conceptions of it.[17] And, in fact, Dworkin's critics have often interpreted the idea very differently. Robert George, for

---

[15] This explanation of toleration fits well with Preston King's description of it. King sees toleration as occurring when one objects both to a state of affairs and (even more strongly) to at least one of the means available for altering that state of affairs. See *Toleration*, chap. 1.

[16] Ronald Dworkin, *Taking Rights Seriously* (Cambridge: Harvard University Press, 1978), p. 273.

[17] Ibid., p. 180.

example, would claim that respect for persons means respecting the potential for a life guided by practical reason, not endorsing every choice persons actually make. Discouraging someone from undertaking a particular use of freedom may actually be a higher form of respect than treating his choice with indifference, if the person is using his freedom in a way that undermines his future capacity for flourishing.[18] Alternatively, equal respect could be construed along democratic lines. Equal respect for moral agency could imply counting each person's opinion equally in deciding what rights individuals have and what limits should be placed on the pursuit of the public good.[19] If we deliberate about the good as a community and my voice counts as much as everyone else's, why is it a sign of disrespect when my position does not prevail? People are moral agents who have not only views about how they want to live their own lives, but also views about right and wrong and virtue and vice that apply to society. There is nothing about the concept of equal respect for persons that necessarily favors the former over the latter.[20]

Similar problems abound when persons invoke ideas like autonomy and well-being. It should already be obvious that the vagueness of such terms has implications that go far beyond the scope of debates about toleration, narrowly defined. The appeal to ideas that are contested in meaning is a pervasive feature of political justification. Because this kind of contestation is so common it raises the problem of skepticism again, this time in a new way. In our initial formulation the charge of implicit skepticism arose because a person refused to act on a moral principle she believes true. In the current formulation it arises because a person is asked, "Why don't you act on the particular conception of the general concept that you believe is correct?" Why, in fact, should persons refrain from doing so unless they are skeptical as to whether their own specification is correct?

In the remainder of this chapter I suggest why we sometimes have a nonskeptical reason not to act on our preferred interpretation of a general

[18] Robert P. George, *Making Men Moral: Civil Liberties and Public Morality* (Oxford: Clarendon Press, 1993), pp. 95–97.

[19] Jeremy Waldron, *Law and Disagreement* (Oxford: Clarendon Press, 1999), pp. 282–312.

[20] Dworkin's argument about external preferences is of little help in the case at hand, since it applies only to arguments that use a utilitarian framework. See *Taking Rights Seriously*, pp. 234–238. Dworkin does acknowledge that moral principles, such as the principle of equal respect, are legitimate justifications for law. See chapter 6, note 32, below. Our focal case involves persons who rightly believe that the action they oppose violates a moral principle. Any attempt to rule out their arguments by drawing a sharp distinction between justice and other aspects of morality will rest on a more specific conception of equal respect, not the general concept, and thus stands in need of further justification. Later chapters will examine Lockean arguments that help to justify a more specific conception.

principle if we adopt a certain kind of legislative point of view. In the next section I examine the way contested principles are used in political argument. Since the legislative point of view, as I employ it, rests upon an analogy between positive laws and moral principles, the concluding section examines that analogy and explains why we would have a nonskeptical reason to reject certain principles because of the way others would interpret and apply them *if* we adopted a certain type of legislative point of view.

Contested Principles and the Legislative Point of View

Some principles are contested on their face, others because of the way they are interpreted and applied.[21] In this section I give a more precise account of the way contested principles are used in political argument and focus on different types of objections that can be made to principles that are contested in this second sense. By doing so we will be able to see when skepticism does and does not enter in as a relevant concern. Since my goal is to draw an analogy to legislative thinking, I will, in this section, move freely between discussions of positive laws that are contested and moral principles that are contested. In the next section I will consider the objection that there is a morally relevant difference between the two that renders the analogy invalid.

Some principles are contested in the sense that opponents reject them outright. There is little disagreement about what the terms in the principle mean but considerable disagreement over whether the principle should be adopted. To use an example that will be prominent later, the principle "The government should promote the true religion" is contested in both senses. There are many people who would deny the principle *even if* there were no disagreement about which religion is the true one.[22] But this principle is also contested in the second sense, in that if it were adopted there would inevitably be disagreement about which religion is the true one.

The best way to understand contestation in this second sense is to say that when persons try to justify a particular law, policy, or state action,

[21] I will frequently refer to concerns about the way a principle will be "interpreted and applied." I use this phrase to indicate disputes both about the meaning of words and phrases in a principle and about whether a particular case is covered by a principle, correctly interpreted. The distinction between interpreting and applying a principle is not a sharp one. I will argue in chapter 5 that "execution" of the law involves interpretation as well.

[22] As will be made clear below, I include under "disagreement" both disagreement about what a term means as well as disagreement about which actual cases are covered by the term. In other words, both disagreements about the definition and those about the referent are included in this analysis.

there will generally be at least one major premise and one minor premise in their argument. The main reason for this is that most people admit that for a principle to count as moral it must have some degree of generality.[23] If it is right for the state to use its coercive power in a given situation, then it should also be right for the state to use its power in all cases that are not different in morally relevant ways. Therefore, there will be a more general major premise that outlines how the relevant actor should act in a set of situations and a minor premise claiming that the specific law, policy, or action is a member of that set. For example, someone defending the establishment of religion might claim that governments should promote the true religion (major premise) and that Islam is the true religion (minor premise). This idea of generality is a prominent feature of law.[24] Prohibitions on bills of attainder, bills that name a particular person, flow from the assumption that the law should treat like cases alike and that, therefore, laws should be stated with some degree of generality.

Contestedness will of course be a matter of degree. It is a persistent feature of political life that those moral terms that are mutually recognized as justifying state action are contested in their meaning and application. Thomas Hobbes gave one reason we can expect disagreement to be endemic on moral and political questions. Considering why principles of right and wrong are more disputed than those of geometry, he claimed that in geometry

> men care not, in that subject what be truth, as a thing that crosses no mans ambition, profit, or lust. For I doubt not, but if it had been a thing contrary to any mans right of dominion, or to the interest of men than have dominion, *That the three Angles of a Triangle should be equall to two Angles of a Square*; that doctrine should have been, if not disputed, yet by the burning of all books of Geometry, suppressed, as farre as he whom it concerned was able.[25]

Debates in politics invariably involve questions of persons' interests that will make it difficult even for those committed to following the truth to be impartial. Disagreement is not, however, simply a product of bias and self-interest. Even if the problem of self-interest could be set to the side, the questions themselves are sometimes very difficult. Also, the fact that people begin from diverse moral perspectives will have an effect on the

---

[23] See, for example, Amy Gutmann and Dennis Thompson, *Democracy and Disagreement* (Cambridge: Belknap Press of Harvard University, 1996) p. 13.

[24] See Lon L. Fuller, *The Morality of Law*, 2d. ed. (New Haven: Yale University Press, 1964), pp. 46–49.

[25] Thomas Hobbes, *Leviathan*, ed. Richard Tuck (Cambridge: Cambridge University Press, 1991), p. 74.

way they interpret principles. One does not have to be a relativist to admit that a person's early upbringing can exert a powerful hold on her later beliefs. So almost all political principles will be contested in this second sense to some degree. But they are not all contested to the *same* degree. We can choose between more and less contested terms. "The government should promote virtue" will be more contested in the second sense than "The government should promote courage." I do not, therefore, claim that only those principles that are not contested at all in the second sense are justifiable. The goal is not to find completely uncontested principles. Rather, the goal is to develop criteria that help persons judge *when* contestation in this second sense provides a sufficient reason to reject a principle as a justification for force.

In political debate, some principles are contested only at the level of the major premise or only at the level of the minor premise, and there is no interaction between the two levels. For example, both sides might interpret the major premise in the same way but simply disagree about whether to adopt it. There might, for example, be debates about abortion where both sides define their terms in the same way and simply have different views about the moral status of the fetus. Conversely, both sides might accept the major premise as correct and simply debate the minor premise on its merits. For example, both sides might agree that the government should promote the true religion and simply disagree about which religion the government should promote. The group that is not in power does not call for toleration, but rather for its own religion to be the state religion. Both of these scenarios happen frequently, and when they do the uncontested major or minor premise will normally be implicit rather than explicit in political debate. If both sides agree that the state should promote the public good and that improving the economy promotes the public good, the actual debate will simply be about whether a proposed policy would improve the economy.

In some cases, however, there is interaction between the two levels. Persons dispute the minor premise and claim this as a reason for rejecting the major premise. This is different from rejecting both the major premise and the minor premise for independent reasons. Our present concern is with instances where a person rejects a premise because of the way that it will be applied.[26] In general, the more vague and abstract a justificatory premise is, the more discretion political actors will have when they apply it to specific cases. The easiest examples involve vague laws. Suppose we

---

[26] A person could, in fact, combine all three kinds of objections, or some subset of them. For example, a person could reject a major premise *both* on its face *and* because of the way it will be applied *and* could reject the minor premise for some independent reason as well.

adopt the principle "Slanderous speech against public officials should be punished" and enact that principle into law. As justification for the law we could point to the unjust infliction of harm that occurs when one person damages another's reputation without cause. A person might dispute the major premise on its face because he believes there is nothing wrong with telling lies that harm another person, but a more effective objection would be that in practice fallible people will have to make difficult decisions about whether particular characterizations of public officials are false; people might be arrested for making what they believed at the time were good-faith criticisms. Moreover, the government might not apply the rule in good faith; it might use the law as a tool to silence criticism.[27]

When we remember that the rule will have to be applied to particular cases, a host of reasons emerge for why we might not want to empower the government to act in certain ways. We might reject a rule because we believe that those who will carry it out will be biased. Government officials regulating political speech will have a conflict of interest, since they will be tempted to apply such laws in ways that help the current regime stay in power. We might reject a rule because the cost of errors, when they occur, will be very high. Many people believe that it is much more harmful to suppress a single true belief than not to suppress many false beliefs. We might also reject a rule because it calls for very difficult judgments that will often be wrong. As we will examine in more detail later, Locke believed that very few magistrates would correctly apply the principle "Promote the true religion." Finally, we must also remember that not all people who invoke a particular principle do so in good faith. We will sometimes prefer a formulation of a principle that grants less discretion to those who will interpret and apply it in order to reduce the dangers of a bad-faith interpretation.

To this point I have simplified the problem by assuming that there is a single major premise and a set of mutually exclusive minor premises in potential competition with one another. The reality will of course always be much messier than that. Suppose we ask what justifies punishing person X and we are told: "The law states that persons who gamble shall be fined fifty dollars (major premise), and a court found X guilty of gambling (minor premise), so he was fined fifty dollars (conclusion)." When we ask what justifies the criminalization of gambling, we may be told: "The state must pass laws that aim to promote the public good (major premise), and making gambling a crime promotes the public good (minor premise)." In this case there are two separate arguments: one an argument of principle purporting to justify a law, and another justifying the application of a law

---

[27] This was the Supreme Court's logic in *New York Times v. Sullivan*, 376 U.S. 254.

to a particular person. In the next section we will take up the question whether there are morally relevant differences between the two types of argument. The point here is that there may be multiple steps to an argument. There may be several different principles that function the way the major premise functions in the simpler cases above. An opponent may object to any of these subordinate "major premises" by claiming that when people in good faith attempt to follow it, they will not necessarily arrive at the minor premise the proponent thinks they will.

When an objection arises that a rule should be rejected because of the way it will be applied, the rule's proponent may decide to reformulate the principle to avoid the objection. One obvious way of doing this is to change the principle from a political to a nonpolitical one. A person might replace the principle "The state should coercively promote the true religion" with "Each person should persuade others to adopt and practice true beliefs about religion." Since in this book we focus on principles that govern the use of force, our concern is with those major premises that direct persons or groups to use force. Were someone to reformulate her position in the above way, it would mean she accepted an argument for political toleration. To such a person, the arguments I develop in this book would have nothing more to say, at least explicitly.

The proponent of the principle could also reformulate it by making it more specific while continuing to maintain that it justifies coercive action. A common argumentative strategy is to claim that because the major premise will be misapplied, it should be amended so that it will be misapplied less often. Consider the following argument: "If the government always correctly identified virtue and was always successful in selecting those policies that would encourage it, there would be no problem with including personal virtue as one aspect of the public good. But in practice if we give the government this power it will abuse that power in paternalistic ways. I do not claim that because we disagree about private virtue the government should not try to promote virtue at all. Rather, I claim that we should replace the principle 'The government should promote virtue' with 'The government should promote virtue except in those matters where an individual's conduct does not directly harm others.'" This is a variation on Mill's argument for not allowing the government to enact paternalistic laws.[28] Thus, one need not always choose between adopting a vague major premise and abandoning it completely.

Once we acknowledge the possibility of reformulating principles so that they are more specific, an objection arises. Suppose I propose the principle "The government should promote the true religion" and my

---

[28] See John Stuart Mill, *On Liberty*, ed. Alburey Castell (Arlington Heights, IL: Harlan Davidson, 1947), pp. 84–85.

opponent objects that such a principle should be rejected because of the way it would be applied, since many persons who do not believe in the true religion would make a mess of things attempting to carry out the directive. I may not, in response, simply collapse the premises. If my opponent points out that there is disagreement about how to interpret the principle "Promote the true religion," I cannot reply by saying, "Well then, my major premise is 'Promote Catholicism' and my minor premise is 'Persecuting Protestants promotes Catholicism.'" It is true that the latter premise is less subject to varying interpretations than the former. Nonetheless, responses of this type are normally unsatisfactory because they run afoul of the requirement of generality. Someone can intelligibly ask, "Why Catholicism?" Unless we can come up with some more general reason, for example, that Catholicism is the true religion or that believing it to be true has very beneficial effects, we have not given an intelligible reason for our actions: we merely impose our will.

Using intelligibility as a criterion raises problems of its own. One can keep asking the "Why?" question indefinitely. Why promote the true religion? Why care about the souls of other people? Why promote the public good? Why be moral? At some point the one being questioned will look at the questioner with a blank stare because he believes that the reason he has just given provides a general reason for acting that the other person ought to accept as a reason. An unavoidable problem in politics is that moments like this are always possible. The Lockean account I will describe in later chapters handles this problem through Locke's doctrine of an "appeal to heaven." The fact that someone else refuses to accept what one sincerely believes is a sufficient justification for action is not a conclusive reason for one to refrain from performing that action. We must admit the danger that people will abuse this doctrine and pursue policies that others rightly reject, but we must also recognize that human fallibility cuts both ways and that there is a cost to giving others a veto power over our actions, which could of course be abused as well. The Lockean doctrine that I will present in the later chapters gives priority to protecting the right of individuals and groups to act according to conscience.

Although it is true that there may be instances where each of the opposing parties speaks a moral language that is unintelligible to others, this is not the norm. The people in dialogue will often have sufficiently similar moral beliefs to carry on an intelligible conversation. They may agree, for example, that human life should be preserved. In fact, the dynamic of contested principles exists in large part precisely because of this kind of normative overlap. Both sides recognize a term or phrase as carrying normative weight and for that reason contest what it means. Words like equality, freedom, and democracy have been termed "essentially contested concepts" partly because they have this feature.[29] To conclude, simply collapsing the premises is not a legitimate strategy because persons have a responsibility to make a good-faith effort to provide reasons that they believe the other side should find intelligible. Not all principles that are intelligible to a person are acceptable to that person. In chapter 4 I discuss theories that take the stronger position that we act only on principles we believe others could not reasonably reject.

The Analogy between Laws and Moral Principles

To this point I have moved rather freely between discussions of contested moral principles and those of contested positive laws. I now examine the analogy between the two in more detail. It is best to begin with the simpler case: the application of the legislative point of view to positive law. Martin Luther King, Jr., gives us an example of someone who thought certain positive laws should be rejected because they would not be adopted from a legislative point of view. In his "Letter from the Birmingham City Jail," he wrote: "There are some instances when a law is just on its face but unjust in its application."[30] Whites often adopted laws that were de jure just but unjust in their application in order to maintain the legal fiction that blacks were treated equally. Whites in the American South often used facially neutral poll taxes and literacy tests to harass, intimidate, and disenfranchise black voters. They used ordinances requiring a permit for parades to prevent marches by denying the permits. When King wrote his letter, he was in jail for parading without a permit. He wrote: "Now there is nothing wrong with an ordinance which requires a permit for a parade, but when the ordinance is used to preserve segregation and to deny citizens the First Amendment privilege of peaceful assembly and peaceful protest, then it becomes unjust."[31] If we consider literacy tests and poll taxes simply in the abstract, we can imagine various arguments for and against them. Supporters could argue that literacy tests encourage a more educated and thoughtful electorate and that poll taxes provide a needed source of revenue for the state. Opponents

[29] W. B. Gallie, "Essentially Contested Concepts," *Proceedings of the Aristotelian Society* 56 (1956), pp. 167–198. I do not mean to endorse one interpretation of this idea that holds that one interpretation of an essentially contested concept cannot be more reasonable than its rivals. I use it merely as a descriptive term to note the fact that we can expect disagreement in some realms to be persistent.

[30] Reprinted in *American Political Thought*, 2d ed., ed. Kenneth M. Dolbeare (Chatham, NJ: Chatham House Publishers, 1989), p. 530.

[31] Ibid.

might respond that such a taxation policy is unjustly regressive and that poverty and illiteracy should not burden the right to vote. In the end, however, one of the strongest arguments against such policies has always been that they will likely be abused. While there may be other objections to such policies, this one is sufficient. The more discretion one gives to officials, the greater the risk from abuse of discretion. One could call for the abolition of poll taxes and literacy tests and for significant reform of the parade permit requirement on the grounds that these laws, as currently written, will be applied in discriminatory ways and that it would be better to reduce local discretion.

If we put ourselves in the position of a legislator deciding whether to vote for the abolition of poll taxes and literacy tests, the skeptical position described above seems rather beside the point. We would not object to a legislator: "Why don't you allow literacy tests, since if you were the one applying the law you would do so in a fair and unbiased manner? Why should the fact that a law with good aims will be interpreted by persons with less than desirable intentions be a reason to reject the law? Are you skeptical that your own interpretation of the laws is actually correct?" Such an objection is nonsense because the legislator knows very well that in practice he will not be the one interpreting his own law. He knows that the laws he adopts will be interpreted and applied by executive and judicial officials who may not share either his goals or his interpretation of the law. A legislator who considers the way others might interpret and apply a law and rejects the law because of the way it would likely be misused is not a skeptic at all, merely sensible.

Because the legislator is concerned with the possibility of error, it does not matter in principle whether the minor premise is disputed on moral, religious, scientific, economic, or technical grounds. The argument rests upon a belief in human fallibility, not skepticism. If the argument relied on skepticism, it would be of the form: "Since there are no right answers in area X, it is wrong for persons to impose their preferred interpretation of X on others." If one believes that there are universally valid, scientific claims but not moral claims, then disputed moral minor premises would be valid, but disputed scientific minor premises would not. The Lockean argument does not have this structure.[32] Scientific, economic, and technical judgments can be difficult and contested, even if we are sure that there is a single right answer to the question we have asked. Admittedly, since contestedness is a matter of degree, if moral principles are more contested than scientific ones, arguments based on contestedness will be successful more often in the former than the latter. To the

---

[32] Richard Vernon also argues that Locke's theory of toleration does not rest on skepticism. See *The Career of Toleration*, chap. 3.

extent that we have greater confidence in technical expertise, than in moral expertise, a real or hypothetical legislator might be more willing to grant the former greater discretion. All this can be granted while still maintaining that such contested political principles must be evaluated from a legislative point of view. For example, a legislator adopting legislation that directs public schools to teach the "truth about human origins" should consider the way those who carry out the directive will interpret it. I take up this example at the end of chapter 3.

While the substantive argument for why persons should assess political principles from a legislative point of view awaits in chapter 2, the current chapter should make it clear why, if the argument is successful, it allows for toleration without skepticism. The distinction between major and minor premises, coupled with the legislative point of view, shows how one can make an argument for toleration without skepticism, and thus how Locke's argument can address both problems at the same time. As a logical matter, denying the minor premise cannot refute the major premise. I will argue in the next chapter that the fact that the minor premise will be abused gives us a reason not to adopt the major premise as a principle to guide our action, but it does not alter the truth value of the major premise, so long as the major premise is only considered as a principle of evaluation.

While it is clear that a legislator contemplating the adoption of a positive law has a nonskeptical reason to assess the law from a legislative point of view, it is less clear that there is a similar obligation on the part of a private citizen deciding which political principle to follow. Again, we can find a powerful illustration from King's "Letter from the Birmingham City Jail." King justified his disobedience to the parade permit requirement by appealing to the principle that there is no moral obligation to obey an unjust law. King's opponents objected that he was inconsistent because he condemned whites for disobeying Supreme Court decisions that they thought were unjust. King wrote, "One may well ask, 'How can you advocate breaking some laws and obeying others?' The answer is found in the fact that there are two types of laws: There are *just* laws and there are *unjust* laws."[33]

Though they did not put it in exactly those terms, King's opponents asked him to consider his principle from a legislative point of view and suggest what would happen if everyone acted on it, including those who disagreed with him about justice. King seems to be saying that the difference between himself and his opponents is that he applies the principle correctly and they do not. A supporter of King could claim there is a morally relevant distinction between a person appealing to a contested

---

[33] King, "Letter from the Birmingham City Jail," p. 529.

principle and a legislator enacting a contested law. When, as in some of the previous examples, we imagine a legislature writing laws that *other* persons (judges, police officers, or juries, for example) will interpret and apply, it makes sense for the legislature to consider the way those judges may misapply their instructions, assuming that a good legislature cares whether its laws actually further those goals they were intended to promote. It is not clear, however, that persons deciding what moral principles to act on are in an analogous position. The most obvious difference is that the person adopting the principle is *the same one* who will interpret it and act on it.

Gerald Dworkin has developed a theoretical objection along these lines. As an example, he considers a law that permits judges to excuse crimes committed while the defendant was sleepwalking. He claims that even if such a law would be foolish because of the way it would be applied (because of corruption or honest error), that says nothing about whether the moral principle "Persons should not be held responsible for actions committed while sleepwalking" is true, or false. If the latter principle is true, then an injustice is done each time the state punishes a bona fide sleepwalker. Dworkin's view will be discussed in more detail in chapter 2, but one of his main arguments is that it is not clear why the fact that someone else would misapply a principle is a reason for me not to try to apply it correctly. If you are not a skeptic and believe that your own interpretation is the right one, should the mistakes of others count as a reason? Dworkin claims that laws and moral principles are not analogous.[34]

Dworkin thinks that, when considering cases like the King example above, there are only two options. We can adopt a skeptical attitude toward claims of moral truth and say that appeals to "just" and "unjust" should be dismissed as mere rhetoric or admit that there is, in principle, no objection to persons appealing to moral principles that are contested in their meaning. The skeptical option is not one I will explore in this book, for reasons I have already indicated. If we accept Dworkin's second alternative, we would justify King's actions on the basis of the distinction between contested laws and contested moral principles. The original objection against King was that he should not adopt the principle "Disobey unjust laws" because it will be abused. The proposed rejoinder is that because a legislature gives instructions to other persons, it has a nonskeptical reason to consider the way the law will be misinterpreted and misapplied by those persons. A group trying to decide how to act politically is not in an analogous situation since the same group that adopts the princi-

---

[34] Gerald Dworkin, "Non-neutral Principles," *Journal of Philosophy* 71 (1974), pp. 499–501.

ple will act on the principle. Unless they are skeptical about their own beliefs, there is no reason why the fact that other groups would misapply the principle gives them a reason not to act on it. King's action, on this account, is justified because the relevant moral considerations that apply to legislators do not apply to someone in King's position.

In the remainder of this book, I argue against this conclusion. All persons insofar as they articulate principles that shape what the law will be should take on what I will call a "legislative point of view." King's actions were justified, but their justification does not depend on the distinction between legislative and nonlegislative situations. I argue that even persons who are not actually drafting legislation should take on a legislative point of view and act as if the principles they adopted were ones that their opponents would attempt to follow as well. The legislative point of view will, to be sure, take on different forms in different institutional contexts. The idea of a legislative point of view applies to many persons other than those we normally think of as legislators. Citizens when they vote, members of executive branches who must actually apply vague legislative directives, judges when they articulate general principles that have the force of law: all of these should act from a legislative point of view. After developing the theory in the next chapter I will argue that King's actions were justified precisely because they could be justified from a legislative point of view.

The present chapter shows that *if* the analogy between laws and moral principles is valid, we have a nonskeptical reason for toleration. But more than that, we have a general moral perspective with implications that go far beyond debates about toleration, narrowly defined. Given the pervasiveness of contested moral terms in political debate, adopting this moral perspective will affect how we look at a wide range of moral problems. In the classic toleration debates one must decide whether to prevent someone from violating a moral principle one believes true. There are, however, many other ways that persons invoke principles that are politically contested in meaning. When persons invoke positive political goals and ideals, like the public good, they appeal to contested principles. Persons also invoke contested principles when they appeal to contested constitutional provisions that define a political actor's jurisdiction. Exploring these more complicated problems will be the task for the remainder of the book. Chapters 2–4 will do this in part by contrasting the Lockean point of view with the main alternatives in the liberal tradition: utilitarianism, contractualism, and perfectionism.

CHAPTER 2

Contested Principles and the Legislative Point of View

If we adopt a legislative point of view, we have a reason to take into consideration the way others would interpret and apply a principle when deciding whether or not to act on that principle. The question is why we should adopt such a point of view if we are not really legislating. That was the essence of the King dilemma in chapter 1: why should he reject the principle "Disobey unjust laws" because other people might apply the principle incorrectly? The objection is a very important one, and in this chapter I will present a Lockean response to it. Before doing so, I want to consider the objection in a more familiar context, since this is in fact one of the principal objections that have been levied against rule-utilitarianism. In the first section of this chapter I argue that rule-utilitarianism is more attractive than act-utilitarianism precisely because it makes use of a legislative point of view and that, in doing so, it resonates with a powerful moral intuition. Rule-utilitarianism, however, is unable to give a satisfactory answer to the above objection. In the second section I present Locke's original argument for taking on this point of view. Locke was able to avoid the rule-utilitarian's dilemma because he grounded the legislative point of view in a theistic theory of natural law. In the third section I examine the core premises that Locke's argument rests on and formulate an analogous version that appeals to similar moral intuitions but which could be endorsed by persons who reject a universal theistic morality. The concluding section applies the Lockean argument to two concrete problems: contemporary debates over hate speech and Martin Luther King, Jr.'s, justification for civil disobedience. Developing the argument from the previous chapter, we see that King's actions were justifiable from a legislative point of view. The Lockean argument provides an important response to those who would justify force on the basis of principles that they would not want persons who disagree with them to interpret and apply.

Rule-Utilitarianism and Contested Principles

The place to begin is with Gerald Dworkin's treatment of this problem in his classic article, "Non-neutral Principles."[1] I use the term "contested"

---

[1] Dworkin, "Non-neutral Principles," pp. 492, 496.

rather than "nonneutral" to avoid misunderstandings based on the larger debates about neutrality and because the kinds of principles I discuss are a broader set than Dworkin's "non-neutral principles."[2] Before proceeding to Dworkin's argument, let us take a hypothetical example (inspired by Dworkin's account) involving a debate over a nonneutral, or contested, principle in its simplest form. Suppose the state is using its coercive power to censor a dissident because the state believes the dissident's views are false. The principle "Censor false views" is contested because whether the view is actually false is precisely what is in dispute between the two parties. Contested principles are one way of responding to the charge of inconsistency. Suppose the dissident charges those in power with inconsistency because they would not like it if those who thought their views were false censored them. The state replies that although it would not like it if its views were censored, that is beside the point because there is an important and morally relevant difference: the state's views are true while the dissident's views are false. The argument again returns to the point at which we started: whether the dissident's views are false is precisely what is in dispute between the two parties. The dissident will hardly regard this as a persuasive reply. Many principles that purport to justify coercion are contested in this way.

Dworkin considers a rule-utilitarian response to contested principles.[3] A rule-utilitarian would argue that a person employing a principle like "Censor false beliefs" makes the unwarranted assumption that persons will always apply the principle correctly. Instead, one should consider the tendency of persons to misapply the principle. Indeed, the claim that the state will accidentally or intentionally censor some true beliefs has always been one of the strongest arguments against censorship. A general rule protecting freedom of speech would have better

---

[2] In the later chapters I will apply the idea of a legislative point of view to sets of problems rather different from the simpler cases discussed in this chapter. Dworkin has in mind principles that directly justify an action. Later chapters will apply the idea of contested principles to conceptions of the public good and problems of institutional jurisdiction.

[3] Dworkin makes another argument related to contested principles that I will not discuss separately. The argument is that although the possibility of misuse may make it unwise to act on a principle, it does not change what is truly right and wrong. Thus if sleepwalkers ought not be held accountable for crimes committed while sleepwalking but legislators disallow the defense for fear that it will be abused and lead to even more injustice, it remains true that any bona fide sleepwalker is treated unjustly when punished for a crime committed while sleepwalking. Dworkin is correct if one talks about moral principles merely as principles of evaluation. If one objects to censorship because the government will likely misuse its power, one is objecting to misuse of power, not censorship. To the extent that moral principles serve as instructions to act, Dworkin's very example admits that the legislators act rightly when they ban the defense. Thus, if one can provide reasons why individuals should assume that the moral rules in question are constructed from a legislative point of view, the fact of misuse becomes relevant to establishing their content. Doing so is the burden of what follows. See Dworkin, "Non-neutral Principles," pp. 499–501.

consequences than one allowing the state to suppress beliefs. Dworkin quickly notes the famous problem with this type of argument. It is not clear how a rule-utilitarian can sustain this position against an act-utilitarian challenge. If a situation arises where a person truly believes, accounting for the possibility that she might be wrong, that breaking the rule will likely produce more utility than following the rule, why on utilitarian grounds should she follow the rule?[4] If utility is really the ultimate criterion, why give greater allegiance to rules than to utility itself? Dworkin concludes that the only reply to contested principles is the skeptical one that denies that there is such a thing as a "really true" principle. Although Dworkin points to an important problem with rule-utilitarianism, his conclusion is too hasty.

The strength of rule-utilitarianism relative to act-utilitarianism is that it forces persons to assume a legislative point of view. Historically, utilitarianism developed primarily as a guide for legislators and has always been most plausible when confined to large-scale political decisions rather than questions like whom to marry and what to eat for breakfast.[5] When a member of Congress decides whether to vote for a law, of course she should consider the tendency of the law to be misapplied in practice. If you assume the legislative point of view, then there are sound consequentialist reasons for being wary of sweeping decrees like "Censor false views" or "Punish false religion" that almost always require a contested minor premise when they are applied and that may often be misapplied.

Although there are many important objections to utilitarianism per se (some of which I think are valid), I do not discuss them here. I focus on an objection that is specific to rule-utilitarianism. Rule-utilitarianism must often assume the legislative point of view without giving a utilitarian reason why individuals should assume that point of view when they have the opportunity to avoid it. This is the case because often one can produce more utility by not assuming the legislative point of view. Here are some examples. Although the legislator as legislator has good reason to act in a rule-utilitarian manner, she does not have a compelling reason when she exercises her power in a nonlegislative capacity. Politicians often have opportunities to exercise power secretly and outside the forum of law. In such situations they may reasonably believe that no one will ever learn of their actions, and that their actions will not serve as a precedent for the actions of others. Likewise, citizens who are supposed to obey the law are not in a legislative position. If citizens believe they can break the law and likely produce better consequences, then on utilitarian grounds

---

[4] Ibid., p. 498.

[5] See Robert E. Goodin, *Utilitarianism as a Public Philosophy* (Cambridge: Cambridge University Press, 1995), chap. 1.

they should do so. Finally, consider citizens voting in a referendum to determine whether force may be used to promote the true religion. If the overwhelming majority is of one religion, they may feel that they can safely ignore the possibility that the law would be used against them. When those who legislate can be sure that they will also control the application of the law to specific cases, they will feel much freer to disregard the legislative point of view and promote utility, or whatever other end they have in mind, directly.

What is needed, but what rule-utilitarianism cannot provide, is a reason to assume the legislative point of view when one is not already there. In the case of contested principles the question becomes why I should let another person's mistakes keep me from applying a valid moral principle. I should account for my own fallibility and for the possibility that misguided people will mimic me, but neither of these is a distinctly rule-utilitarian calculation. An act-utilitarian would consider them as well, and act-utilitarianism does not require a legislative point of view.

Locke, Proast, and Contested Principles

Locke's dispute with his contemporary, Jonas Proast, also revolved around the use of a contested principle to justify the use of force. Proast claimed that the magistrate should use force to promote the true religion. This principle is contested because it is rarely invoked unless there is disagreement about which religion is true.[6] In his *Second* and *Third Letters*, Locke constantly replied that Proast could not simply assume that his theory would only authorize magistrates to use force who supported the true religion. In the first *Letter*, Locke wrote: "For it must be remembered that the Civil Power is the same every where and the Religion of every Prince is Orthodox to himself." Any power, he continued, that is granted to the magistrate in one country to root out idolatry must be given to all magistrates, many of whom believe in false religions (*Letter*, 42–43). Locke and Proast seem to be arguing past each other in the following way. Proast believed that the magistrate had a duty to believe the true religion *and* to use his power to promote that religion wisely. Proast held that magistrates used their power justly when they fulfilled both conditions; he was presenting an evaluative argument for assessing whether the magistrate's power had been used rightly or wrongly. A magistrate who believed a false religion or who failed to use force in support of the true

---

[6] One could imagine a situation where everyone agreed about the true religion but disagreed about whether the state should enforce it. This could only occur if the true religion did not contain within itself an authoritative teaching about whether the state should enforce it.

religion was evaluated negatively, and his use of force (in the former case) was ruled unjust. Thus, from an evaluative point of view, Proast saw Locke's objection as pointless because he held that the use of force by magistrates of a false religion was a sin. Many commentators have felt that Locke simply misses the strength of Proast's argument. Jeremy Waldron writes of Locke's objection:

> Notice that this is a good argument only against the following rather silly principle: (P1) that the magistrate may enforce *his own* religion or whatever religion *he thinks* correct. It is not a good argument against the somewhat more sensible proposition (P2) that a magistrate may enforce the religion, whatever it may be, which is *in fact* objectively correct.[7]

Waldron and Proast interpret Locke's objection similarly, and as they interpret it, it is indeed a failure. Proast suspected that Locke was a skeptic who denied that we could know religious truth.[8]

In his *Third Letter*, Locke noted that he and Proast both accepted the law of nature as a justification for the use of force. Locke wrote elsewhere that a person in the state of nature may take it upon himself to enforce the law of nature (*Treatises*, 2.7). Magistrates retain the power to enforce the law of nature in civil society (*Treatises*, 2.128, 129, 135). Proast claimed that by the law of nature the magistrate had the authority to promote the public good, and that promoting the true religion would promote the public good.[9] Locke elsewhere disputed this claim on the grounds that only consent could give the magistrate such an expansive power.[10] But on two occasions Locke takes up Proast's position simply as a claim about the content of natural law. If there was a natural law provision of the sort

[7] Jeremy Waldron, "Locke, Toleration, and the Rationality of Persecution," in *Liberal Rights: Collected Papers 1981–1991* (Cambridge: Cambridge University Press, 1993), p. 99.

[8] There is a grain of truth in Proast's suspicion. Locke did not believe that we could have "knowledge" of true religion, but only because he had an extremely strict notion of what counts as knowledge. He also did not think we could have "knowledge" of any historical facts (*Essay* 4.16.6–8). Nonetheless, the evidence for such facts could be so great that the probability is high enough to give us a full assurance of its truth. Locke thought that there were rational grounds for having a full assurance of the truth of Christianity.

[9] Jonas Proast, *A Third Letter Concerning Toleration*. (Oxford, 1691), p. 31.

[10] For an exploration of the themes in this article based primarily on Locke's theory of consent rather than his theory of natural law, see Vernon, *The Career of Toleration*. My interpretation of Locke is similar to Vernon's on some central points, particularly Locke's claims that principles that guide political action should be principles that are reasonable when interpreted and acted on by the persons in question and that different standards of reason apply to political reasoning and personal ethics (pp. 48–49). Vernon, however, does not spend much time examining the role that this argument plays within Locke's theological framework and thus fails to notice that this is an argument that also applies to the

Proast claimed, Locke's position would be in danger since Locke agreed that the magistrate has the authority to enforce natural law. More than that, Locke's early *Essays on the Law of Nature* (123) listed failure to worship God as a breach of natural law. Locke needed to provide a reason why such breaches should not be punished. In effect, he needed to distinguish two branches of natural law: one that humans should enforce, and one that they should not. Locke tried to show that not all valid moral principles are justifications for the use of force.

Locke contended that enforceable laws of nature were principles to which persons could appeal when justifying the use of force.[11] He also held a voluntarist theory of moral obligation that claimed that laws of nature were real laws and that God was the legislator (*Essay* 1.3.6). Locke further held that God was perfect, and that any claim that attributed an imperfection to him was therefore false. Laws of nature are promulgated to all persons, and therefore all have an obligation to obey them. They must also be clearly promulgated (by reason) to be binding. Proast would likely have agreed with all of these assumptions, and none of them requires a commitment to skepticism. Given these assumptions, Locke could rule out certain principles that are possible candidates for the status of natural law in the following way. Someone claims that a principle P is an enforceable natural law. If it is the case that if all persons attempt to follow P as a law of nature the result is hindering the goal that P was intended to promote, one must infer a lack of wisdom or foresight on the part of the legislator who enacted P. But God, by definition, does not lack wisdom or foresight so the previous reasoning must be false. P cannot, therefore, be a law of nature.[12] Importantly, a principle can sometimes be reformulated so that it passes this test simply by omitting the directive to

---

justification of force through natural law. Vernon's argument applies only to political decisions, not to the use of force in general, and at base it rests on the validity of using a contractual approach to settle the permissible functions of government (see pp. 23–24, 32–33, 150). Vernon acknowledges (p. 150) that Locke's account does not solve all of the objections associated with contractualism. A classic statement of these objections is found in Hanna Pitkin, "Obligation and Consent" (I and II), in *American Political Science Review* 59 (1965), pp. 991–999, and 60 (1966) pp. 39–52. By focusing on natural law, we set aside the question of what the parties in a dispute did or should consent to from their situated perspectives and instead ask what rule a legislator should adopt.

[11] For the purposes of this book, a law of nature is a rule that is normative rather than descriptive and that is in principle universally knowable and applicable. This does not mean that all persons actually know, accept, or obey the rule in question. It does mean, however, that if one claims "P is a law of nature," one is committing oneself to the *possibility* and the *desirability* of P's being known by *all* persons to be a binding normative rule. See *Treatises*, 2.7.

[12] To be sure, this position rests on a controversial understanding of God. In particular, it assumes that God is concerned with the instrumental rationality of His principles.

use force. Thus, one could believe that there is a natural law duty to worship God properly but not a duty (or permission) to punish those who fail to worship God properly.

Part of the reason Locke's modern interpreters have generally missed this argument is that the clearest examples occur in the dark recesses of the seldom read *Third Letter* and in the uncompleted *Fourth Letter*.[13] Locke argued that if Proast's principle was known to be a natural law and acted upon by the magistrates of the world, true religion would be undermined because most of them embrace error. Locke claimed that it was wrong to evaluate the question by looking at the application of force in a specific instance. He admitted that in particular cases the use of force might promote the true religion. Instead, he asked Proast to consider two different frameworks: one where religion was a part of the public good the magistrate might pursue, and one where it was not. The former would be counterproductive in promoting true religion and so Locke denied that God, through natural law, adopted it. Locke rejected the claim that God would grant magistrates a power that was self-defeating in this way. Instead, he asked Proast to think of the consequences of his principle when applied in practice by all governments.

According to Locke, Proast's position, that the magistrate is obliged to use force in support of the true religion, is equivalent to the position that the magistrate is obliged to use force in support of the religion he believes to be true.[14] Proast's reply was that his theory only gave a posi-

---

[13] Locke's clearest statement is as follows: "[Y]ou [Proast] have recourse to the general law of nature; and what is that? The law of reason, whereby every one is commissioned to do good. And the propagating the true religion for the salvation of men's souls being doing good, you say, the civil sovereigns are commissioned and required by that law to use their force for those ends. But since by this law all civil sovereigns are commissioned and obliged alike to use their coactive power for the propagating the true religion, and the salvation of souls; and it is not possible for them to execute such a commission, or obey that law, but by using force to bring men to that religion which they judge the true; by which use of force much more harm than good would be done towards the propagating the true religion in the world, as I have showed elsewhere: therefore no such commission, whose execution would do more harm than good, more hinder than promote the end for which it is supposed given, can be a commission from God by the law of nature" (*Works*, 6:213). Additional passages are given in appendix 1.

[14] *Works*, 6:143. Dworkin objects that the two are not equivalent because I could intentionally attempt to believe a false proposition on which I would then be obliged to act. See "Non-neutral Principles," p. 497. Here we must distinguish a second way in which one principle reduces to another, namely, when the first is necessarily an example of the second. There are two different versions of the principle "Enforce the religion you believe is true": one where there is an additional duty to avoid belief manipulation of this sort, and one where there is not. The consequences of acting on the principle "Enforce the true religion" would be equivalent to the former, but not the latter. A Lockean theory assumes the former interpretation, and there are presumably moral grounds why persons ought not engage in belief manipulation of this sort. In any case, any person who attempted to act on the principle "Enforce the true religion" would have to interpret that principle.

tive evaluation of the magistrate's use of force when force was used in support of the true religion. At first glance Locke seems simply to be equivocating on the difference between the subjective and objective meanings of "obliged." Mistaken magistrates think they are obliged to promote their own religion when, in fact, they are not.

In fact, it is Proast who conflates two distinct evaluative standpoints. Where a law leaves a possibility of disagreement as to its proper interpretation and application, there are *two* distinct and relevant standpoints of evaluation: (1) evaluation of the law and the legislature that drafted it, and (2) evaluation of the way in which those who must interpret and execute the vague law conduct themselves.[15] Proast correctly noted that we sometimes evaluate how a person has conducted himself, given the framework in which he operates. In this sense all magistrates are not equally orthodox because God will judge who is right and who is wrong. But Proast confuses this with evaluation of the framework as a framework. The framework specifies which issues may or may not be settled by the use of force, and when we consider a framework we must face the fact that on Earth there is no natural judge of orthodoxy. Therefore, if we adopt the principle "Magistrates should promote the true religion," in fact they must all adopt the principle they believe true, but many of them may be wrong. In theistic natural law language, evidence that the framework is bad is evidence that the framework is not God's. Proast treats principles of natural law as principles of *evaluation* without realizing that they are practical principles of *action* as well. Locke assumed that God was aware of the fallibility of human judgment and that he adopted a framework that took this fallibility into consideration because the point of natural law was the promotion of God's purposes. Thus, if the purpose of religious worship is proper worship of the true God, and if most magistrates fail in this regard, and if force actually is an effective means for altering belief, then if each magistrate applies the principle the purpose of the principle would be undermined.

Because God relates to the law of nature as a legislator, He cannot treat the law of nature merely as a set of principles of evaluation. The law of nature is also an instruction to fallible persons to act in certain ways, and as a rational legislator God considers the imperfections of the beings who will execute the law on Earth. When there is disagreement about the content of natural law, human beings must also attempt to assume a legislative perspective, not because they have the authority to issue binding

---

[15] Richard Vernon, in *The Career of Toleration*, pp. 60–61, also notes that there are two standards of evaluation but emphasizes the distinction between situations of reasoning and situations of power and thus interprets Locke's argument as one restricting arguments in the public realm. Construed this way, the argument ultimately stands or falls with Locke's contractualism (p. 63.) Again, my interpretation of Locke works from his theory of natural law, not his theory of consent.

commands but in order to interpret God's commands correctly. Unlike the rule-utilitarian who attempts to justify his preoccupation with rules on grounds of utility, Locke justified his concern with rules out of respect for God and the equality of men under God. Locke's political theory rests on a moral picture that could be termed "juridical equality." He believed that God had created men free and equal and that one man could not use force against his equal unless God had commanded it.[16] Locke believed that God had endowed men with reason, and thus all men had the ability and duty to judge as moral agents.[17] Yet when they attempted to use force to make their judgments binding on others, they were trying to make themselves *judge over* their fellow men.[18] Because of their equality, one man could only make himself judge over another if their common superior, God, had authorized it. Any claim that the authorization came through natural law would have to be a claim about the content of a general and accessible rule that applies to all persons.

Locke's concern with consequences not only rested on different grounds than rule-utilitarianism but also looked at consequences in a different way. Consider the paradigm case in Locke's time. Suppose the king of England believes strongly that the Anglican religion is true and is considering using his power to suppress Catholics. Any good consequentialist will consider the tendency of one person's acts to influence or set precedents for the behavior of others. If the king has good reason to believe that the king of France will begin to persecute Protestants when he learns that the king of England is persecuting Catholics, then the king of England has a sound consequentialist reason not to persecute Catholics. If the king is a utilitarian, whether act or rule, he will look at the probable consequences of his action. If the king of England can persecute a few

---

[16] This is implicit when Locke writes in the *Letter* (p. 26) that the civil magistrate has no authority over souls because "it appears not that God has ever given any such Authority to one Man over another, as to compell any one to his Religion." It is also present in Locke's description of the perfect equality of the state of nature (*Treatises*, 2.7).

[17] "Person" is for Locke a "Forensick" term designating someone who can take moral responsibility for his actions (*Essay*, 2.27.26). Moral responsibility and moral agency are, in a deep sense, constitutive of the very idea of personhood for Locke. "For though Men uniting into politick Societies, have resigned up to the publick the disposing of all their Force, so that they cannot employ it against any Fellow-Citizen, any farther than the Law of the Country directs: yet they retain still the power of Thinking well or ill; approving or disapproving of the actions of those whom they live amongst, and converse with: And by this approbation and dislike they establish amongst themselves what they will call *Vertue* and *Vice*" (*Essay*, 2.28.10).

[18] Locke writes, "He that thinks another man in an error, judges him, as you phrase it, alienated from the truth, and then judges of truth and falsehood only for himself. But if he lays any penalty upon others, which they are to lie under till they embrace for a truth what he judges to be so, he is then so far a judge of truth for those others" (*Works*, 6:174). See also Vernon, *The Career of Toleration*, p. 60.

Catholics here and there and be quite sure that no one else will ever know, the consequentialist reason for toleration disappears. Unless there is some empirical reason to think that his behavior will serve as a precedent for others, he has no reason to adopt a legislative point of view and act as if he is enacting a rule that others will follow. It may often be the case that a state, province, or city can enact laws within its own borders and have little reason to think that its action will serve as a precedent for similar actions by other states, provinces, or cities.[19]

Locke's argument looks at consequences in a different way. It considers hypothetical consequences, not probable ones. Locke's king is supposed to ask what the consequences would be if all magistrates attempted to obey the principle that he personally is about to obey, regardless of whether his action will change the likelihood that they actually do attempt to obey the principle. Hypothetical consequences are consequences analyzed from a legislative perspective, in this case from the perspective of God as He decides whether or not to issue a command to all magistrates. The king is then bound to act according to the rule that is reasonable from God's perspective, not his own. If it is not reasonable from God's perspective, then it is not what God commanded since God is always reasonable. There is a world of difference between asking what the consequences would be *if* everyone acted on my principle and asking how my acting on the principle will *actually* affect the actions of others.

Locke's position does allow some contested principles to justify the use of force.[20] "Juries should convict guilty people" is contested since the fact of a trial guarantees disagreement about whether the person in question is guilty. It is not being contested per se that makes a principle illegitimate. Rather, it is the tendency of the contested principle to undermine its purpose when fallible persons attempt to interpret and apply it. The question is always whether there is another rule that would better promote the end in question. For example, Locke was well aware that there would be

[19] Interestingly, Proast makes an objection along these lines. He claims it is beside the point if true religion would gain in other countries if they adopted a principle of toleration because what is in question is whether England should adopt such a policy. See Proast, *A Third Letter*, p. 9.

[20] This is an important point. It is potentially misleading to think in terms of a neutral/contested dichotomy. It is better to think of more and less contested principles. The Lockean argument is not intended to move us from contested principles to principles that are so clear that they could not *possibly* be contested in their application. Instead, the argument will help us choose between competing contested principles. Dworkin also notes that it is better to think of a continuum of more and less neutral principles. Insofar as his goal is merely to show that not all contested principles are illegitimate, I do not disagree with him (see *Nonneutral Principles*, p. 493). But posing the question that way constructs a straw man since there might be a general reason for rejecting contested principles, but that reason might be only prima facie. Moreover, there are good grounds for giving distinct attention to those contested principles that purport to justify force.

disagreement over how to apply the principle "Use force to protect life, liberty, and property." Even this principle, which Locke clearly thought *could* authorize force, is potentially contested. If one endorses the rule, one must accept that some of those who apply it will apply it wrongly: that, for example, they will use excessive force or defend property that is not really theirs. Locke was under no illusions about the fact that sometimes persons will disagree with each other on a matter that both think involves a fundamental right, and that in such cases there is no appeal but to heaven. The desire to reduce these inconveniences provides an incentive to leave the state of nature. But in the state of nature there is no better rule to adopt because if people cannot defend themselves there will be even more injustice. God enacted this principle as the lesser of two evils. Locke's position is thus able to capture the essential rule-utilitarian insight, that we should consider the tendency of rules of conduct to be misapplied, without resting the argument on utilitarian grounds or applying it in the same way.

The Secular Analogue of the Lockean Argument

Many contemporary readers will feel that Locke's different grounds are more of a problem than a solution. To those who reject a theological and voluntaristic theory of natural law, Locke's theory will seem unpersuasive. Nonetheless, there is an analogous version of the argument that such readers could accept on plausible secular grounds. One important distinction is between the formal and substantive aspects of Locke's theory of natural law. The latter has to do with the substantive provisions that Locke thought would or would not authorize force, and I will not concern myself with them here. Thus, objections to Locke's views on suicide or property are irrelevant. What I want to defend is Locke's formal criteria for determining which true substantive moral principles are also valid justifications for the use of force. A Lockean theory must endorse four formal criteria: moral agency, moral equality, generality, and publicity. There are a variety of positions that could endorse these four criteria, the Rawlsian one being perhaps the best known.[21]

Moral agency implies that we recognize other persons as moral agents who must do their best to interpret and obey those moral principles that apply to them. This is a fairly minimal form of the claim. It does not, by itself, require us to permit others to act on their moral beliefs in all cases. Rather, it implies that they can be held accountable for the moral decisions that they make. The principle of moral equality holds that force

[21] Rawls, *Political Liberalism,* chap. 1.

stands in need of justification. I cannot use force against someone who is my moral equal simply because I want to do so. I must appeal to some higher principle that stands above both of us. In Locke's original formulation the grounds for moral agency and equality rested primarily on our equality as rational creatures created by God, but there are prominent contemporary theorists who argue for these same premises on secular grounds.

The third and fourth criteria, publicity and generality, though not uncontroversial, are hardly uncommon in contemporary political theory. Publicity requires that the persons who are obligated by moral principles be able to know those principles so that they can act on them. Secrecy should not be necessary for the principle to succeed. Generality requires that persons believe that the same moral principles that apply to them also apply to those with whom they have a dispute. The two sides do not have to agree on what the correct rule is, but they do need to believe that whatever the correct rule is, it applies to both sides. Locke went one step further in holding that the law of nature is universal. To the extent that moral rules have universal scope, they can be used to arbitrate disputes between nations and cultures. Even persons who believe that moral systems are relative to particular cultures could still employ the Lockean criteria to guide political debate within a culture if most people in the culture accept the necessary background assumptions. Again, numerous contemporary theorists argue for both of these formal requirements.[22]

The idea of reciprocity combines many of the above ideas, since if we regard others as moral agents under a common set of moral principles, those moral principles provide a way of insuring that we treat others as we would treat ourselves. What stands behind all of these formal criteria is an underlying moral picture that sees persons as equals under a common set of rules that they are all obligated to interpret and obey. I will use the phrase "juridical equality" to refer to this set of moral premises that gives people reason to take on a legislative point of view. Locke's unique contribution comes from a fifth criterion that is derived from this moral picture: reasonableness. People who endorse the other criteria should endorse this one as well. Because reasonableness is a criterion that is also common in contemporary political philosophy, it is important to distinguish the Lockean conception of it from other conceptions. The Lockean conception refers to reasonableness from a legislative point of view. Once we accept that there is a moral framework that specifies when persons may or may not use force and that fallible persons will attempt to interpret and apply those principles, we should desire a framework that in

---

[22] See, for example, Gutmann and Thompson, *Democracy and Disagreement*.

practice furthers its ends. Just as a reasonable legislator takes into account the tendency of a vague law to be misunderstood, so persons should adopt the perspective of a reasonable legislator when arguing about the content of the framework. One need not accept Locke's claim that God legislates the moral law to accept this criterion. Even persons who believe that humans construct the moral rules that govern them should realize that construction is a legislative act and should try to construct a framework that will achieve its goals when fallible persons attempt to obey it. Persons may adopt the legislative perspective because they think it the best way to *discover* true moral principles, or because they think it is the best way to *construct* those principles, or because it is the *interpretive tool* that makes the most sense in political debates among persons who affirm liberal political principles.[23] In any case, they have a nonconsequentialist reason to assume the legislative point of view grounded in a moral picture that sees their fellow fallible citizens as moral agents under a common set of moral rules. Taking the legislative point of view means that when contested principles are used to justify force, persons should ask whether they would want others to act on the same principle that they propose to act on, recognizing that others may interpret and apply controversial terms very differently.

The Lockean position represents an alternative to utilitarian and Kantian approaches to contested principles. As I will explain in more detail in chapter 4, there is a weak version and a strong version of the Lockean position. The weak version of the argument simply presents a nonconsequentialist reason why persons should adopt the legislative point of view. Once a person has adopted that point of view, she is free to adopt those substantive principles, consistent with the requirements of juridical equality, that she believes true or valid. A rule-utilitarian could thus adopt the weak version of the argument and still claim that the principle of utility is a public and general framework that she would want others to interpret and apply. In the weak interpretation, a rule-utilitarian would simply regard the Lockean view as giving a nonconsequentialist reason based on respect for persons to assume the rule- rather than act-utilitarian perspective. Since one of my purposes is to present the general

---

[23] Here I follow Walzer's distinction among moral inquiry as discovery, invention, and interpretation. Walzer compares these to executive, legislative, and judicial roles in government. See *Interpretation and Social Criticism* (Cambridge: Harvard University Press, 1987). I will argue in chapter 5 that this is a misleading division insofar as interpretation is, in practice, a part of legislative and executive activities. Interestingly, Walzer uses Locke's *Letter* as an example of social criticism as he reinterprets the requirements of personal salvation (pp. 52–56). In a sense, Locke does the same thing in the *Third Letter*: he takes an accepted set of beliefs about natural law and draws from them a new interpretation of how one interprets natural law.

theory in a way that a number of different liberal theories could affirm it, this is an important advantage. The stronger version of the argument would reject utility as the substantive principle to guide choices made from a legislative point of view. In its place, a Lockean thinker would reflect on the best interpretation of Locke's natural law position, particularly his claim that the fundamental law of nature requires that, as much as possible, mankind be preserved. Although I do not attempt to defend the stronger position, I explore Locke's fundamental law in more detail in chapter 3. For present purposes the important point is that the Lockean view differs from rule-utilitarianism in that it does not *require* that one use the principle of utility as the way to assess better and worse outcomes from the legislative point of view.

Like Kantians, Lockeans ask persons to take on a legislative point of view, not because doing so will produce the best consequences but simply because it is their duty to do so. Taking on the legislative point of view is a way of expressing respect for other persons. As Locke would have put it, we are all equally judges even if we are not equally good at judging.[24] But the Lockean position differs from the Kantian one in what it looks at from the legislative point of view. At least on the most common interpretation, Kantians ask whether the principle if generalized would contradict itself or thwart a fundamental end of humanity. The Lockean position is much more willing to consider contingent and empirical consequences.[25] One need not show that the principle is logically contradictory or that it thwarts a fundamental end of humanity, only that the principle would undermine its stated end if fallible persons attempted to obey it. Moreover, contingent and contextual facts like the degree of disagreement will play an important role. Locke believed there was much more disagreement about the fundamentals of true religion than about the fundamentals of natural law, a contingent state of affairs. Yet this state of affairs takes on moral implications in Locke's theory. The more disagreement there is over how to apply a principle, the more wary we should be of using it as a justification for force. Indeed it would be surprising if a political morality could avoid concerning itself in some way with the uncertainties and contingencies that surround so many political decisions. Utilitarians are right about at least that much. What the Lockean argument

---

[24] See *Works*, 6:153, 221. See also Vernon, *The Career of Toleration*, pp. 59–60.

[25] Vernon articulates part of the difference in noting Locke's concern with whether principles will be interpreted correctly in practice rather than a concern with whether there would be a logical contradiction if the principle were correctly acted on by all. See *The Career of Toleration*, p. 46. I would also call attention to the Kantian consideration of whether the principle conflicts with a necessary end, which is a stricter requirement than the Lockean one. Compare, for example, Jeffrie G. Murphy, *Kant: The Philosophy of Right* (London: Macmillan, 1970), chap. 3.

does is put an additional moral constraint on the way we consider the consequences of the principles we adopt.

Admittedly, there is such a wide range of interpretations of Kant that some interpretations do suggest something like the Lockean position. Some Kantians are more willing to allow contingent facts to figure in the application of Kantian principles. To the best of my knowledge, the closest a Kantian comes to the Lockean position is Thomas E. Hill, Jr., in his article "How a Kantian Might Think about Terrorism." He argues that from the Kantian legislative point of view, legislators consider the way a principle will be abused and misapplied. He writes: "A legal system or moral code that said, without careful qualification, 'Authorities may risk killing one person whenever they think that they can thereby save more than one,' would invite abuse and probably cost more lives in the long run."[26] Even if Kant is interpreted such that this is a permissible moral consideration, it is still importantly different from the Lockean position.

First, as Hill quickly notes, a Kantian cannot take the idea of an impartial legislator trying to preserve human life as a sufficient condition for adopting a principle since a Kantian has a much more stringent concept of what is called for to respect the dignity of each person.[27] While a Kantian of Hill's variety could endorse the Lockean argument, he would find it insufficient. Whereas the Kantian position Hill describes is a full moral theory, the Lockean legislative point of view, as I present it, is deliberately partial. I present it as a necessary but not a sufficient condition. The advantage to presenting the theory in this way is that it generates a general moral perspective that can frame disagreements between people who do not share a more controversial set of assumptions, such as the full Kantian theory.

Not only does the Lockean position not rest on Kantian foundations, it also represents a different way of conceiving of the legislative point of view. The Kantian position is often understood to require that a position be acceptable from the perspective of each agent affected by that action. Hill, for example, writes that "Each legislator would favor the policy when looking at it from his or her own perspective (abstractly conceived) and also when reviewing it from the perspective of each other person."[28] The idea that principles must be acceptable to all persons, at least all reasonable persons, is prominent among contemporary theorists influenced by Kant. As I will argue chapter 4 when I consider the theory of John Rawls, the Lockean position shows respect for persons and the

---

[26] "How a Kantian Might Think about Terrorism," in *Dignity and Practical Reason in Kant's Moral Theory* (Ithaca: Cornell University Press, 1992), p. 216.

[27] Ibid., pp. 216–217.

[28] Ibid., p. 215.

ideal of reciprocity in a different way, by asking what principle we would want all to interpret and obey rather than what principle all could accept. Suffice it to say that even those readings of Kant that are closest to the Lockean position I defend are importantly different. As with utilitarianism, I do not attempt a refutation of the entire Kantian position. Instead I suggest, first, a way the Lockean view could supplement that position and, second, a way it could serve as a meaningful alternative to it.

Two Illustrations

With the main theory in place, two concrete examples will clarify how the Lockean legislative point of view would function in practice. I consider first contemporary debates about hate speech. Such debates make use of contested principles and thus should be examined from a legislative point of view. This first illustration provides some important clarifications and qualifications to the above argument. I then return to Martin Luther King, Jr.'s, dilemma, discussed in chapter 1, and show that his actions could be justified from a legislative point of view.

Hate speech is generally defined as speech that causes injury to another on the basis of some protected category, such as membership in a particular racial group. The implicit assumption is that membership in the protected category does not constitute a reason for making derogatory remarks toward the persons in question. "Hate speech ought to be punished" is a contested principle because those accused of it generally do think that membership in the category in question merits condemnation. Whether they are right or not makes all the difference. Membership in the group "dead-beat dads" may well constitute a justification for public condemnation while membership in a racial group certainly does not. There is thus a principled ground for differential evaluation of the two expressions of condemnation. At the level of moral evaluation, we would certainly have different opinions of those who try to shame dead-beat dads into paying up and those who attempt to shame African Americans out of a neighborhood. The issue is what happens when we move from the principle "Hate speech should be condemned" to the principle "Hate speech should be punished by the state." The former is a principle of evaluation, the latter a principle of political action.

Suppose a small town is considering adopting legislation that would make hate speech a crime. The justificatory principle in question is "Hate speech ought to be punished." Suppose that the small town in question is composed almost totally of fundamentalist Christians and that, given the majority view, the principle application of the hate speech law would be to prosecute blasphemy against the Christian religion. If the citizens accept the principles implicit in juridical equality, and they would be more likely to accept Locke's theological version of the argument than a secular reformulation of it, they should ask themselves whether they would want other governments to interpret and act on the same principle. This means they should consider the fact that others might construe the same principle to ban some Christian attempts at proselytizing. It might also be used to prevent Christians from denouncing homosexuality. These considerations would give the community a reason to reject hate speech laws, even though there is no actual empirical link between their decision to adopt the law and the decisions of other communities on whether to adopt similar legislation. Moreover, the same argument would give a secular community that accepted juridical equality a reason to reject the law as well.

One question this example raises is how one determines the appropriate comparison group for the generalization. Should citizens ask whether they would want other cities in the county, the state, the nation, or the world to adopt and interpret the principle in question? Which level they pick will make an important difference in their evaluation since one generally encounters more diversity of interpretation the larger the sample. The generality of the principle should depend upon the extensiveness of the original moral claim. If the principle claims to oblige only some particular subset of the world, then that subset is the appropriate sample group. For example, a principle might claim to apply only to people who hold a particular office. Of course persons who claim a restricted principle of this sort should be ready to rebut the accusation that they restrict the application of the principle on arbitrary grounds. If the proposed principle is "Hate speech should be punished in the town of X," the proponent must give reasons why residence in town X is morally relevant. Needless to say, this is only a necessary and not a sufficient condition. Many principles could pass this formal test, which should be rejected on other grounds.

Which leads us to a second important qualification. The persons who will apply the Lockean criteria are fallible. They will sometimes hold false substantive beliefs, and they will sometimes apply the formal criteria incorrectly. The Lockean approach assuredly does not eliminate the problem of disagreement. One of the strengths of the Lockean approach is its recognition of this fact. This recognition is found in the Lockean doctrine of the state of nature. For present purposes, persons are in the state of nature when they have no higher earthly judge authorized by them or by their common superior to render judgment when disputes arise. In the state of nature we should assume the legislative point of view and ask what rules we would want others as well as ourselves to enforce. In that state, there will be times when two persons disagree and when each of them thinks the other has violated an enforceable rule. In such circumstances there is no appeal but to heaven: that is, each must follow his or her conscience. Even in civil society, the state of nature remains as a possibility if the state consistently uses its power for evil purposes.

But disputes of this kind do not always occur outside the boundaries of organized politics. When citizens or legislators deliberate about what the law should be, they are in an analogous situation. Each person will have to decide whether she should want the law to enforce her understanding of morality or whether she should restrict herself to noncoercive means of bringing people to accept her position. Whether the choice takes place in the setting of institutionalized politics or not, the Lockean criteria can help guide her deliberation. They constitute necessary conditions that a principle must meet for a person to claim in good faith that the principle is an *enforceable* moral law. Because I accept that all persons have an equal right to make moral judgments, I must consider the consequences of allowing my fellow citizens, or human beings, to interpret the same principle that I adopt. The rules that authorize the use of force must be reasonable when interpreted through the moral lenses of publicity and generality. Put another way, they are reasonable from the perspective of the legislator of the framework, not from the perspective of individual agents within the framework.

The Lockean argument applies whenever the use of force is in question. Since the actions of the state almost always involve direct or indirect coercion, the Lockean argument helps to clarify the way concerns about coercion influence the development of a normative *political* theory. There may be many circumstances in personal ethics where the legislative point of view is inappropriate. When questions of coercion arise, the political metaphor is very appropriate. Whether or not we are acting in the arena of organized politics, we should think of principles that authorize force as laws and ask whether they make sense as laws that apply both to us and to other persons. The adoption of political principles is not simply about reaching our own best judgment on truth or morality and then acting upon it, but rather about respecting the fact that force must be exercised though a common framework that we share with our fellow citizens and ultimately human beings. We must be aware of our own fallibility and of the fallibility of our fellows and realize that we make a moral mistake if we use political force without taking both into account.

Focusing on the way coercion triggers special moral considerations may also provide insight into the dispute over the liberal "right to do wrong."[29] The liberal idea of a right to do wrong is best understood as a claim right that prohibits the use of a certain means, coercion, in certain circumstances; it is not a claim that persons who engage in wrong actions

---

[29] See Robert George's criticism in *Making Men Moral*, pp. 110–128.

do not deserve blame. The confusion occurs when we fail to distinguish the two evaluative standpoints. From the first standpoint, which evaluates the morality of the actions of individual agents, there is never a right to do wrong. One aspect of the first standpoint, however, is the claim that it is morally wrong for persons to use force if the principle of action on which they act cannot be justified from the second standpoint, the legislative standpoint.[30] If liberals "merely" establish such a claim right, they have made an important argument. The Lockean position claims that without skepticism we can hold that there are valid standards of moral evaluation that we should not enforce even if in the specific case doing so would be effective.

With these clarifications in mind, we are now ready to return to the example of Martin Luther King, Jr., with which we began in chapter 1. The dilemma was how to justify breaking laws he thought unjust while condemning others for breaking laws they thought unjust. One proposed solution was that King, as a private citizen, was not obliged to take on the legislative point of view. While legislators must consider the way fallible persons will interpret their directives, private individuals direct only themselves and thus have no reason, aside from skepticism, to take someone else's errors in applying a principle to be a reason to reject that principle. This argument should be rejected because all persons, whether private citizens or not, should take on a legislative point of view when trying to affect the application of state power. Thinking of the moral principles that justify force as part of a common framework that we share with others is an important way of showing respect for them as moral agents. King, because he invoked natural law, should have been particularly receptive to this requirement. The very idea of natural law presupposes the idea of universal and public principles of action that all must interpret and obey.

When we look at King's argument closely, we can argue that he was, implicitly, employing the legislative point of view. The Lockean view differentiates principles of evaluation from principles of action. Principles of action are assessed from a legislative point of view. Once a principle of

---

[30] The distinction between principles of evaluation and principles of action is somewhat similar to Derek Parfit's distinction between ideal theory and practical act theory. See *Reasons and Persons* (Oxford: Oxford University Press, 1987), pp. 99–100. On pages 30–31 he describes the closest practical parallel, collective consequentialism, to the Lockean argument and mentions a subsequent discussion. Collective consequentialism requires us to perform the action that would produce the best consequences if all performed it. The Lockean position is less vulnerable to objection since it need not rest on a consequentialist foundation, and since it assumes that what is right for us to do is determined from a legislator's vantage point. It can be both wrong (evaluatively) for someone to do X and wrong (evaluatively) for me to stop him from doing X. The legislator supplies different criteria for judging the actions of others and deciding which principles we should act on ourselves.

action is accepted, we can then evaluate how well others and ourselves have interpreted and applied it. For that second step, we make use of our full moral theory. When King invokes natural law to differentiate himself from the segregationists by stating that the laws he disobeys are unjust and the laws they disobey are just, we can take him to be making the second kind of criticism: the problem is not that they are following the wrong principle (disobey unjust laws) but that they incorrectly apply the correct principle.

The legislative point of view is implicitly present in the way King selects the principle on which he acts. When considering what general rule people ought to attempt to follow, King is again able to distinguish his own position from that of the segregationists. He writes:

> I hope you can see the distinction I am trying to point out. In no sense do I advocate evading or defying the law as the rabid segregationist would do. This would lead to anarchy. One who breaks an unjust law must do it *openly*, *lovingly*, (not hatefully as the white mothers did in New Orleans when they were seen on television screaming "nigger, nigger, nigger") and with a willingness to accept the penalty.[31]

His reference to the problem of "anarchy" shows that he considered what would happen if fallible persons attempted to follow a rule that permitted anyone to disobey laws that they thought unjust with no further stipulations. King would want all people, even his enemies, to adopt the rule "One may disobey unjust laws if one does so openly, lovingly, and with a willingness to accept the penalty." King argues, I think persuasively, that such a rule is desirable even though some persons will use it to disobey laws that are not unjust. Forbidding all disobedience to the law because some will abuse the principle would be much worse.[32]

King's example thus provides another important clarification of the earlier argument. When we attempt to change the way state power is used, we should do so only on the basis of principles of action that are reasonable from a legislative point of view. It is in this sense that the errors of others can provide us for a reason to be tolerant, to not act on a principle we believe correct. Adopting the legislative point of view does not, however, preclude us from making use of our full moral theory in evaluating whether our own actions or the actions of others correctly apply that principle. It is entirely appropriate to criticize someone by saying that he or she acted on the right principle but interpreted it poorly. What is inappropriate is selecting the initial principle without considering

---

[31] "Letter from the Birmingham City Jail," p. 530.

[32] I leave to the side the question of whether King's principle is too restrictive.

whether we would want others to interpret it and act on it also, given the likely differences in how they will do so.

Locke asks us to think of principles that justify force as part of a common framework. When our principle includes disputed terms, we must ask whether allowing each person (or official) to interpret that principle to the best of her ability and then use force on behalf of that belief is superior to an arrangement where force is ruled out and we must content ourselves with persuasion. Locke's argument rests upon a substantive and therefore controversial set of premises. For him, many of those substantive commitments were based on his commitment to Protestant Christianity. This is a fact of some contemporary importance in that Lockean arguments (this one and others) may be persuasive to persons with similar religious beliefs. But even within academia, where such persons are a minority, the key premises for Locke's formal argument are still widely held. The analogical reading of his argument shows that persons with very different conceptions of morality could also accept it. When we are considering political principles, principles that will authorize the use of force, there are additional considerations that do not apply to moral evaluations or to noncoercive actions that flow from those evaluations. Political principles must take into account the imperfections of those who will implement them; they are guides to action as well as principles of evaluation. These considerations express an important part of what is distinctive in the relationship between normative political theory and ethics.

This chapter has applied the idea of a legislative point of view to the simplest case, that in which persons justify their actions by direct appeal to a moral principle. In Locke's thought, however, not all appeals to principle are the same. One can justify force by appealing to natural law, but one can also justify force by appealing to consent. Only consent can authorize the government to act on a person's behalf in pursuit of the public good (*Treatises* 2.87–89, 95). The public good is, however, a paradigm example of a contested idea. In chapter 3, I take up this particular example of a contested principle and examine the way the idea of consent functions as an intervening variable. In particular, I argue that the legislative point of view suggests a different way of understanding the role that consent plays in a Lockean account of the concept of the public good.

Legislative Consent and the Public Good

Invocations of "the public good" are a paradigm case of contested principles. In many instances people who disagree about the public good are disagreeing not merely about whether a given policy will actually produce the results that its proponents claim it will produce, but also about whether results of that sort should bear the honorific title "public good." Some restrict the public good to material benefits like health, physical safety, and economic prosperity. For others it may involve a common national identity, virtue, or even religious piety. When the two sides in a disagreement invoke different conceptions of the public good to justify or condemn state policy, we have a classic instance of contested principles. Simple statements like "Result X would promote the public good" will beg the question when what is really in dispute is which conception of the public good to use in evaluating result X. Given the importance of "the public good" as a justification for policy, it is perhaps the most important contested phrase in political debate. It is important precisely because citizens are constantly trying to renegotiate the extent of the government's reach. At any given time there will be some persons who want the state's power to reach into new areas and others who think the state's reach is already too long.

Debates over the public good assume the rejection of what Cass Sunstein has called "naked preferences," instances where a majority imposes its will simply because it has the raw power to do so.[1] Rule by sheer force of numbers can confer no more legitimacy than the principle "Might makes right." Instead, citizens should think of themselves as under a moral obligation to appeal to some moral principle or public value to justify coercive laws. It should go almost without saying that states cannot and should not always legally enforce this moral obligation.[2] The principles need not always be explicit. Often debate can take place where the end in question is so clearly a part of the public good that the only question is the best means to achieve that end. The important point is that

---

[1] Cass R. Sunstein, *The Partial Constitution* (Cambridge: Harvard University Press, 1993), pp. 27–29.

[2] Even setting the problem of knowing a person's true motives to the side, a law of that sort would be open to such incredible abuse that it would fail its own test. Reasonable persons would not affirm it from a legislative point of view.

persons be able to defend their proposals when someone objects that they are nothing but naked preferences. This requirement is consistent with the part of Locke's theory I described as "juridical equality" in the previous chapter. One consequence of the idea of juridical equality is that force must be justified by an appeal to principle. One cannot simply appeal to will, to the fact that one wants to use force.

This principle holds for majorities as well as for individuals. Even if we accept majority rule as the principle by which disagreements will be settled, juridical equality still places a moral obligation on persons to vote on the basis of principled reasons. This does not mean that the government can act only to protect rights (for example, the right to life, liberty, and property). Another type of principled justification is the claim that a proposed law will promote the public good, the common good, or the public interest. Lockean arguments can provide valuable insights for persons who must decide between competing conceptions of the public good.

The difficult question is whether the public good can specify anything distinctive as a normative concept or whether it is doomed to be nothing more than a useful piece of political rhetoric. If the term "public good," is to be of any use at all, it must mean something more specific than "good." A key problem for political theory is figuring out what "public" adds to "good." One approach is to claim that the public good is the subset of goods that governments may promote through coercive laws. The word "may" becomes crucial. If it means those goods that governments are physically capable of bringing about, then the only problem that the *public* good presents us with is one of instrumental rationality. There may be disagreements about the good itself, but adding the word "public" only poses one additional question: can state power bring about the state of affairs we regard as good?

Proast made this argument against Locke during their exchange. He claimed that the magistrate should use his sword to procure all of the benefits that he could. If we could agree that a certain state of affairs was good, the only objection to using state power to achieve it would be practical (for example, that it could not be achieved or that achieving it would cause unacceptable harms in other areas). This argument bears a clear similarity both to utilitarian and to some neo-Thomist views of political power. On utilitarian grounds all entities, the government included, should use their power to create the best state of affairs (measured in terms of happiness, well-being, pleasure, satisfied preferences, or some other comprehensive consequentialist category). Utilitarians would have to say that if there were a true religion promising eternal life to its adherents and the use of force could create even a small net increase in the number of persons obtaining eternal life, then the state should use force. Some neo-Thomists have argued that government may in principle use force to promote virtue. Piety presumably is such a virtue. Both might recognize reasons why it would be unwise to engage in religious persecution, but they would not rule out such a policy in principle as an end of government.

Although this position is still alive, it is hardly uncontroversial. There have been many attempts to qualify further the idea "public good," so that it actually restricts the government from pursuing certain ends for reasons other than impracticality. Amidst the various attempts to specify it, the phrase "public good" has proved vague. Does it mean something that is good for every single person, or simply for most people? If defining "public" is difficult, it is easy in comparison to "good." Is it defined objectively or subjectively, and if the former, how is it given content? Some writers have tried to formulate precise definitions of this and other related terms like "public interest,"[3] but these are somewhat artificial and impose more coherence on the term than it actually has in public debate. Probably the only uncontroversial uses of the term are in contrast to acts that are manifestly for private gain. A politician embezzling tax dollars for personal use is the paradigm case. Given the confusion that surrounds the term, a political theory that is able to help structure deliberation about what is and is not a part of the public good is certainly desirable. Locke, in his dispute with Proast, was forced to justify his more restrictive use of the term "public good" and in the process developed an argumentative model that may be of use in contemporary debates. In the discussion below, the phrase "public good" will denote those goods that the public may legitimately pursue through the use of coercive laws.[4] Understood in this way, the definition of the public good is clarified by inquiring into the legitimate ends of government. Moral principles will define the legitimate ends of government and thus the public good. The task of this chapter is to develop principles that can guide legislative deliberation concerning which conception of the public good to endorse.

When legislators deliberate about the scope of the idea "public good," they also face the issue of toleration. Because government actions

---

[3] See Brian Barry, *Political Argument* (Berkeley and Los Angeles: University of California Press, 1990), pp. 173–236.

[4] There is thus an asymmetry between rights and the public good. Locke believed that all persons have a right to enforce the former in the state of nature while the latter can only be enforced by a legitimate magistrate. Once there is a magistrate, however, he becomes responsible for both except in rare circumstances. Once in a legitimate state, the magistrate's duty to uphold the public good will include his duty to protect rights. Admittedly, another approach would be to define the public good more broadly and note that at times we may have to refrain from promoting the public good out of a concern for individual rights. The former approach is adopted because it is closer to Locke's usage and because it emphasizes that rights protection is one aspect of the public good.

are generally coercive and in any case are financed by coercively collected taxes, moral considerations related to the use of force are applicable when the government tries to promote a positive goal as well as when it uses the criminal law to punish a particular behavior. Admittedly, coercion is a matter of degree. It is more coercive to force someone to attend a church than to force someone to contribute a moderate sum to the support that church. Both, however, are coercive actions. One cannot, as Joseph Raz sometimes seems to suggest, morally separate the raising of money and the spending of money, thinking of only the former as coercive.[5] The fact that one action is less coercive than another may make us less wary of it, but it is still an example of "being judge over" rather than mere judging.[6] When we claim that the government should force people to contribute money for a particular good, we are authorizing coercion and should think in terms of a legislative point of view. As we will see in the next chapter, that does not mean that the government may never pursue "perfectionist" goals. It does mean that the legislative point of view is relevant when pursuing positive goods as well as when enforcing rights.

Just as the claim "X is wrong" does not prove the state has a right to punish X, so the claim "X is good" does not prove the state has a right to promote X. It provides a reason, but not one that is sufficient by itself. Just as in the criminal law toleration takes place when the government rightly decides not to punish an action that it rightly condemns, so also toleration takes place when the government rightly decides not to promote a good of which it rightly approves. It is not hard, for example, to imagine an argument where someone claims that both the decision not to punish religious dissent and the decision not to establish a national church are acts of toleration. It is not surprising, therefore, that Locke's analysis of toleration is of use in what might, at first glance, seem an unrelated matter.

It is probably already clear from the preceding chapter what one of the main claims of this chapter will be: when considering conflicting conceptions of the public good, persons should take on a legislative point of view. That is, they should not advocate policies based on a very broad understanding of the public good on the assumption that their preferred conception of the public good will prevail in application. They should act as if they are legislators setting forward an understanding of the public good that diverse persons will interpret and apply to specific cases. In-

---

[5] "Facing up: A Reply," *Southern California Law Review* 62 (1989), p. 1232–1233. Raz does admit that "most government actions rely on coercion as a means of ultimate enforcement" (p. 1232).

[6] See discussion of juridical equality in chapter 2.

deed, most of the arguments for such a claim have already been made in the previous chapter.

It would not, however, do justice to Locke's thought to move there directly. Locke distinguished between two kinds of justifications for the use of force. Sometimes one could justify the use of force by direct appeal to natural law. There was, however, no right by the law of nature to use force in support of the public good. Indeed, in the state of nature there was as yet no constituted "public" whose good one might promote. When persons did come together to form a political society, the government that emerged acquired not only the previously held right of punishing violations of natural law but also the new right to promote the public good. The crucial intervening idea is consent. Consent was not necessary in the state of nature for one person to enforce the law of nature against another, but it was necessary to create a political society with the authority to employ collective force on behalf of the public good. Although it is important, as in the previous chapter, to examine moral considerations that attach to the use of force in general, it is also important to ask whether there are additional moral principles that apply specifically to legislative deliberation in an established state. The analysis of the last chapter takes deliberation in a state of nature as its starting point and then reasons by analogy to established political society. This chapter focuses on moral considerations that are unique to established political society. Locke clearly thought that the idea of consent was particularly relevant to such societies.

Almost all recent scholars who have tried to make a case for the continuing relevance of Locke's thought on toleration take his arguments about what persons should or could consent to as the starting point for their arguments. Many of their arguments often boil down to the claim that it would not be instrumentally rational for persons to consent to give the government the authority to act in some area of life, particularly the area of religion. Put another way, Lockean arguments about consent provide reasons for restricting the scope of the public good so that it does not, for example, encompass religious ends. And, in fact, if one looks solely at the *Letter Concerning Toleration* there is some justification for this emphasis. Locke does indeed spend most of his time arguing that persons would not consent to give such a power to the magistrate because, for example, force is ineffective in securing genuine belief anyway. This is Locke's most famous argument, and most commentators find it insufficient to make a robust case for toleration. Much of the literature consists of persons trying to find more promising but still consent-based arguments in Locke's thought that are not dependent on the claim that force cannot produce genuine belief.

My goal in this chapter is to articulate the way the analysis of natural law and the legislative point of view discussed in the previous chapter relates to consent and the public good. My approach relies in large part on two distinctions. First, theorists use consent theory for at least two different purposes. Sometimes consent is proposed as a solution to the problem of political obligation, to explain why citizens have a moral obligation to obey the law. At other times theorists use it to clarify the legitimate ends of government by asking whether real persons have consented or hypothetical persons would consent to the government pursuing some particular end.[7]

The second distinction involves what we understand the act of consent to entail. Often by an act of consent we understand a morally binding agreement between two or more sides. For consent to bear any moral weight it must be voluntary; the persons must be free to withhold consent as well. The person who withholds consent must be able to opt out of the agreement by doing so. Thus, if citizenship requires consent, then a person can avoid the unique responsibilities that attach to citizenship by withholding consent. I refer to this type of consent as "contractual consent." If the ends of government are determined by what hypothetical persons would accept, then contractual consent implies that any of the hypothetical persons can exercise veto power by withholding consent. But there is another way of understanding consent that presupposes a solution to the problem of political obligation that I call "legislative consent." When a bill is put before a congress or parliament, or when citizens vote in a referendum, those who support the proposed legislation can be said to consent to that legislation. In this context it is already taken as given that there is a public, that there will be some collective decision, and that there is a prima facie obligation to abide by that decision. In this context withholding consent does not allow one to opt out of the collective judgment. Thus, the citizen who decides not to vote in the referendum is still bound by its results. Here consent carries with it more the connotation of *approval* than agreement. It is the sense of the word when we say that a bill becomes a law "with majority consent." For example, Article 2, Section 2, of the United States Constitution gives the president the right to appoint high-ranking officials with the "advice and consent" of the Senate. Since the Senate is conceived of as an established entity, consent here simply means the consent of a majority of the Senate. Consent *between* president and Senate is of the contractual variety since each has a

---

[7] Failure to distinguish these different uses of consent partially explains the ambiguous relationship that Andrew R. Murphy finds between contractualism and toleration. See "The Uneasy Relationship between Social Contract Theory and Religious Toleration," *Journal of Politics* 59 (1997), pp. 368–392.

veto, but the Senate's *act of consent* simply requires a majority vote. In this latter case of legislative consent, senators, when they vote, register their opinion about what the position of the Senate as a whole should be.

These two distinctions are important in the present case because my defense of Lockean ideas is partial. I want to defend Lockean ideas about the proper ends of government, the public good, without defending Locke's theory of political obligation. There are notorious difficulties with that theory. Briefly, there is either a robust notion of what counts as consent or there is not. In the former case we would have to conclude that there has never been a nation in which a clear majority of persons have given meaningful consent and thus every state that has ever existed has been illegitimate with respect to most of its inhabitants. A weaker version of consent (for example, a tacit consent signified by mere residence within the country after the age of majority) does allow us to think of most persons as having consented, but consent of this weaker sort is of dubious moral weight, because it is not really consent at all.[8] While I will not refute Locke's theory of political obligation, I will not defend it either. I will set to the side the question of political obligation and how states come to be legitimate. My claim is that it is more helpful to think in terms of legislative consent than contractual consent when considering the scope of the public good.

It is true that Locke thought contractual consent was necessary to solve the problem of political obligation, of explaining how particular people come to have special obligations to particular political communities. But it is also the case that when he talks about the extent of the reach of legitimate governments, he talks about consent in the legislative sense. He claims, for example, that governments may not take property from the people without "their consent, that is, the consent of the majority" (*Treatises*, 2.140). While it is true that Locke used the citizens' contractual consent to justify their obligation to abide by the decisions of the majority (*Treatises*, 2.96–98), many people since Locke have found other solutions to the problem of political obligation more persuasive. Persons who do so may nonetheless find Locke's account of legislative consent helpful for the distinct problem that it addressed: the problem of the ends of government.

It might be objected that we distort our discussion of the ends of government when we separate it from discussions about political obligation because how one answers the latter question, will have implications for the former question. This objection, however, fails to distinguish between overlapping grounds and overlapping questions. The claim that a

---

[8] See A. John Simmons, *On the Edge of Anarchy: Locke, Consent, and the Limits of Society* (Princeton: Princeton University Press, 1993), pp. 197–201.

person's freedom may only be limited by his own consent, if true, would have profound implications for both questions. By limiting myself to the latter question, I do not prevent others from invoking underlying moral principles that have implications for *both* the question of political obligation and the question of the limits of the ends of government. I merely set to the side those moral principles that apply only to the question of political obligation. I present a formal framework to help assess whether underlying principles are relevant to defining the public good.

A second objection might be that I cannot set the problem of political obligation to the side now since that problem figured prominently in the discussion of King in the previous two chapters. If it is consent in the contractual sense that is relevant when discussing questions of political obligation, how is an argument based on legislative consent relevant to King's situation? King clearly thought that there was a prima facie obligation to obey just laws and even an obligation to submit to the punishment of unjust laws. He clearly thought, therefore, that there was some solution to the problem of political obligation even if he did not think the solution was Locke's. As will become even clearer in chapters 5 and 6, the legislative point of view can be used in a variety of contexts. It is perfectly possible to use the legislative point of view to evaluate proposed exceptions to the prima facie obligation to obey the law without defending a contractual consent account of the sources of that obligation. I present the legislative point of view without resting it on a particular comprehensive moral theory precisely to make this possible.

Unfortunately, most of the Locke literature has ignored the two distinctions described above. It has generally addressed the problem of defining the proper ends of government based on a contractual, rather than legislative, understanding of consent. Framing the problem in that way puts too much emphasis on the question of what agreement instrumentally rational individuals would reach. Lockean consent understood from the legislative point of view is a broader concept. In the Locke literature the central question has been whether instrumentally rational persons would agree to allow the government to promote what it believes is the true religion. If you can show that it would be irrational for such persons to consent to that end, then the end is illegitimate. Since Locke does not develop an elaborate set of moral constraints on consent in the *Letter Concerning Toleration* in the way that Rawls does in *A Theory of Justice*, there are two main strategies.[9] One can question the efficacy of force to actually change belief, or one can question the likelihood that the govern-

---

[9] Rawls, for example, constrains agreement by making persons negotiate behind a veil of ignorance so that they are unable to bias agreement toward rewarding those attributes they happen to possess. See chapter 4 below.

ment will use force on behalf of the correct beliefs, or some combination of the two. This is the question that dominates the discussions by Waldron, David Wootton, Susan Mendus, and Richard Vernon. I argue below that these approaches do not fully capture Locke's response.

If we move from the question "What would citizens agree to?" to the question "What should citizens approve of?" we must still ask what moral criteria should guide approval. Locke's solution was for each to ask, "To what ends does natural law direct the government?" Citizens and legislators would approve of the best understanding of natural law that they could. My analogous claim is that when citizens and legislators deliberate about the public good, they should understand the public good to be determined by moral principles, and those moral principles should be constructed or discovered from a legislative point of view. Thinking of the public good as mediated by consent is consistent with thinking of the public good as defined by moral principles constructed from a legislative point of view. This claim allows the analysis of the previous chapter to apply to the public good as well. But there is a second claim that I wish to advance. As we explore the consent argument understood in terms of legislative consent, we will find additional formal criteria that apply specifically to legislative deliberation. Disputes about how to promote the public good, unlike disputes about the punishment of simple moral wrongs, presuppose a public and some method of collective decision making. In this chapter I will thus examine formal criteria that are uniquely applicable to deliberation about toleration in an established state.

The organization of this chapter is complicated by the fact that it is in this chapter most of all that I interact with the secondary literature on Locke. Whereas Locke's legislative point of view has not been widely discussed by scholars, his theory of consent and its relationship to toleration has been. This is a complication since my main purpose in this book is to develop a Lockean argument that will be of interest to a larger audience than just Locke scholars. My approach will be to distinguish two types of debates in the Locke literature. The first type concerns questions about whether an argument attributed to Locke actually makes a successful case for toleration, while the second concerns whether a particular position can fairly be attributed to Locke. Questions of the first type should be important even to people who are not Locke scholars and can shed light on the limits of consent theory as a way of establishing the proper limits of toleration. Questions of the latter type are important in that I claim my own position is genuinely Lockean, that it derives from theoretical positions Locke actually advanced, even though I do not endorse all of Locke's other positions. I take up questions of this latter type in appendix 2. There I offer additional textual support for what will be a controversial interpretation of the relationship between consent and the ends of government and the role of the fundamental law of nature in Locke's political thought.

In the next section I argue against interpretations of Locke that take the problem of consent to be one of deciding what instrumentally rational persons should accept or have accepted. In the concluding section I put forward formal Lockean arguments that restrict the scope of the public good. I argue, as in chapter 2, that an analogous version of the Lockean argument is applicable to contemporary debates about the public good.

Problems with Contractual Consent

A crucial question in the Locke literature is whether Locke has a good response to the following objection from Proast:

> Doubtless Commonwealths are instituted for the attaining of all the Benefits which Political Government can yield. And therefore if the *Spiritual* and *Eternal* Interests of men may any way be procured or advanced by Political Government; the procuring or advancing of those Interests must in all reason be reckon'd amongst the Ends of Civil Society, and so, consequently, fall within the compass of the Magistrate's jurisdiction."[10]

Is there such a thing as a good the government may not procure because it is in principle outside of the government's legitimate ends? Locke did not deny that the eternal and spiritual interests of persons are real goods; in fact, he claimed that they are the most important goods imaginable (*Letter,* 36). He did not, therefore, restrict the ends of government based on skepticism, as some contemporary liberal accounts do.[11] He did believe that as a matter of fact the use of force in the case at hand would cause more harm than good and would probably cause more people to turn away from the true faith than to join it. He also wanted, however, to show that force should not be used even if there were a particular situation where it seemed likely to produce the desired outcome.

Locke's position was that one's ability to produce a good outcome is not a sufficient ground for the use of force because force requires author-

[10] Proast, *The Argument of the Letter concerning Toleration Briefly Consider'd and Answered* (Oxford, 1690), pp. 18–19.

[11] As Vernon and others have argued, Locke did not believe that disagreement over religion was a barrier to the individual possessing a full assurance that his own faith was correct. See Vernon, *The Career of Toleration*, chap. 3.

ity. The grounds for this belief were discussed in the previous chapter. The use of force is a presumed breach of juridical equality and needs justification. Locke acknowledged that consent was one possible source of justification, but he wanted to deny that this collapsed into Proast's position. He denied that we ought to consent to the use of force for as much good as possible. To do this he had to show that there was something other than our expectation of good that constrained the content of our consent. Because Locke believed that persons by nature were free, equal, and independent, he concluded that the public good that the state may pursue must be something to which individuals so described would rationally consent.

Many have thought that this approach could not meet its objective. Waldron argues that everything rests on the rationality of persecution, on the belief that true faith cannot be coerced. This fact would simultaneously make it irrational for persecutors to use force *and* irrational for subjects to consent to allow the government to use force in matters of religion. But if we were to discover evidence that suggested that persecution was effective in promoting true religion in some circumstances, consent to force in matters of religion would not be irrational. Even if only arguments can change belief, force can regulate which arguments people hear. Empirically, Locke himself realized that coercion was often effective, at least in producing outward conformity. Thus the fact that force promotes only outward conformity would be no objection to someone who thought outward conformity valuable for its own sake.[12] Locke acknowledged that coercion might be effective in this way when he observed that the clergy was more likely to conform to the wishes of the king than vice versa (*Letter*, 37–38). Given that force might be effective, we should be irrational if we did not take every precaution to avoid believing a false religion.

Wootton and Vernon have both devised responses to Waldron that try to show that what it is rational for persons to consent to allow the government to do is not identical to the question of whether persecution is rational. Both bring out elements that are certainly part of Locke's argument but are nonetheless incomplete. Both, in different ways, try to redeem Locke's argument by focusing on the possibility that the government may be wrong rather than the claim that force cannot alter belief. Wootton argues that Locke has two distinct lines of argument that supplement the claim that true faith cannot be forced. The first is that we cannot contract something that we generally cannot control when the costs of failure to comply will be very high. For this reason Locke does not need to show that force is *never* effective in changing religious beliefs,

---

[12] See Waldron, "Locke, Toleration, and Persecution."

only that it is ineffective in the vast majority of cases. Wootton argues that I would not consent to allow someone to use force to get me to believe in his religion because it would be unlikely, though not impossible, that the force would really change my beliefs, and to suffer religious persecution is a great harm that I would avoid. Second, I would not consent because the government is likely to be wrong. It may be rational to allow the government to make choices when settling property disputes between my neighbor and me because the government will be more impartial and the use of force will likely be effective against noncompliance. In the case of religion, the magistrate is no more impartial, and it will be difficult to detect cases of noncompliance, and even more difficult to use force to remedy them.[13]

Both of these points help to explicate Locke's argument, but they are still vulnerable to Waldron's objection. Let us take the second argument first. If we imagine a king making everyone adhere to his religion, to which he has given no more thought than anyone else, few would consent to such a power. But suppose that there is a different model. Part of the reason that government policies are not picked at random from the opinions of the average citizen is that political deliberation often leads to better decisions. Locke's argument relies on the fact that kings are no less liable to error than the average person. Proast replied that if we think the legislature (whether a king or parliament) is more likely to be right than wrong when passing laws for the promotion of our civil interests, we should also think that the legislature might be able to promote our spiritual interests.[14] If political deliberation is no more likely to be right than an individual deciding alone, this undermines the justifications for government action in secular spheres as well.

Wootton mentions the most obvious answer to this challenge, which is that in arbitrating property disputes the government is more impartial than the disputants are, while in matters of religion everyone is a party to the dispute. This view is more effective in justifying the authority of judges than of legislators. When legislators deliberate about whether to raise taxes, they are deliberating about laws that will affect them as well. There is a sense in which they are no more impartial on the question than anyone else. The need for impartial *arbitrators* is part of the justification for government, but the need does not help us distinguish between *legislative* deliberation about religious versus secular ends. Moreover, impartiality is a more helpful concept with respect to interests than beliefs. Indeed, on the question "Is X the true religion?" there is no impartial *belief*

---

[13] See Wootton's introduction to John Locke, *Political Writings* (London: Penguin, 1993), pp. 94–110.

[14] Proast, *A Third Letter*, p. 39.

one could adopt, though there might be interests that could bias one's attempt to answer the question. The fact that I have not yet formed an opinion on something does not guarantee that I will be impartial when I do consider it; impartiality is not equivalent to either agnosticism or ignorance. I take up Locke's solution to this problem at the end of this section.

If we believe that political deliberation is more likely to be right, we can imagine someone reasoning as follows:

> I consent to allow the government to undertake a deliberative process concerning the use of state power regarding religion. This will include both an inquiry into which religion is most likely true and into the use of force most likely to be effective in causing people to seriously consider the arguments in favor of that religion. I know that I may disagree with the majority and that even after the threat of sanctions has inclined me to listen to their arguments I may not be persuaded. The fact that they are more likely to be right will not be sufficient for me to believe them if in the actual case I do not find their reasons the most compelling, but it is sufficient for me to believe that I should be compelled, if I am unwilling in the future, to listen closely to their arguments, since my eternal fate hangs in the balance.

If we agree that true religion is of surpassing value, that the majority is more likely to be right, and that some forms of coercion might cause a net increase in those adhering to that religion, then there is no reason not to consent to allow the government to be involved in matters of religion. We can also now see the response to the first objection. It may be the case that we generally cannot control our beliefs. Nonetheless, what we are contracting to do is not to believe something, but rather to allow force to be used so that we will consider arguments. If the former argument falls, this one also falls.

Richard Vernon develops two additional arguments to bolster Locke's theory of consent. The first speaks to the problem of redundancy. If our consent should be determined by our assessment of what is right or good, then it is what is right or good that determines the ends of government; consent does no additional work. This objection goes back at least to Hume. Vernon's response is that consent relates to the difference between prospective and retrospective assessments of states of affairs. Even if we could take a pill that would cause us in the future to sincerely hold a specific belief, we would not take it because we would, prospectively, only want to hold that belief for relevant reasons.[15] Thus even if force could cause us to hold a set of beliefs, we would not want to

---

[15] Vernon, *The Career of Toleration*, pp. 22–23.

hold them because we were forced; we would only want to hold them because there were good reasons.[16] There are two problems with this argument. The first is that it is not sufficiently critical of the reasons that ground our current opinions. If in state X only relevant reasons influence my beliefs and in state Y some new pressure (which is not a relevant reason for belief) is introduced that makes me more likely to believe something else, then Vernon's argument would hold. But suppose that in state X many of my beliefs are already influenced by irrelevant pressures. Now the introduction of new pressures is ambiguous. It might be that they lead me further astray, but they might counteract some of the old irrelevant pressures and leave me freer to base my judgments only on reasons that are actually relevant. If in state X my beliefs are largely determined by apathy and indifference, then the introduction of sanctions could cause me to spend some time thinking more seriously about my beliefs. This is the sort of answer neo-Thomists often give for morals legislation. The fact that I will be punished for something is not a reason for changing my opinion about its validity, but it might serve to counteract other passions, like lust or greed, that are similarly irrelevant to opinions about truth.

The second problem is that it is not obvious what constitutes a relevant reason for holding a religious belief. Different religions have different answers to the question of what are appropriate grounds for holding a religious belief. Even within the Christian tradition alone there is sharp disagreement about what reasons count as appropriate reasons for belief. Does faith rest on reliable witnesses to historical events or a direct encounter with Jesus? One can imagine religions in which force is thought to play a constructive role in altering belief. "Relevant reasons for belief" is itself a contested concept.[17]

Vernon's second argument poses the question of why not consent to be forced to be right. This was the objection to Wootton's position earlier in the chapter. Vernon uses the Rawlsian language of the original position[18] and asks whether persons in that state would allow some subset of persons (for example, those with red hair) to impose a religion if there was some sign (red hair) that certain persons, rather than others,

---

[16] Susan Mendus similarly claims that we would not want beliefs that were sincere but not authentic. If we only arrive at a position because someone manipulated what we could read or hear, our belief may not be authentic. See *Toleration and the Limits of Liberalism*, pp. 30–35.

[17] See, for example, Moshe Halbertal, "Autonomy, Toleration, and Group Rights," in *Toleration: An Elusive Virtue*, ed. David Heyd (Princeton: Princeton University Press, 1996), p. 109, on the conversion of St. Paul.

[18] The original argument is of course John Rawls, *A Theory of Justice* (Cambridge: Harvard University Press, 1971).

possessed the truth. He responds that signs of truth might be infallible or convincing or both. We would only consent if both were the case, and clearly both are not. We would not consent if the marks of truth were fallible because those who ruled might be wrong. We would not consent if the marks of truth might be such that we fail to recognize them (how red does red have to be?), because then we might select the wrong persons as rulers.[19] This argument, however, assumes that we would require certainty. If our goal in the original position is to choose the position most likely to be right, it would be enough to show that there are signs of truth that are sufficiently reliable and convincing that entrusting power to those we believe to be truth bearers will most likely bring us closer to the truth. The logic of risk aversion would actually cut the wrong way for Vernon since the "maximin" strategy seeks to avoid the worst outcome, and the worst outcome is believing the wrong religion (and suffering the eternal consequences of doing so), not earthly persecution.

The problem is that we can imagine cases where (1) a collective decision is more likely to be right, (2) coercion would make people more likely to adhere to that religion (if only by suppressing seductive false views and encouraging persons to listen to rational arguments), and (3) the magnitude of the potential eternal consequences of our actions make it rational to accept temporal harms for even a small increase in our chances of going to heaven. Most of our attention has focused on (1), and the difficulty is explaining why governments are bad judges in the sphere of religion but good judges in other spheres of disputed belief, such as justice.

Locke's argument has generally been missed because part of the argument is presented in the *Letter* and part of it is presented in the *Third Letter* in response to Proast's objection. Proast claimed that if governments were such bad judges of religion we would not trust them with our civil interests either.[20] Locke presents an argument for why political deliberation is more reliable about some topics than others. It is important to clarify what we mean by political deliberation. The question whether discussion and debate improve our chances of arriving at true religion is distinct from whether *political* deliberation is more effective than nonpolitical deliberation at bringing us to the true religion. A church council can deliberate on a religious question and make a pronouncement without coercing those who disagree. What Locke denied was that the political deliberation of the state on a religious question was more likely to be

---

[19] Vernon, *The Career of Toleration*, pp. 63–64.
[20] Proast, *A Third Letter*, p. 39.

right than was nonpolitical deliberation. Rejecting deliberation in a *political* forum does not entail advocating atomistic inquiry.

Locke believed that all human deliberations were subject to error because of human frailty. Our passions and desires often interfere with our inquiry. One of the passions most likely to corrupt our judgment about the truth is the lust for power. If holding belief A leads to a position of power while belief B (because it is unpopular) leads to a position of weakness, there will be a natural human tendency to want A to be true. All too often, persons will be biased toward a position because they think it is the position others want them to adopt. Locke believed that the clergy in England exhibited just this tendency. When religion is politicized, the members (particularly leaders) of the national church obtain power. Locke recounts in recent English history "how easily and smoothly the Clergy changed their Decrees, their Articles of Faith, their Form of Worship, everything, according to the inclination of those Kings and Queens" (*Letter*, 38). Moreover, we should not forget Max Weber's warning that politics is a place for those who are willing to get their hands dirty. The specter of violence is always present in politics, and violence is not particularly conducive to thoughtful deliberation. When questions of truth are mingled with the pursuit of power and threats of violence, the pursuit of truth is compromised.

The danger with this argument is that it might prove too much. The desire for power is an ineliminable part of politics, and so the conclusion one would arrive at is that all political deliberation is suspect. Locke's response is that political deliberation aimed at preservation differs from political deliberation about true religion. When asking whether deliberation should be politicized, there are two different dimensions to consider. One is the appropriateness of the means to the end. Locke could plausibly argue that coercive laws were a more appropriate response to acts of violence than to errant opinions. The second is the tendency of the means to corrupt deliberation itself. Locke assumed that a properly conceived legislature would be required to pass laws of general applicability, laws that would restrain both the legislators and others. This restriction decreases the likelihood that political deliberation about temporal security will be biased.

> For though men of all ranks could be content to have their own humours, passions, and prejudices satisfied; yet when they come to make laws, which are to direct their force in civil matters, they are driven to oppose their laws to the humours, passions, and prejudices of men in general, whereby their own come to be restrained: for if law-makers, in making of laws, did not direct them against the irregular humours, prejudices, and passions of men, which are apt to mis-

lead them; if they did not endeavor, with their best judgment, to bring men from their humours and passions, to the obedience and practice of right reason; the society could not subsist, and so they themselves would be in danger to lose their station in it, and be exposed to the unrestrained humors, passions, and violence of others. (*Works*, 6:504)

"But in matters of religion," Locke wrote, "it is quite otherwise" (6:505). If individuals, when they deliberate about true religion, go astray in doctrine because they fail to restrain their own prejudices, they will not suffer any consequences in this world. Deliberation becomes political when it is given the force of law; in civil matters the knowledge that the decision will be general and backed by force creates an incentive for legislatures to try to counteract the passions that lead men astray; in religious matters, those who are in the majority have nothing to lose from giving their own prejudices free rein.

Consider, for example, an argument made by the influential theologian John Hick. He argues that particular religious beliefs, ranging from the claim that God exists to Christian debates over whether all persons will ultimately be saved, are potentially verifiable. They are amenable to "eschatological verification." If they are correct, it will be clear that they are correct at some unspecified future end time. Whatever one thinks of this sort of argument as a ground for religious belief, one can say that arguments that only admit of eschatological verification are poor candidates for political deliberation since legislators cannot expect any temporal consequences to a right or wrong answer. There is no feedback loop to offset the corrupting aspects of politics.[21]

George Sher attributes to Mill an argument similar to the one I here attribute to Locke. He claims that Mill's argument is primarily about motivation: the threat of being forced out of office is necessary to make persons seriously consider the good, and that threat is lacking in cases where there are no clear-cut tests for judging success. Sher admits that there is much truth in this objection but claims that it does not show that moral motivation is only possible via self-interest and that the argument is too weak to justify a principle of neutrality. Setting to the side whether this is the correct interpretation of Mill, it is not a good argument against Locke's version since, as will be discussed in the following chapter, Locke does not attempt to derive a general requirement of neutrality. What Sher misses is the idea that politics itself already creates pressures on deliberation that makes political deliberation, absent correcting

[21] See John Hick, *A John Hick Reader*, ed. Paul Badham (London: Macmillan Press, 1990), chaps. 5 and 8.

pressures, more likely to be errant than the same deliberation in a less politically charged context. It is not that absent selfish motives we will not think hard about the good, but rather that political pressures will bias us toward politically popular answers in cases where there is not a more objective measure of whether our answers are correct.[22]

This argument has implications for topics other than religious toleration. The more general point is that sometimes there is disagreement not only about what to do but also about how to assess whether what was previously done was successful. Where there are accepted standards of assessment, there will be a partial corrective to the natural tendency of politicization to corrupt deliberation. Where such standards are absent we should be even more wary of contested principles as justifications for force. If one insists on interpreting the Lockean argument in terms of what instrumentally rational persons would consent to, this is a crucial move in his argument. It is a mistake, however, to see this way of framing the problem as Locke's most important contribution. This insight can still be employed from two different points of view: legislative or nonlegislative. In the section that follows I argue that Locke's understanding of consent as it relates to the scope of the public good is better understood as legislative consent making use of a legislative point of view than as contractual consent based on the instrumental rationality of individual agents.

Locke's Legislative Consent and the Public Good

Although Locke argued that political forums were ill suited for deciding questions of religious truth, it is wrong to think that his conception of the public good reduced to whatever it would be instrumentally rational for individuals in the state of nature to accept.[23] The whole purpose of a legislative point of view is to encourage persons to make judgments from

---

[22] See *Beyond Neutrality: Perfectionism and Politics* (New York: Cambridge University Press, 1997), pp. 130 and 137–138.

[23] Of course Locke does sometimes make the negative version of this argument, that if it is manifestly not in a person's interest in the state of nature to consent to something, then that person must not have consented to it. For example, "It cannot be supposed that they should intend, had they a power so to do, to give any one, or more, an *absolute Arbitrary Power* over their Persons and Estates" (*Treatises*, 2.137). Locke's argument here is overdetermined since he also thinks persons have no such power to give because natural law commands them to see to their own preservation (2.135).

a perspective that is not simply their own situated perspective. The problem is that the legislative point of view, as described in chapter 2, applies most naturally to cases where natural law is at issue, since it is there that Locke could most plausibly ask persons to take on a legislative point of view. God is, according to Locke, the legislator of natural law. It is not immediately obvious why a similar perspective is relevant to Locke's thought when the subject is consent rather than natural law. Consent, thought of as a promise to abide by some agreement, seems to be the paradigm case where the individual's situated perspective is *precisely* what is relevant. When I give my consent, it is only myself that I bind, and thus it is only my perspective that is relevant.

This objection holds only if it is consent in this contractual sense that is the relevant form of consent. Recalling the distinction made at the beginning of this chapter, I argue that when Locke is considering the scope of the public good, it is legislative consent, not contractual consent, that is relevant. Locke did not believe that the scope of the public good was determined by a bargaining process between individuals constrained only by the negative prohibitions of natural law like "Do not steal." If it were, different states would have different ends depending on what the outcome of the negotiation process was at the time of their founding. When Locke discusses the ends of government, there is no hint that he thinks we need to engage in historical research to find out what the actual parties to the contract decided. Instead he claims that the state may only act if its goal is to promote the fundamental law of nature. He claims that the legislative power is "limited to the publick good" and "hath no other end but preservation" (*Treatises*, 2.135). The goal of preservation is precisely the positive goal specified by Locke's fundamental law of nature. In the *Letter Concerning Toleration*, Locke briefly summarizes the forces that drive men into political society and notes that "arms, riches, and multitude of citizens" is the appropriate governmental remedy for the threat of invasion. One can see how he justifies particular goals the government can pursue, such as a strong economy, because they contribute to fulfilling the command of the fundamental law of nature, namely, that mankind be preserved. If the fundamental law of nature defines the scope of the public good, then the public good should also be defined from a legislative point of view. In this reading, consent is used not to determine the result of a bargain between instrumentally rational individuals, but rather for each person to register his belief about what natural law, constructed from a legislative point of view, requires. I make the textual arguments for this view in more detail in appendix 2.

Although I concentrate on legislative consent as part of the solution to the problem of the ends of government, I do not deny that contractual consent plays an important part in other aspects of Locke's theory.[24] As mentioned above, contractual consent remains Locke's solution to the problem of political obligation (*Treatises*, 2.95). Moreover, because our natural and proper state is one of freedom, it is not enough for the people to consent to an initial contract. Instead, the ongoing (express or tacit) consent of the people is required for the government to remain legitimate. Any other arrangement would reduce the people to a state of slavery (*Treatises*, 2.96–99, 138–140, 240).

Thus, while it is the case (as Locke often says) that governments have only those powers that they are granted by contractual consent, it is also the case that natural law makes prior restrictions on what persons can consent to when forming civil society. In other words, when people "consent" to the ends of government, they are simply stating their belief about what the fundamental law of nature requires, they are not consenting in the sense of entering into a contract. This latter sense of "consent" is present in Locke's theory of political obligation but not in his theory of the ends of government.

If it is the law of nature that does most of the work in setting limits on the ends of government, then the crucial question becomes how Locke justifies the limited goal of comfortable preservation instead of the more ambitious goal of creating the best, most pious, or happiest citizens. Why, for example, could the fundamental law not be "Maximize the good"? Part of the reason has to do with the formal criteria that any natural law must meet, criteria that give us a reason to reject some particularly expansive notions of the public good. The first formal test was developed in the previous chapter. In Locke's theory, natural law is given its content from God's legislative point of view. Thus, when we put forward arguments about what we think natural law requires, we also do so from a legislative point of view. In particular we must ask how fallible persons will interpret and act on the principle we put forward. So if we claim an expansive understanding of the fundamental law of nature, we must also consider the way other persons would interpret and apply the principle. Although the goal of preserving mankind is not without possible ambiguity, it is considerably less open to disputed interpretation than the goal of maximizing virtue. That one principle is less contested

---

[24] Rogers M. Smith notes that there is a potential tension between understanding consent as constrained by natural law and consent as the source of political obligation. The more constrained consent is, the less work it does in justifying political obligation. See *Liberalism and American Constitutional Law* (Cambridge: Harvard University Press, 1985), pp. 42–45. It is thus important to emphasize that my purpose here is not to solve the problem of political obligation, but to examine the structure of Locke's argument for determining the legitimate ends of government. This might be a first step toward a better understanding of Locke's theory of political obligation.

than another provides only a prima facie reason for accepting it, but it is a reason nonetheless.

In this chapter we have noted an additional consideration. We should take special note of the tendency of politicization to corrupt deliberation since it is more likely to do so in some spheres than others. Again we can think of this in terms of a legislative point of view. The legislators who determine policy should imagine a super-legislator (in Locke's theory, God) who decides what sort of jurisdiction to grant them. If there is an area such as religion where politicized deliberation leads to worse results than nonpolitical deliberation, then that area is off limits to legislators. They adopt His legislative point of view when debating the extent of their own powers. These same arguments would apply to the citizens who elect legislators as well.

Understanding the Lockean arguments through the legislative metaphor is better than trying to understand them as an agreement reached by instrumentally rational individuals. The ideas of rationality and reasonableness do not as such tell us *the perspective from which* outcomes are assessed. Just as rule-utilitarianism cannot provide us with a reason to take on the legislative point of view when we could produce better consequences by not doing so, in the same way instrumental rationality by itself does not give an agent a reason to assess consequences from anything other than his own situated perspective. But reasonableness in Locke's theory means more than that. Natural law is the very epitome of reason, and it is rational in the first instance from God's perspective rather than our own. We are asked to forgo actions that are instrumentally rational from our perspective but unreasonable for God to command as an instruction to all similarly situated persons.

Locke's understanding of reasonableness and rationality is thus closely connected with his support for what I have called juridical equality. It is reasonable to recognize our fellow human beings as moral agents like ourselves who must interpret the moral principles that apply to them. We may not use force against them simply because we desire to do so. We understand there to be a common set of substantive moral principles that apply to both of us that both of us must interpret and obey. A person who ignores these principles is unreasonable from a Lockean perspective even though his action may be unimpeachable as a matter of instrumental rationality, as in the case of a person who effectively gratifies some personal desire by the unjust use of force against another. Consent, understood as what instrumentally rational persons would agree to, fails to capture this dimension of Locke's thought.

Instead we should use a different notion of consent that focuses on belief rather than interests, judgment not will. The instrumental rationality model asks what agreement would be in a person's interests. The legislative model asks, "Which articulation of the fundamental law of nature do you support?" The citizen or legislator who supports a particular interpretation can be said to consent to that interpretation. Consent here refers to the considered moral opinions of persons about what principles should define the public good. It does not presume agreement between parties about that good. Indeed, keeping with the legislative metaphor, disagreement is to be expected. The legislative picture of citizens deliberating about the fundamental law of nature under the constraints of the legislative point of view captures an important and underappreciated aspect of Locke's thought.[25]

Someone could object that by emphasizing the formal aspects of Locke's theory, the defense of toleration remains contingent. Suppose governments in general *are* better judges of religious truth than is the average citizen. If so, an individual might endorse the contested principle "Governments promote the true religion" and want all governments to apply it as best they can. Two things can be said in response. First, the Lockean argument presented in this chapter about the way politicization can affect deliberation does at least give a reason to think that governments will not be better judges in some areas even if the argument does not have the force of a geometric proof. Second, one must ask, "By what criteria do you judge the government a better judge?" In fact, the world is filled with people who disagree about whether the government is the better judge or not, and the question is how we decide between them. There is something question-begging about using results-driven criteria to decide who should judge when part of what is in dispute is what should count as a positive result.[26] All too often, persons disagree both about substantive matters and about which procedure to use in settling the question, or even about whether there should be a common decision procedure at all.

In such situations, we cannot decide the question by infinite appeals to higher and higher levels of abstraction. That it is to say, all solutions that one side could accept may invoke contested principles that the opposing side rejects. As noted in chapter 2, such situations are always possible in political life. When they occur, we have to muddle through as best we can. A Lockean theory assists us by providing principles to help us muddle. We should insist that any proposed solution respect the fact that persons have moral views not only about substantive questions, but also about the proper procedures for answering those questions. Since there are disagreements about what results should count as evidence that the

---

[25] I am indebted to Jeremy Waldron for this idea of Locke's legislature as a place of deliberation about the content of natural law. See *The Dignity of Legislation*, chap. 4.

[26] See Jeremy Waldron, "Judicial Review and the Conditions of Democracy," *Journal of Political Philosophy* 6 (1998), pp. 346–354.

government is a better judge, we should not make results-driven arguments on the assumption that our preferred standard for judging results will prevail. We should apply the Lockean criteria both to procedure and to substance. At the end of the day, even this does not guarantee agreement. It does, however, provide meaningful guidance as to how we should approach situations of this sort.

Still, it should be admitted that this portion of the argument does not provide a completely noncontingent defense of religious toleration. Any argumentative strategy will have its strengths and weaknesses. In this book I have chosen to focus on a formal argument about the principles that justify force and have stayed away from trying to settle deeper foundational questions. The advantage to proceeding in this way is that it is possible to articulate a more general moral perspective that persons who hold a variety of conflicting substantive views could employ. Practically this is an appealing strategy since it is often rather hard to argue people out of their existing foundational views, and in any case disagreement about such issues seems likely to persist. The more general argument can also apply to a wider set of problems than religious toleration. The drawback is that the general moral perspective does not determine a single specific outcome, such as an iron-clad defense of religious toleration. It constrains but does not uniquely determine our choices. It provides an argument for religious toleration, but it is an argument that does, in fact, depend on contingent facts about the world.

It is thus worth pointing out that if one was to supplement the argument for a legislative point of view with additional substantive positions that Locke also held, the defense of toleration would become more secure. The substantive Christian beliefs that Locke held and that Proast shared made the argument considerably easier. To the extent that one believes that the true religion itself commands toleration, toleration becomes a perfect duty. If sincere belief, rather than outward conformity, is the central aspect of religion, the use of force becomes less effective. If one pictures religious seeking as an individual duty rather than a collective one, then the idea of transferring responsibility for that decision to a collectivity becomes perverse.[27]

For present purposes though, the most important Christian aspects of Locke's thought are captured in his basic moral picture of the relations between persons. Lockean moral thinking does not begin by positing some good, whether monistic or plural, and then engage in practical reasoning about what set of actions is most likely to promote it. Instead, the

[27] Many Protestants believe that the search for religious truth is conducted as part of a community of believers, but that each individual has a duty to believe according to her own conscience.

most fundamental reflections are about the juridical relationship we stand in with respect to one another. Locke's fundamental moral picture is of individuals who as equals stand before a God to whom they are responsible. To this point I have focused on the political implications of this moral picture, but it has religious implications as well. The equality of status between persons places the burden of justification on those who would make themselves judge over others. But insofar as juridical equality shapes one's view of the relations between a person and God as well as between person and person, a second consequence follows. Locke believed that if we really accepted that description, that burden would be insurmountably high when persons try to make themselves judge over others in matters of religion. Locke thought that it followed from this picture of the world that the vertical relation between a person and God takes priority over the horizontal relationship between person and person. It is only with respect to goals that concern us as people that we can even presume to judge one another. Clearly, someone who envisioned a more hierarchical picture of persons and God would disagree. The point here is that before something can even be proposed as a law of nature and subjected to Locke's test, it must be consistent with a more basic picture of the juridical relationship that we stand in with respect to one another.

This religious dimension of Locke's thought is not, however, of primary importance for the current discussion. Instead, I claim that persons who do not accept Locke's theology could accept and apply an analogous version of the Lockean legislative point of view. Locke's crucial claims are that our consent (in the legislative, not contractual, sense) determines the public good, that when we consent to some conception of the public good, we offer our best interpretation of the fundamental law of nature, and that we should consider contested conceptions of the public good from a legislative point of view since they are determined by the perfect legislator, God. The analogous claims are that the public good will be defined by the consent of those who have legislative authority, that some moral perspective will frame their deliberation about which moral principles will define the scope of the public good, and that when citizens and legislators decide which of several competing principles to endorse, they try to do so from a legislative point of view. By the legislative point of view, I mean to imply three things here. First, citizens will ask whether the moral principle is consistent with the background assumptions of juridical equality, with generality, publicity, moral equality, and moral agency. Second, they will not take the necessity of a political solution as given; a decision not to act is still a collective decision. They will first step back and ask whether this is the sort of issue where politicizing deliberation leads to inferior results. Third, they will ask whether they would want other persons to interpret and act upon the conception of the public good that they put forward, realizing that others will interpret it differently. As in chapter 2, I leave open the question of whether they will understand themselves to be constructing or discovering the relevant moral principles when they take on the legislative point of view.

Since our concern is again with the formal aspects of Locke's theory of natural law, we can set to the side the question of whether his formulation "as much as possible mankind is to be preserved" is the correct one. Although we could certainly do much worse, I will not try to defend it as the best. On Locke's understanding the state could act not only to prevent one citizen from injuring another but also to prevent starvation and enemy attack. These additional considerations justified considerable government regulation in promoting things like public virtue, wealth, military strength, and optimal population size insofar as these intermediate goals served the end of making the state more secure from foreign invasion and famine.[28]

The primary question is whether the general Lockean perspective should be adopted when persons attempt to justify a particular conception of the public good. For this question, one common objection is beside the point. That objection states that Locke is misguided in trying to specify the ends of government because those ends are always subject to change and should be subject to change. No one denies as a matter of fact that the ends of government have changed and will change in the future. The line will never be set in one place never to move again. Even if everyone acknowledged a fundamental set of eternal moral principles, changing empirical circumstances would require some changes in the ends that governments pursue. All of this is perfectly consistent with asking how we should think about what ends government may pursue at any given time.

Just as we cannot proceed directly from "this is wrong" to "this may be punished," so we cannot proceed directly from "this would be good" to "the state may use force to pursue this." The underlying considerations that restricted the enforceable content of natural law were the recognition of the equality of persons as moral agents (none of us by nature has a right to command others) and a recognition that the use of force makes one person judge over another. This led to a presumption against the use of force expressed by the condition that we should only claim that a principle is an enforceable moral rule if we would want our fellow citizens to be able to interpret that rule and to act on their interpretation. The same presumption holds when considering the public good. When we move to the use of consent in political society, the same moral considerations apply. What we are giving approval to is the use of force and a body that will be judge over our fellow citizens. Lockean criteria can help regulate

---

[28] I defend this interpretive claim in appendix 2.

the positive goals we put forward as well as the negative injunctions we enforce.

In the previous chapter, we noted that a community might decide not to implement hate speech laws out of a concern for how other communities would interpret and apply the same principle. In that example the question was whether the state should attempt to punish genuine moral wrongs, bona fide cases of hate speech. It is only a short step to note that the same type of reasoning can occur when citizens or legislatures engage in debate about the appropriate ends of government. Before one adopts the position, "The government should promote virtue," one should take into account the fact that it is not necessarily one's own view of virtue that will be put into practice. One should ask whether we would want this as a subject for general deliberation and would be willing to abide by the results. Framing the question this way does not prove that the government should be completely unconcerned with virtue, but it might force us to make our formulations more specific. When we are deciding what ends the government should pursue, we cannot forget that it will be pursued as part of a common policy with our fellow citizens. When we are pressed to justify government action in some area and we do so by claiming that the government may pursue goods of type X (where the action in question is a member of X), we should ask whether we would want our fellow citizens to pursue our general understanding of the good X according to their specific interpretation.

This theoretical approach has widespread implications for contemporary political problems. When conservatives argue that the public schools should teach family values or that state law should promote sexual morality, they should do so only if their support is not contingent on their preferred conception of values and morality prevailing. The same applies to liberals who would like to use state power radically to restructure the family. Consider, in particular, debates over creationism in United States public schools. One could reasonably claim that the public good is promoted if public schools teach students the truth about human origins. Evolutionists and creationists would both accept that claim, but of course they have very different views about what the truth actually is. We have, therefore, contested interpretations of the public good.

Suppose creationists are attempting to introduce creationist textbooks into a local school system. A creationist who adopted the Lockean legislative point of view would have to ask whether she would want each school district to teach its own view of human origins, realizing that this means that in many school systems elsewhere evolutionists will teach their view. This *might* cause the creationist to believe that skipping the subject altogether would better promote the public good. It *might* cause an evolutionist to come to the same conclusion. Whether it would actually do so would depend on the balance of arguments considered from a legislative point of view. On the other hand, a peaceful version of the "appeal to heaven" is also possible where both affirm the principle, fully aware of the future conflicts it will create. Moreover, both sides would have to give reasons why, from a legislative point of view, allowing each school district to decide is more conducive to the public good than an alternate institutional arrangement with a state or national standard. Even if one recommended allowing a team of experts to set a national curriculum, that team would have to be accountable to some governmental body, and we should evaluate the proposal from a legislative point of view. In this case that would mean considering the possibility that our opponents might be appointed to the board. Chapter 6 will argue that when disputes arise about the allocation of power between different government institutions or levels of government, the disputes should be resolved from the standpoint of a hypothetical constitutional framer. In this case one would ask what level of government one would allocate this authority if one were a constitutional framer.

The important point is that one may not simply appeal to the fact that one's view is the local majority and one thinks the local majority is right. The Lockean view asks us to respect the right of others to act as rational decision makers even when we do not think that they are using their reason particularly well. At least in a democracy, being smarter (or thinking you are) does not give you the right to force others to obey your will. Speaking of magistrates whose religious beliefs were errant, Locke wrote, "I do not say they judge as right, but that they are by as much right judges" (*Works*, 6:221). The argument that Locke applied to heads of state applies by analogy to citizens in a democracy. Each has a right to act as a deciding agent even if all are not equally good at doing so. The Lockean legislative point of view would not eliminate the conflict between creationists and evolutionists, but it would ask them to think in terms of a general solution and to treat their opponents as persons whose beliefs make a moral claim. It would ask them to take human fallibility into account when adopting a conception of the public good. This case illustrates the fact that people may believe that a principle should be adopted even though it is contested. There are many problems where individuals will realize that *any* solution will require state action and that choosing between contested principles is the only viable option. The hope is that when citizens, policy makers, politicians, and judges deliberate about the content of the public good, they will do so from a legislative point of view that recognizes their fellow citizens as equal moral agents.

In political deliberation, there are questions of jurisdiction that are prior to questions of the good. The belief in the equality and agency of persons implies that we should consider the fact of disagreement between persons when formulating the ends of government. We should not propose a goal as an end of government on the assumption that our favored interpretation of that goal will carry the day. Liberalism need not be based on a skepticism about the good; it rather implies that our recognition of agency and equality restricts the pursuit of the good when the means that we will employ is force. The Lockean legislative point of view can thus both guide choices about direct appeals to right and guide individuals as they give their consent to particular conceptions of the public good. This legislative point of view provides a distinctive way of addressing the problem of disagreement from within a liberal perspective. In the next chapter, I illustrate this by comparing the Lockean position to two very different liberal theories, the neutralist contractualism of John Rawls and the liberal perfectionism of Joseph Raz.

CHAPTER 4

Beyond Neutrality and Perfectionism

Two Liberal Approaches

As we saw in chapter 2, Martin Luther King, Jr.'s, civil disobedience was justifiable from a legislative point of view. His principle was that persons should disobey (openly, lovingly, and with a willingness to accept punishment) those laws that are unjust. This was a principle he advocated knowing full well that persons with deficient conceptions of justice would sometimes apply it. The requirement that we accept the punishment for breaking the law was a way to temper the anarchy that might result if fallible people were at complete liberty to disobey all laws that they thought unjust. King's case is particularly interesting because he justified his views about which laws were just and unjust by appeal to a moral position that was not held by all at the time and is rejected by most contemporary political theorists. His case raises the question of what counts as an adequate political justification, of whether one may simply appeal to a principle because one believes it to be true or whether one must also believe that others will accept the principle.

King appealed to a theistic natural law theory to justify his actions. He defined a just law as "a man-made code that squares with the moral law or the law of God."[1] The sources he quoted were theologians: Augustine, Aquinas, Buber, and Tillich. Following Buber, he claimed that the pattern of racial discrimination indicates that whites in their relationship with blacks have substituted an "I-it" relationship for an "I-thou" relationship.[2] King's opponents treated blacks as objects rather than as persons who are equal moral agents. Because Locke's original argument also used a theistic natural law theory, a synthesis of the two is fairly easy. But insofar as King makes a religious appeal, he seems to be making an appeal on grounds that persons from some other religious (or irreligious) traditions cannot accept.

---

[1] King, Jr., "Letter From the Birmingham City Jail," p. 529.

[2] The named audience for King's letter was other clergymen, but as a public letter published in newspapers it was clearly aimed at the larger public as well. In any case, King frequently used religious arguments in public settings.

King's approach stands in sharp contrast to that of John Rawls in *Political Liberalism*. He and other proponents of political liberalism claim that persons should be able to justify political actions on the basis of freestanding political principles that all reasonable persons could accept rather than on the basis of a particular comprehensive view, such as utilitarianism or Christianity, that it is not reasonable to expect all persons to endorse. It is not the fact that King used a religious argument that is the problem, for if he had appealed to utilitarianism the objection would be the same. The problem is that he takes a particular position on the grounding of ultimate morality and claims a right to act politically on the basis of that principle because it is true. Rawls and others believe that reasonable people can disagree about such matters and that people should not be coerced on the basis of principles with which they reasonably disagree.

There are two very different understandings of political justification at work here. Following Thomas Nagel, we can think of these two liberal approaches to the problem of disagreement as "convergence" and "common standpoint."[3] Convergence theories justify political power by showing that a given use of power is acceptable from the perspectives of the different parties involved, whatever those perspectives happen to be. Nagel holds up Hobbes as the paradigm convergence theorist since he claims that obedience to the sovereign promotes the interests of persons, taking the interests of persons as they are. Hobbesian subjects owe obedience because it makes sense from their own perspective, not because it makes sense from some impartial perspective. At the other extreme are persons who make use of a common standpoint that all persons *ought* to use in settling political disputes. According to this account, if all persons employed the correct standpoint in the right way, they would all agree. In practice this unanimity will not exist, but a person has done his moral duty if he has taken on the common standpoint to the best of his abilities. Nagel holds up utilitarianism as a paradigm example of this second approach since it calls on each person to view choices from the perspective of someone trying to maximize the total amount of happiness and minimize unhappiness. Some versions of perfectionism would also fall in this category insofar as they insist that we may judge human flourishing from a single correct standpoint and that we may formulate laws on the basis of that understanding.

The pure convergence approach is not a particularly promising one for liberal theory, and the fact that Hobbes's theory is the best illustration of that approach should tell us why. Although Hobbes played a very important role in the development of liberal thought, he was not a liberal.

---

[3] "Moral Conflict and Political Legitimacy," *Philosophy and Public Affairs* 16 (1987), pp. 218–221.

Brian Barry, making a distinction similar to Nagel's, has characterized Hobbesian justice as "justice as mutual advantage."[4] The problem with this approach, as Barry points out, is that there are no antecedent standards of morality or fairness that define what is a legitimate goal or a legitimate use of power. This way of thinking about justice quickly devolves into the following, rather unsavory, principle: "to each according to his threat advantage."[5] When a robber and victim negotiate as to how much money the latter should give the former, the fact that the former has gained a bargaining advantage by threatening the latter with harm is normally thought of as a morally relevant fact. But on the pure convergence approach, their "agreement" would still be binding so long as both agreed that "your money for your life" was a mutually beneficial arrangement.

The pure common standpoint approach is more promising, but not without difficulties. Many of the objections to utilitarianism are to its specific content rather than to the claim that there is a standpoint from which we can make and enforce valid moral claims on others. Nonetheless, liberal theorists have increasingly explored options that take as their starting point the aspiration toward principles that can be endorsed by persons who do not share a common moral perspective. The problem with the pure common standpoint approach, according to this critique, is that it fails to satisfy the moral demands of *political* theory. An adequate political theory must give moral weight to the fact of disagreement; it cannot simply be a matter of an individual deciding what she thinks is right and acting from her own perspective since a political theory must be applicable to people who do not share the same moral perspective.

Nagel points out that many theories are mixtures of the two approaches and cites Rawls as an example.[6] Although it is true that many are mixed, one aspiration or the other will be dominant, and which is dominant will affect the conclusions to which the theory points. A convergence theory that incorporates common standpoint elements will use antecedent moral principles to constrain agreement. A common standpoint theory that incorporates convergence elements will give weight to the fact of disagreement and the diversity of views that people actually hold. Depending on which moral aspiration is given higher priority, there will be a corresponding tendency to view neutrality favorably or unfavorably. Of particular interest in this chapter are the views that the state should not favor a particular conception of the good life and that it should not endorse a

---

[4] Brian Barry, *Justice as Impartiality* vol. 2 of *A Treatise on Social Justice* (Oxford: Clarendon Press, 1995), pp. 31–46.

[5] Rawls, *A Theory of Justice*, p. 141.

[6] Nagel, *Moral Conflict*, pp. 219–220.

particular comprehensive moral or religious doctrine. I will refer to these positions as "liberal neutrality" and "political liberalism," respectively. The two positions are closely related, and many thinkers, such as Rawls, endorse both. By "perfectionists" I mean those who reject the doctrine of liberal neutrality and believe that the state can favor particular ways of life because they contribute to human flourishing or well-being. By taking this position they also commit themselves to the view that the state may base its policies on controversial views of the good.

Theories that emphasize convergence prioritize the perspective of those persons *affected* by an action and ask whether they could accept the principle that justifies the action from their own perspective. If one assumes persistent disagreement about the good, convergence theories will often see neutrality as the only solution all could accept. Theories that emphasize a common standpoint will prioritize the perspective of the person *deciding* which action to perform and will concentrate on correctly specifying the moral considerations that should guide her choice. If the fundamental problem is framed in terms of "what should I do" rather than "what could others accept," neutrality becomes a less helpful solution.

In this chapter, I compare the Lockean legislative point of view, developed in the previous chapters, with two distinct strands of contemporary thought: liberal neutrality and liberal perfectionism, taking Rawls as a spokesman for the former and Joseph Raz as a spokesman for the latter.[7] I argue that Rawls is typical of mixed theories that give great weight to the ideal of convergence while Raz is more typical of those theories that give great weight to a common standpoint. The Lockean legislative point of view is a common standpoint approach that is nonetheless able to give moral weight to the fact of disagreement. Locke wrote before people thought in terms of a dichotomy between convergence and common standpoint theories. He wrote before people thought in terms of a dichotomy between neutralist and perfectionist thought. It is partly for this reason that his thought is of continuing importance today. In the concluding section I argue that this approach gives us a way to account for moral disagreement by moving beyond the current neutralist-perfectionist debate.

Rawls and Reasonable Agreement

The most influential example of a mixed theory that gives priority to convergence is found in the political philosophy of Rawls. His ideas are complex, and the summaries below will not do full justice to them. Al-

---

[7] I will focus on Rawls's theory as presented in *A Theory of Justice* and *Political Liberalism* and Raz's as presented in *The Morality of Freedom* (Oxford: Clarendon Press, 1986).

though our main interest is in his expression of liberal neutrality in *Political Liberalism*, the underlying tension was already present in *A Theory of Justice*, and it will be helpful to begin there. In the earlier work, Rawls appeals to a doctrine of hypothetical consent. He famously argues that we should imagine persons in an "original position" where they will decide what principles of justice will serve as the basis of political justification in their community. Each person is behind a "veil of ignorance" that prevents that person from knowing such facts as his wealth, talent, family situation, race, and conception of the good. Each desires to have as much as possible of certain primary goods, such as wealth, but is aware that whatever decision is reached must be reached unanimously. From this Rawls extracts his two favored principles of justice, which can then serve as the standard against which the basic structure of a society may be judged.[8]

In this view, one does not justify principles by saying that persons have in fact consented to them, but rather by saying that they would agree to them under certain hypothetical conditions. Hypothetical consent theories can emphasize either approach to political justification depending on how the original choice situation is described. The choice situation may be defined in such a way that all persons must reach an agreement, or it may be defined in such a way that the range of possible agreements is merely narrowed. The distinction in the previous chapter is relevant here. Theories that understand consent contractually will generally, and almost by definition, emphasize the aspiration toward agreement, whereas those that understand consent legislatively will not. Since legislative approaches do not expect agreement, they need not be constructed in such a way that agreement is guaranteed. Rawls's approach is of the contractual sort.

To see this, let us look more closely at the way Rawls uses the "veil of ignorance" to constrain the choice of political principles. Part of what makes Rawls's argument in *Theory* attractive is that it filters out sources of power that cannot be justified on grounds of fairness alone. Might does not make right, and most of the information that the veil of ignorance excludes has the effect of making it impossible for those with superior might to bias the rules in favor of those with their characteristics. Rawls asks persons to choose principles of justice behind a veil of ignorance that prevents them from knowing facts such as their strength, their race, their intelligence, and their wealth. It also prevents persons from knowing how many others have the same characteristics as themselves, hence persons cannot know whether they will be in the majority or minority.[9] The best

---

[8] Rawls, *A Theory of Justice*, pp. 11–22, 54–64, and 118–160.
[9] Ibid., pp. 136–142.

justification for these restrictions is precisely the fact that they model the intuition "might does not make right" and they prevent persons from using their superior strength to threaten others into an unfair bargain. Rawls supplements this with a second intuition about justice, which is that persons have no right to advantage based on characteristics they have from the "natural lottery." That one is born rich or talented is, from a moral point of view, arbitrary. As Rawls puts it, "Somehow we must nullify the effects of specific contingencies which put men at odds and tempt them to exploit social and natural circumstances to their own advantage."[10]

But as Rawls develops his argument, it becomes clear that another consideration is at work. Why is it that Rawls prevents people from knowing their conception of the good in the original position? We might think that it is so that the majority cannot gain an unfair advantage by choosing principles of justice that favor its conception of the good since one might think that whether one's conception of the good is also held by the majority is also a matter of luck. But this is not a sufficient argument. We could accomplish *that* goal simply by preventing people from knowing whether those who agreed with them about the good were in the majority or the minority. For example, a Christian would have to decide whether to adopt a policy of religious toleration without knowing whether the majority would be Christian and, even if they were, what variety of Christian. Unlike the principle "Might does not make right," the claim "The good is irrelevant to justice" does not claim overwhelming support from our antecedent moral intuitions about justice.[11] The reason for the exclusion stems from a much more controversial claim about the nature of justice. It is here that Rawls's aspiration toward principles that all could accept takes center stage. A few pages later Rawls indicates that the theory must be constructed so that there is a determinate solution. Why must there be a determinate solution? My sense is that it is because if there is not we will be unable to justify force by saying "you would consent to this under fair choice conditions." By omitting all knowledge that distinguishes one person from another, one is able to insure unanimity, a result Rawls terms "of great importance."[12] The constraints are added not only to exclude information that is unfair, but also to insure agreement at least under ideal conditions. It is only because Rawls places so much emphasis on agreement as a constituent part of justice that the

---

[10] Ibid., p. 136.

[11] Waldron, for example, considers the possibility that each theory of the good is paired with a particular theory of justice, in *Law and Disagreement*, pp. 162–163.

[12] Rawls, *A Theory of Justice*, pp. 139–142.

original position must have a determinate solution rather than simply functioning as a constraint on disagreement.

The moral aspiration toward agreement is even more pronounced in *Political Liberalism*. In this more recent work Rawls explores the question of how fair cooperation is possible between persons who disagree about fundamental religious and philosophical matters. He claims that liberal democracies are characterized by three facts that have important implications for democratic theory. He first claims that "the diversity of reasonable comprehensive religious, philosophical, and moral doctrines found in modern democratic societies is not a mere historical condition that may soon pass away; it is a permanent feature of the public culture of democracy." Second, he argues that "a continuing shared understanding on one comprehensive religious, philosophical, or moral doctrine can be maintained only by the oppressive use of state power." Third, and finally, he claims that "an enduring and secure democratic regime, one not divided into contending doctrinal confessions and hostile social classes, must be willingly and freely supported by at least a substantial majority of its politically active citizens."[13] From these claims he derives the conclusion that there must be a political conception, consistent with liberal democracy, that can be endorsed by a variety of comprehensive doctrines. This does not involve the claim that all doctrines are equal and that debate about the strongest grounds is irrelevant. It is merely the claim that people will often be able to endorse a common set of political principles despite the fact that they disagree over the proper grounds for those principles.

The Rawlsian approach could be described as "nonfoundationalist" in that it does not rely upon a particular foundational approach, such as utilitarianism, Kantianism, or Christianity, but rather might be endorsed by some versions of each of these. A Rawlsian theory of justice therefore becomes a *political* theory in the strict sense; it prescribes political norms but remains completely agnostic on metaphysics. It does not take a stand one way or the other on the existence of God, the truth of moral realism, or the validity of scientific naturalism, and it can be endorsed, potentially, by people who disagree with each other on these divisive questions. An overlapping consensus can develop, to use Rawlsian terminology, around political principles despite the fact of moral disagreement. These freestanding political principles should be acceptable to all reasonable persons and can therefore serve as a basis for political justification.

[13] Rawls, *Political Liberalism*, pp. 36–38.

By "reasonable persons" Rawls means persons who "are ready to propose principles and standards as fair terms of cooperation and to abide by them willingly, given the assurance that others will likewise do so." They seek to "cooperate with others on terms all can accept." Furthermore, reasonable people recognize what Rawls calls the "burdens of judgement." Rawls lists a variety of reasons for the claim stated earlier that disagreement over moral questions is endemic and that there will always be a plurality of reasonable comprehensive doctrines. For example, the evidence may be complex and conflicting, we may disagree about the relative weight that should be assigned different considerations, people's evaluations may be shaped by their past experiences, and so on. A reasonable person, according to Rawls, acknowledges this fact of reasonable disagreement. "[R]easonable persons will think it unreasonable to use political power, should they possess it, to repress comprehensive views that are not unreasonable, though different from their own."[14]

The claim that Rawls's main aspiration in *Political Liberalism* is one of convergence is liable to be misunderstood since it is sometimes thought that his doctrine of "overlapping consensus" is a convergence theory. On the contrary, the theory of overlapping consensus does not make people's actual beliefs about justice the starting point or make the validity of principles of justice dependent on their being accepted by other persons.[15] He does not claim that a theory is correct only if an actual consensus forms around it. He is not simply taking people's moral beliefs as given and creating a least common denominator morality. The question of an overlapping consensus is raised only after persons have adopted principles of justice and must determine whether such principles could, over time, generate moral support from reasonable persons. If his was a pure convergence theory, he could not ask people to set aside their comprehensive doctrines for political purposes. The doctrine of overlapping consensus does not make the content of morality depend entirely on what people actually agree to. There is a particular moral perspective that people are asked to take on when considering basic political questions, but it is not a perspective grounded in a particular comprehensive conception. Although the theory of overlapping consensus is a partial manifestation of the aspiration for convergence, it is not the source.

Rather, Rawls gives priority to convergence in the *content* of his moral perspective. In *Political Liberalism*, Rawls is more explicit about the social role he expects principles of justice to play. Principles of justice must be able to justify force to the other, from the other person's

---

[14] Ibid., 49–50, 54, 56–57, 60.

[15] See ibid., pp. 140–143, and Selina Chen, "Liberal Toleration in the Thought of John Locke and John Rawls," Ph. D. diss., Oxford University, 1996, chap. 4.

perspective, provided it is a reasonable perspective.[16] It is this aspect of his theory, rather than his theory of overlapping consensus, that reveals his true commitment to convergence. The moral perspective he advocates turns the idea of reasonable convergence into a moral aspiration. Throughout *Political Liberalism* he directs us to adopt principles that all (reasonable) persons can accept. A striking feature of much contemporary liberal thought is its emphasis on variations on the claim that we strive for principles that others cannot reasonably reject.[17] If this is our aspiration, and if we believe that people reasonably disagree about religion and philosophy, it is not hard to see how Rawls ends up with his theory of public reason. If there is moral disagreement about comprehensive conceptions of the good and our goal is a theory that all could accept, then neutrality with respect to the good quickly emerges as the only solution we could propose that we could reasonably expect other people who share our moral motivation for principles acceptable to all to endorse.[18]

It is true that political liberalism remains agnostic on persons' reasons for endorsing the political principles. There is nothing to *stop* someone from endorsing Rawls's principles because he believes they correspond to moral principles that hold regardless of what agreement persons would reach. Although Rawls prefers to think of moral principles as the outcome of construction, he does not prevent persons from thinking that the process of construction is a heuristic device that helps us discover principles that would hold regardless of what *we* accept. Although Rawls presents his theory so that these options are not ruled out, it is clear that what actually drives the project of political liberalism is the desire for principles that all reasonable people could accept. He makes it clear that as a political theory, *Political Liberalism* is constructed based on practical reasoning about the question: what are fair terms of cooperation that all could accept as free and equal citizens?[19] Although we may regard the principles that emerge as right because they correspond to an antecedent moral theory, this is something of a happy coincidence. The real question turns on how we distinguish fair terms of cooperation. Is fairness defined only in terms of moral intuitions that exist independently of the aspiration toward agreement, or is that aspiration a fundamental part of what justice requires?

---

[16] Rawls, *Political Liberalism*, pp. 35–39, 60–61.

[17] See, for example, Barry, *Justice as Impartiality;* Gerald F. Gauss, *Justificatory Liberalism* (Oxford: Oxford University Press, 1996); and Thomas M. Scanlon, "Contractualism and Utilitarianism," in *Utilitarianism and Beyond*, ed. Amartya Sen and Bernard Williams (Cambridge: Cambridge University Press, 1982), pp. 103–128.

[18] *Political Liberalism*, pp. 192–194.

[19] Ibid., p. 3.

Because Rawls's position has this aspiration, it is not a coincidence that the first edition of *Political Liberalism* contained a moral (but not legal) ban on appeals to comprehensive conceptions of the good. The implication was that it was improper for people like Martin Luther King, Jr., to appeal to religious premises in public debate. Since then Rawls has tried to reformulate his theory in such a way that it does not prevent people who believe in a comprehensive moral doctrine like King's from endorsing political liberalism. There is no difficulty in explaining why Rawls thinks that civil disobedience was justified in King's case. Rawls would claim that the system of racial oppression King fought against violated the principles of justice that Rawls describes in *A Theory of Justice*. The system did not provide fair equality of opportunity for blacks and certainly did not permit only those inequalities that make the worst off group better off.[20] Not only is such a system unjust according to Rawls's preferred theory of justice, he could also claim that it is not even reasonable since it does not propose fair terms of cooperation for both whites and blacks. Because Rawls believes there are adequate public reasons to defend King's action, the only real problem is with the method of public justification that King employed. Here Rawls has made a concession that he believes solves the problem. Persons may make appeals to comprehensive doctrines, as King did, provided that in due course they are willing and able to provide public reasons that do not depend on a particular comprehensive doctrine.[21] Since in King's case such public reasons could have been offered, his actions were justified.

Rawls realizes that there are far too many people who, like King, believe in a comprehensive (and often religious) moral perspective for a theory that excludes such people to be viable. His goal is thus to formulate a political theory that both secular and religious persons can endorse. In his introduction to the paperback edition of *Political Liberalism*, Rawls claims that the central question of the book is most sharply put as follows: "How is it possible for those affirming a religious doctrine that is based on religious authority, for example, the Church or the Bible, also to hold a reasonable political conception that supports a just democratic regime?"[22]

Rawls's attempt to include people like King in his overlapping consensus either fails or is incomplete. First, there is a difference between convergence in the act and convergence in principle. It may well be the case that, in the specific instance considered here, King's theory of natural law pronounces unjust political practices that Rawls would describe as

---

[20] Rawls, *A Theory of Justice*, pp. 60–65, 371–377.
[21] Rawls, "Introduction to the Paperback Edition," *Political Liberalism*, p. lii.
[22] Ibid., p. xxxix.

unreasonable. But we would hardly expect this always to be the case. Although it is impossible to say exactly how King would respond to Rawls's theory, a literal reading of King's remarks suggests that he takes the just, not the reasonable, to be the relevant standard. Rawls makes it clear that the two terms are not interchangeable; if they were, it would defeat the entire project of political liberalism.

Second, any theory that wins the support of, to use Rawls's example, Catholics and Protestants must come to terms not only with the fact that their moral views are shaped by revelation, but also with the fact that many of them affirm the natural law tradition that King (and Locke) affirmed. They claim that there are universal moral principles that ought to be recognized by all people and that those who fail to recognize them are unreasonable. Although a natural law theory may provide spaces in which agreement and convergence carry moral weight, in the final instance such theories owe their greatest allegiance to a common standpoint. They believe that the reasons that ground natural law are accessible to all and sufficient to justify state action. Rawls would have to describe natural law theorists as unreasonable since they claim that there is a single moral framework that all persons can reasonably be expected to endorse. For present purposes, we can set to the side the viability of natural law theory from a philosophical standpoint and merely note that there are enough people who hold views with roughly this structure (with widely varying degrees of sophistication and under various titles) that the exclusion of them would threaten the possibility of a widespread overlapping consensus. In other words, there will always be potential conflict between Rawls's requirement of public reason and the belief that there is a common standpoint, be it natural law or utilitarianism, which others are unreasonable to reject. Although in some cases the two positions may come to the same conclusions, there is no reason to believe this will always be so. Rawls's theory is thus a mixed theory that gives higher priority to the ideal of convergence. Rawls's theory must thus be either further supplemented or further amended to accommodate people like King who appeal directly to moral truths.

In the Lockean theory I am defending, the priorities are reversed. To avoid misunderstanding I need to emphasize again that we are at present considering only one aspect of Locke's thought. As discussed in chapter 3, Locke was as contractualist as they come with respect to the problem of political obligation. His theory of natural law placed moral constraints on contractual consent but still required actual agreement before a person became a member of a particular political society. That aspect of his thought is not our concern here because with respect to political justification his theory of natural law is more fundamental than his theory of consent. To review briefly, Locke justified political power in two primary ways, by appeal to natural law and by appeal to consent. But as I argued in chapter 3 (and appendix 2), the former is logically prior to the latter. We cannot consent to those things that are outlawed by natural law. A promise to commit murder is not binding. Moreover, it is the theory of natural law that justifies the doctrine of consent itself. Locke believed that specific persons could only take on the obligations of a citizen by their own consent because he believed that by nature persons were free, equal, and independent. The moral claim that promises are binding is part of his theory of natural law and does not depend for its validity on whether people agree to it. Natural law provides a framework in which actual consent settles important problems such as political obligation and, as we will see in the next chapter, the institutional form of the legislative power. Natural law grounds the obligation to keep promises on which contract theory rests. Natural law grounds and defines the space in which consent legitimates political power.

The most important way in which Locke reverses the priorities is seen in the way he handles situations where there is deep disagreement. Natural law provides a sufficient justification for the use of force while consent does not. As mentioned above, any contractual agreement is void if inconsistent with natural law. On the other hand, Locke's doctrines of the executive power in the state of nature and the appeal to heaven in civil society allow individuals to use force directly on the basis of their assessment of natural law, irrespective of consent (*Treatises*, 2.6–13, 20–21, 91, 240–241). If two people or groups find themselves at odds over what each considers a matter of fundamental justice, each is entitled to appeal to and act on its own conception of justice even if the other side rejects that conception.

With respect to this aspect of his theory, Locke's understanding of political justification is therefore different from Rawls's. It gives appeal to a common standpoint (natural law) priority over appeal to a shared agreement. The different emphases in their theories lead Locke and Rawls to different justifications for toleration. Locke's theory takes the perspective of the actor and applies the principle of reciprocity to others acting in a similar capacity. Since an actor's substantive views about what justice requires should guide his conduct, Locke tried to show how a correct understanding of those substantive views is consistent with toleration. Locke argued that natural law, correctly understood, does not command religious persecution. Such an interpretation of natural law is unreasonable. The justification of toleration from the potential persecutor's point of view is a persistent feature of Locke's theory. Others have noted that Locke's most famous argument for toleration, his claim that true belief cannot be forced, justifies toleration based on what is rational for the persecutor, not what is fair to the persecuted.[23] Locke has been criticized in this respect, but these criticisms have failed to distinguish two questions. One is whether a theory of toleration that focuses on the acting agent's perspective is, by this fact alone, morally suspect. The second is whether a theory that looks only at instrumental rationality from the perspective of the agent is morally suspect. The latter is, admittedly, incomplete at best. But the Lockean argument under consideration here is very different from the instrumental argument that true belief cannot be forced, although it shares an emphasis on the acting agent's point of view. The Lockean argument here assumes not only instrumental rationality, but also moral beliefs about generality, publicity, equality, and moral agency. It emphasizes the acting agent's point of view in that, at the end of the day, one acts on one's own assessment of what natural law requires, whether others agree or not. The content of that theory, however, is determined by the agent's judgment about what is required by a legislative point of view.

Rawls justifies toleration very differently. Consider the following argument:

> For example—I cite an easy case—if we argue that the religious liberty of some citizens is to be denied, we must give them reasons they can not only understand—as Servetus could understand why Calvin wanted to burn him at the stake—but reasons we might reasonably expect that they, as free and equal citizens, might reasonably also accept. The criterion of reciprocity is normally violated whenever basic liberties are denied. For what reasons can both satisfy the criterion of reciprocity and justify denying to some persons religious liberty, holding others as slaves, imposing a property qualification on the right to vote, or denying the right of suffrage to women? . . . Those who believe that fundamental political questions should be decided by what they regard as the best reasons according to their own idea of the whole truth—including their religious or secular comprehensive doctrine—and not by reasons that might be shared by all citizens as free and equal, will of course reject the idea of public reason.[24]

Rawls argues that the principle "promote the true religion" fails to respect reciprocity because the person affected could reject it, from his (reasonable) perspective.

---

[23] See Waldron, "Locke, Toleration, and Persecution," pp. 113–114, and (more sympathetic to Locke) Mendus, *Toleration and the Limits of Liberalism*, chap. 2.

[24] "The Idea of Public Reason Revisited," *University of Chicago Law Review* 64 (Summer 1997), p. 771.

Actually, what we have here are two competing accounts of reciprocity. Both positions see a need for public justification, for moral principles that take others seriously as moral agents, and for principles that express a moral point of view by being public and general. But there are different ways of expressing the reciprocity that is necessary for public justification. Reciprocity at its simplest requires treating others as we would be treated, but there are different perspectives from which we can employ this insight. The Lockean perspective is legislative; the Rawlsian is contractual. The Lockean perspective respects reciprocity by asking whether we would allow others, as free and equal citizens, to interpret and act on the principle that we act on as well. The image is of a legislative assembly where there will be disagreement, but where each person supports her best interpretation of the principle in question. The Rawlsian approach respects reciprocity by asking whether others could *accept*, as free and equal, the principle we propose.[25]

This difference in conceptions of reciprocity corresponds to differences in the way the two approaches treat appeals to comprehensive conceptions. For Locke, comprehensive conceptions are fundamental, and thus one does not ask persons to bracket them for political purposes. Instead, one takes premises that are already in the other person's comprehensive view and tries to draw different conclusions from them. Alternatively, one can attempt to persuade them to adopt the necessary background assumptions. That possibility notwithstanding, Locke's position will only appeal to those persons whose comprehensive conceptions include juridical equality and who therefore have a reason to act from the legislative point of view based on their own comprehensive doctrine. Given the potential for disagreement between persons who do and do not share this perspective, the state of nature remains a possibility, and likewise the direct appeal to foundational moral principles. Each person has a responsibility to judge and act on what she believes are true moral principles by way of a legislative point of view. Locke's perspective asks people to incorporate a respect for others as disagreeing moral agents into those beliefs about true moral principles. Locke expects disagreement about natural law, and the legislature is the place where this is worked out.[26] In this respect the Lockean position joins contemporary critiques of Rawls. From different perspectives, Waldron and Sandel have criticized Rawls on the grounds that we should not expect any less disagreement

---

[25] See the discussion of legislative and contractual consent in chapter 3.

[26] See Waldron, *The Dignity of Legislation*, chap. 4. Key texts for Waldron's position include *Treatises*, 2.87–89, 123, 136.

about rights than about the good life.[27] The Lockean position assumes disagreement about both.

For Rawls, because there is no foreseeable time when we will all accept the same comprehensive conceptions, we bracket them as much as possible. At the end of the day he will allow us to appeal to such principles against those who insist on being unreasonable. If someone claims that everyone should adopt a particular comprehensive doctrine, Rawlsians can make use of their own substantive views to try to refute the claim.[28] For Rawls this kind of an exchange is evidence that something has already gone wrong. In the Lockean view, substantive debates about morals are what we expect. The legislative point of view does not, by itself, have a determinate solution.

I think it is clear, then, that Locke and Rawls relate to the problem of disagreement in different ways. Each gives greater emphasis to a different aspect of the liberal tradition, and there is in fact a tension between the two aspects. The differences between them, and the fact that the Lockean argument under consideration is derived from his writings on religious toleration, is interesting given the fact that Rawls, in *Political Liberalism*, invokes the earlier idea of toleration as a model for a new and broader philosophical toleration.[29] He claims that just as in past times persons agreed to bracket some of their religious beliefs in the public sphere, so also we should now bracket all of our comprehensive doctrines. While religious toleration began as a modus vivendi, with people accepting it as a second best alternative to religious hegemony, people gradually came to support religious toleration as a matter of principle.[30] Rawls hopes that a similar pattern will emerge for comprehensive beliefs generally. Although there are no doubt some arguments for religious toleration that might make for a credible analogy, Locke's argument for a legislative point of view is not one of them because of its very different justificatory structure.

Although there is a tension between Locke and Rawls at the justificatory level, it is still possible to combine parts of their theories. For that reason there are two different ways the Lockean position I describe could relate to political liberalism. If one takes the Rawlsian position to be correct, if principles of justice must be those that all can reasonably be expected to endorse and there is no comprehensive doctrine that meets this requirement, then the Lockean argument functions as a supplement to the

---

[27] Waldron, *Law and Disagreement*, pp. 151–163, and Michael J. Sandel, "Book Review: Political Liberalism," *Harvard Law Review* 107 (1994), pp. 1782–1789.

[28] *Political Liberalism*, p. 152.

[29] Ibid., pp. 9–10, 154.

[30] Ibid., 159–160.

Rawlsian theory, helping to fill in an important gap. On this view, we should put forward principles as justifications for force only if they meet two conditions: we believe that all reasonable persons could accept them, *and* we would be willing to let other reasonable persons interpret and act on them. The second condition would prevent persons from evading the requirements of public reason by adopting vague principles that are supported by public reasons and then making use of their own contested comprehensive viewpoint in the application of those vague principles to specific cases. The reason that the Lockean position can function as a supplement is that Rawlsians accept the basic assumptions on which the theory rests: moral agency, equality, generality, and publicity. The main difference has to do with the perspective from which the idea of reciprocity is employed. Since Rawls takes political principles as things that are constructed, it is quite natural to claim that the principle should be reasonable from the perspective of the one doing the constructing, that is, from a legislative point of view. We should construct principles that will not be self-defeating when persons who hold various comprehensive doctrines interpret and act on them.

On the other hand, the Lockean legislative point of view can play an even more important role for persons who reject Rawls's doctrine of public reason, particularly those who believe that there is a single moral framework that all persons ought to accept. Even Rawlsians who do not believe this can make use of the Lockean argument when debating persons who do believe it. If the substantive doctrine endorses all of the basic moral intuitions, then one can claim that persons should adopt the Lockean legislative point of view. Although this will not ensure that persons are ruled only by principles that they accept, it will still cause people to be much more cautious about imposing their contested beliefs on others. It still forces persons to respect other persons as moral agents under a common moral framework. It still gives a reason for toleration. And it does all of this without asking people like Martin Luther King, Jr., to forgo direct appeals to controversial foundational beliefs about justice and the good.

Another advantage to the Lockean approach, taken as an alternative, is that it does not require us to make difficult judgments about what terms someone else could reasonably reject from his or her own perspective. Gerald Gauss has argued that there is no way to avoid difficult and controversial debates about epistemology, debates about what counts as justified belief, if the idea of "reasonable rejection" is to be practicable.[31] As a matter of application it is easier to know how others would be likely to

---

[31] This is the main thesis of *Justificatory Liberalism*. Although Gauss is sympathetic to the aspiration toward principles that all accept, he demonstrates the complexity of actually determining what counts as justified belief and reasonably rejected belief.

apply a principle than to determine whether people have, within their own belief system, adequate grounds for belief. It is easier to know what someone thinks about something than it is to prove that a belief is unreasonable, given the person's other beliefs.

If we take this second approach, we undercut one of the main reasons for thinking liberalism requires neutrality. Both restrictions on appeals to a comprehensive conception and the goal of political principles that are neutral with respect to foundations often rest on the aspiration toward moral principles that all accept. If the relevant moral question is "on what principle would I want others to interpret and act," there is nothing privileged about neutrality. One might come to the conclusion that on a certain issue a principle of neutrality is the principle on which we would want others to act. One might, for example, think that because so many people have mistaken ideas about religion, one would rather have all states adopt a policy of separation of church and state. But if one adopts a policy of neutrality in a particular sphere, it is because the balance of arguments in that sphere happen to favor it, not because there is an antecedent commitment to neutrality. In any case the reasons for advocating neutrality will themselves presuppose a controversial moral framework.

But this seems to imply the following rather counterintuitive conclusion: Locke, the theorist of toleration who claimed that the state should not act for religious ends, rejects neutrality and is therefore a perfectionist. This claim is misleading because it imposes an anachronistic distinction on Locke's thought, namely, that anyone who rejects neutrality is a perfectionist. Locke, as a natural law theorist, could not be an advocate of neutrality in the sense that Rawls is precisely because Locke allows persons to appeal directly to moral principles that are defined independently of the principle of fair agreement. While one may no doubt define terms in such a way that Locke is labeled a perfectionist, doing so obscures important differences between Locke and contemporary liberal perfectionists. In the next section, I argue that although there are important similarities between Locke and liberal perfectionism, the Lockean position recognizes the moral significance of disagreement in a different way. In particular, the use of a legislative point of view should cause perfectionists to be more cautious when deciding whether to use state power to promote perfectionist values.

Raz and Human Well-Being

There is more than one road to liberal conclusions, and there is a prominent school of thought that claims that the liberal emphasis on neutrality is misguided. Raz's defense of liberal perfectionism in *The Morality of*

Freedom is a classic example, claiming that liberalism cannot avoid endorsing a substantive comprehensive theory.[32] Perfectionists deny the claim that the government must be neutral between competing conceptions of the good life. They also generally oppose the claim that we must bracket our fundamental beliefs for political purposes. One might claim that only controversial views about the good need to be bracketed (anti-perfectionism), or one might claim more broadly that all comprehensive conceptions should be bracketed (political liberalism). By denying the first claim, perfectionists also deny the second, since views about the good are generally rooted in larger religious and philosophical conceptions.

There are important similarities between the perfectionist position and the Lockean view I am exploring. Indeed, some of the arguments I have developed in this chapter are similar to Raz's critique of Rawls. Raz, for example, asks why commitment to agreement must be so important that it outweighs every other good that comes into conflict with it. He claims that there are goods that are even more important than achieving agreements that all could accept, given the fact of reasonable pluralism.[33] Any society will have to make judgments about which uses of freedom are valuable, about what paths of life to encourage and discourage, and a substantive view of the good is needed to do this. He claims that liberalism must spring from a commitment to freedom as a constituent part of human well-being. There is no way to avoid judging the value of different ways people may use their freedoms because the state will inevitably encourage some ways of life more than others.

As McCabe and others note, it is ambiguous in *The Morality of Freedom* whether Raz means that the best autonomous ways of life are always more valuable than the best nonautonomous ways of life, or whether this is only so in liberal societies.[34] Which he means has obvious implications for the range of cases to which his theory applies. Raz, in his subsequent work, has favored the more limited claim.[35] McCabe argues that Raz may need the stronger claim for his argument to be persuasive. I will proceed on the basis of the strong claim since it is more typical of perfectionism. The objection I will advance is applicable to either version for reasons

[32] See also William Galston, *Liberal Purposes: Goods, Virtues, and Diversity in the Libeal State* (Cambridge: Cambridge University Press, 1991); George Sher, *Beyond Neutrality: Perfectionism and Politics* (Cambridge: Cambridge University Press, 1997); Wall, *Liberalism, Perfectionism, and Restraint*; and Stephen Macedo, *Liberal Virtues: Citizenship, Virtue, and Community in Liberal Constitution* (Oxford: Clarenton Press, 1990), pp. 260–263.

[33] Raz, *Morality of Freedom*, pp. 124–130.

[34] David McCabe, "Joseph Raz and the Contextual Argument for Liberal Perfectionism," *Ethics* 111 (2001), pp. 493–495.

[35] "Facing Up: A Reply," p. 1227.

that I explained in chapter 2 when discussing the criterion of generality. Even if someone rejects universal moral claims, the argument can still be applied at the domestic level.

Raz's theory is a common standpoint theory in that it calls on people to take a particular view of freedom and human well-being because it is the best view. It is not a pure common standpoint theory, however, because it does account for the different perspectives from which people act. Although we are to take on the perspective of one trying to promote human well-being, we cannot do this effectively if we ignore the fact of pluralism and the fact that autonomy to pursue divergent ways of life is necessary for well-being. The common standpoint is more limited than in utilitarianism in that there is no perspective from which all goods may be comprehensively ranked.[36]

I choose Raz as my subject in order to simplify the argument by keeping it among those who count themselves as liberals. There are, however, nonliberal perfectionist positions that still accept the necessary moral intuitions about generality, equality, publicity, and agency. Insofar as they do, the arguments below apply to them as much as to Raz. Combined with the discussion of rule-utilitarianism in chapter 2 and the discussion of Rawls above, this completes the analysis of the relationship between the Lockean legislative point of view and the dominant strands in liberal thought: utilitarian, contractualist, and perfectionist.

There are a number of similarities between the Lockean account I have developed and Raz's account. One similarity is their mutual emphasis on the importance of truth claims and the belief that agreement, real or hypothetical, is not the highest good. Raz repeatedly attacks neutralist conceptions of liberalism for thinking they can defend neutrality without presupposing a larger substantive framework that will be controversial. Raz holds that human well-being is the ultimate criterion and that we should not adopt a principle of neutrality if that means people will experience worse lives than they otherwise might. Neutrality might be the appropriate policy in a particular area—the separation of church and state is one possible example—but that is only because in that particular area neutrality best promotes well-being. While it may be regrettable that the government acts on a perfectionist principle that some persons have reasonable grounds for rejecting, it is not clear that this is such a bad occurrence or so wrong that it outweighs every good that governments might be able to bring about in such cases.

This distinction helps to explain why Locke, who argued that governments should refrain from pursuing a particularly important good

---

[36] Raz, *Morality of Freedom*, pp. 340–345.

(religious salvation), was not a neutralist in the modern sense. His writings as a whole show a clear willingness to allow the government to encourage virtuous ways of life where doing so would be beneficial to the public good.[37] Put another way, Locke allowed the government to pursue goals like virtue for instrumental reasons. He believed that a principle such as "Governments should promote virtue where doing so will promote the public good" would be acceptable from a legislative point of view, whereas allowing governments to require adherence to a particular doctrinal confession would not be. This partly reflects the fact that it is easier to regulate behaviors than acts (something a reasonable legislator would take into account), and it partly reflects Locke's views on what was and was not necessary for a stable and well-ordered society. I am not here defending or rejecting Locke's specific claim, but merely illustrating that the legislative point of view does not, by itself, rule out perfectionist goals. Locke did not advocate neutrality in all spheres, but only in areas where doing so was the most reasonable course of action from a legislative point of view.

Another reason it may seem strange to claim strong similarities between the Lockean and perfectionist positions is that Locke is often thought of as one of the paradigm theorists of negative liberty. According to one version of the distinction, negative liberty values the mere absence of restraint, whereas positive freedom examines the actual value of the exercise of freedom. Since Locke is often thought of in this way, and since Raz's view of freedom is central to his larger argument, it will be helpful to compare Raz's view of freedom with Locke's. Although my partial presentation of Locke's theory does not require us to accept his account of freedom, spelling it out will give an indication of the potential similarities between his position and that of Raz.

Raz believes that liberalism must be based on a positive conception of freedom rather than a negative doctrine of neutrality. Freedom, he argues, is a constituent part of human well-being.[38] There are a plurality of mutually exclusive good lives to be led. This does not mean that all ways of life are equally valid. Raz believes we can pronounce some ways of life better than others. What he denies is that we can rank them all on a single scale of goodness. Governments will have to make judgments about which uses of freedom are worthwhile and support those while discouraging others.[39] According to Raz, freedom is not good in and of

---

[37] See John Marshall, *John Locke: Resistance, Religion, and Responsibility* (Cambridge: Cambridge University Press, 1994), pp. 376–383.

[38] Raz, *Morality of Freedom*, p. 91.

[39] Ibid., chaps. 14–15.

itself; instead, it adds value to a life when it is used for good ends. The freedom to do evil is not, itself, of value.

Locke held a similar conception of freedom. Rather than being a supporter of negative liberty in the Hobbesian sense, Locke was working from a conception of freedom that focuses on the positive aspects of what the law can accomplish. According to Locke, just laws do not restrict freedom. For example, Locke referred to people's beliefs about virtue and vice in a given community as a "law of opinion" since there were reputational sanctions for deviating from it (*Essay*, 2.28.10–12). If opinions about virtue and vice in a given community are sound, the freedom of people is not restricted. Locke's position was that legitimate law does not restrict but rather increases the freedom of the subject. "*The end of Law is not to abolish or restrain, but to preserve and enlarge Freedom*: For in all the states of created beings capable of Laws, *where there is no Law, there is no Freedom. . . .* Freedom is not, as we are told, *A Liberty for every Man to do what he lists . . .*" (*Treatises*, 2.57). If I live in a society where lying is absolutely taboo, I may feel that my freedom to lie is restricted. Restrictions on the freedom to do evil are not, on Lockean grounds, restrictions we should worry about very much.[40] What we gain by living in such a society is immeasurably greater: a freedom to enter into meaningful commitments, to plan our lives around stable expectations.

In Hobbes it is quite true that liberty is defined negatively, as freedom *from* restraints.[41] Any law that restricts our choices makes us less free. Less freedom is often exactly what we should want since the absolute freedom of the state of nature carries such a high cost. It is perfectly rational, according to Hobbes, to part with much of our liberty in exchange for greater security and peace. Locke, on the other hand, differentiated sharply between liberty and license (*Treatises*, 2.6). True liberty is always understood alongside a set of moral principles that augment rather than diminish liberty. Locke could say this because he valued aspects of positive liberty as well: the liberty *to* make promises, or the freedom *to* enjoy the property to which one is morally entitled. I think the miscategorization stems from an overemphasis on Locke's negative formulation of natural law, "Do not deprive another of life, liberty, or property." The incorrect assumption is that one is free so long as one is not deprived of these

---

[40] A partial exploration of Locke's concepts of freedom, and natural law appears in Thomas Baldwin, "Toleration and the Right to Freedom," in *Aspects of Toleration: Philosophical Studies,* ed. John Horton and Susan Mendus (London: Methuen, 1985), pp. 36–52.

[41] "By Liberty is understood, according to the proper signification of the word, the absence of externall Impediments: which Impediments may oft take away part of a mans power to do what hee would; but cannot hinder him from using the power left him, according as his judgement, and reason shall dictate to him." Thomas Hobbes, *Leviathan,* p. 91.

three things. As stated in the previous chapter and in appendix 2, the fundamental law of nature is a positive command, not a negative prohibition. We are freer when we obey this positive command than when we do not. Locke recognized a kind of unfreedom stemming from the agent's own irrationality rather than some external impediment. Deviation from the law of nature was the paradigm example of such an irrationality.

Locke's thought stands in a complex relationship to two strands of positive freedom. One view of positive freedom is something like "ordered liberty." The assumption is that there are rational constraints built into the very idea of freedom and that irrational acts are unfree. As we saw in chapter 3, rationality for Locke is not simply instrumental rationality, it also includes the recognition of others as juridical equals. Locke would certainly have agreed that there was something irrational about demanding property rights for yourself and denying them to others. Laws that prevent us from rejecting reciprocity in that way and that prevent us from acting irrationally are not, therefore, constraints on freedom. In this respect there are similarities in Locke's thought to Kant's later notion of positive freedom. But it would be anachronistic to impose a Kantian interpretation on Locke. Locke would have given similar standing to prohibitions on suicide, though for reasons different from those Kant would have given.[42] The prohibition on suicide cannot be explained in terms of reciprocity.

The second strand of thought is teleological. Locke was quite willing, in the *Essays on the Law of Nature*, to make use of teleological arguments (even invoking Aristotle) about the proper purposes of man as one source of data for filling in the content of natural law (*Political Essays*, 81–88). Locke simply did not draw a sharp distinction between teleological and nonteleological arguments. His support for positive freedom is thus closely connected with his theory of natural law, which designates some actions as irrational and not befitting a human being. The freedom to be inhuman was not a freedom Locke was concerned to protect.

Although there is an important truth in the Lockean position that we should not be particularly concerned with protecting the liberty to do evil, the doctrine of toleration presupposes that in some cases the state must grant such a liberty. This is part of what is attractive about a Lockean theory. It can simultaneously do justice to the claim that not all exercises of freedom are equally valuable (or morally valuable at all) and still generate reasons for toleration. By insisting that the rules that govern

---

[42] To oversimplify, Kantians refrain from suicide in order to respect themselves; Lockeans, in order to respect God. Compare Kant's discussion in the *The Metaphysics of Morals*, trans. Mary Gregor (Cambridge: Cambridge University Press, 1996), pp. 176–177, and Locke's discussion at *Treatises*, 2.6.

what is permitted and what is not be public and general and that they be reasonable when interpreted and acted upon by fallible persons, Locke opens up a space for the doctrine of toleration. We must always be wary of principles that are unobjectionable if perfectly applied but dangerous in practice. Although there is no moral wrong when a person is discouraged from doing evil by potential sanctions (reputational or physical), we must still ask what general principles we would want persons to use in deciding when to apply sanctions and take into consideration the tendency of contested principles to be misapplied.

The Lockean position I describe is thus similar to Raz's in that they both employ (or at least allow for) a conception of freedom in which its value is judged according to some external standard. For Locke the standard is natural law; for Raz, it is human well-being. Both Locke and Raz advocate liberal conclusions without advocating a blanket neutrality about the good. There is, however, an important critique of Raz when we look at his theory from the legislative point of view. The crucial question concerns what happens when we think about Raz's fundamental value of well-being from a legislative point of view. Because different people have different understandings of both well-being and autonomy, a government empowered to promote these goals might well act on the wrong understanding. Raz gives two reasons why such a state will not become a manipulative "big brother."

> First, one needs constant reminders that the fact that the state *considers* anything to be valuable or valueless is no reason for anything. Only its being valuable or valueless is a reason. If it is likely that the government will not judge such matters correctly then it has no authority to judge them at all. Secondly, the autonomy-based doctrine of freedom rests primarily on the importance of autonomy and value-pluralism.[43]

He goes on to explain that the importance of autonomy means the government will have an obligation to insure that people have meaningful choices to make.

Raz's first argument immediately recalls the debate between Locke and Proast over whether Proast could defend correct applications of his principle without accounting for the way his principle might be misapplied. Raz's position is more sophisticated than Proast's in that he grants that the government has authority over persons only in situations where the government will be a better judge than the individual. Raz introduces this idea in his earlier discussion of political obligation, but it has implica-

---

[43] *Morality of Freedom*, p. 412.

tions for the reach of government as well, and it is in this latter context that we are interested in it.[44] He claims that we should always act on the basis of the reasons relevant to a given situation. This raises the question why we should ever not act on what seems like, to us, the best reasons. This is of particular importance for understanding why we should obey the government when its edicts do not correspond to our own judgment of what is right. Raz claims that there are certain circumstances where a person may legitimately believe that accepting another's judgment as authoritative will make it more, not less, likely that that person acts on the correct reasons. In such situations Raz claims we have an obligation to obey the law. He also claims, in the passage quoted above, that we can use this as a criterion for determining the scope of the government's authority.[45]

Although Raz is to be commended for building into his theory a criterion that accounts for the relative competence of different actors to make different judgments in different areas, his theory is still very much one that works from the viewpoint of the situated agent rather than from a legislative point of view. His approach is very individualistic: whether the government has authority varies not only from area to area but from person to person. If person A is a better judge in area X than the government but person B is not, then the government has authority over B but not A. Each individual must judge the extent of her own obligation. Because Raz frames the problem primarily in terms of political obligation, he does not attend as he should to the question of what principles the government should use in determining its proper scope. Drawing on Locke's argument, we can say that even if governments should legislate only in areas where doing so makes it more likely that individuals will act on the right reasons, if we make this a principle of political action then governments will legislate wherever they think that they are better judges, and governments may overestimate how often this is the case. Unless the legislative point of view is taken to be a moral requirement, we must worry that the king of England will reason that he is a better judge of true religion than the average person while thinking that king of France is much worse. Therefore, wise governments should legislate quite freely on matters that they would not want less wise governments even to touch. To adopt this attitude is precisely the opposite of what the legislative point of view requires. Either it fails to respect others as moral agents with an equal right to act on the principles that apply equally to all of us, or it fails to consider what principles would be reasonable as a framework

---

[44] Ibid., chaps. 3–4, especially pp. 53–57 and 70–80.

[45] Chapter 5 will explore Locke's account of why someone might not act on his preferred understanding of natural law.

that such people would actually apply. Taking on the legislative point of view is also an effective way of accounting for the tendency of persons and governments to overestimate their own competence. We are often more accurate judges of the fallibility of others than of our own.[46]

If we replace Locke's more restrictive goal of comfortable preservation with the more ambitious one that Raz offers, we should remember that ambition has a price. We must think of the directive "promote well-being" as the directive that all governments should take as the basis of their understanding of the public good. We must also respect the fact that each person is a moral agent who can and should engage in deliberation about what constitutes human well-being, for if well-being is put forward as a principle of action (rather than evaluation), the citizen cannot do otherwise. Many, perhaps most, of the persons who will implement the proposal will disagree with Raz about the nature of human well-being. There will be similar disagreements about the proper understanding of freedom. None of this prevents Raz from using his own theory as a standard of evaluation; it only shows the consequences of his theory as a generalized principle of action. The practical consequence of adopting the legislative point of view would likely be adopting a more specific and restricted understanding of the public good that would be less subject to conflicting interpretations. Whether it would be as restrictive as Locke's formulation of the fundamental law of nature, which directs us to promote human preservation, is of course an open question.

Raz could argue that these concerns are substantially alleviated by his second argument, which claims that recognizing autonomy as a central aspect of well-being mitigates the paternalistic tendencies of perfectionism. This might, for example, prevent the king of England from imposing a religion insofar as a religion's being freely chosen is a necessary condition for its contribution to well-being. Similar arguments could be made in areas other than religion. In effect Raz is narrowing the principle from "Promote well-being" to "Promote autonomy-friendly understandings of well-being" on the grounds that the latter would be less liable to abuse. Notice that such a move would employ a different justificatory approach. Once one admits that authorizing governments to pursue well-being as such would lead to too many errant applications of the principle, one has already adopted the legislative point of view. It is no longer simply a matter of showing that the government pursuing a particular goal in a particular case will contribute to well-being, of showing that the government is a better judge in this *particular* instance. Such a reformulation would be a tacit acceptance of the Lockean framework and of the present

---

[46] See Tuckness, "Rethinking the Intolerant Locke," *American Journal of Political Science* 46 (April 2002), pp. 288–298.

argument, which is that the content of the good needs to be defined more specifically. Of course it remains an open question whether even the more restricted goal above is one that we would want fallible governments and majorities to pursue. Disagreements about the nature of autonomy and of its relative importance for human well-being would make "autonomy-friendly understandings of well-being" contested as well, albeit to a lesser extent.

The difference between a Lockean approach and Razian perfectionism rests in the structure of moral argument. Both are committed to the importance of freedom, but in different senses. A Lockean theory is in the first instance concerned with the juridical relationship between persons, and this is captured by the requirement that we formulate a conception of the public good that we would want others both to interpret and to carry out. This does not imply that truth is not a reason for action; it instead specifies the normative consequences that follow from a particular truth, namely, the truth of juridical equality. For Raz, the idea of freedom is not linked to the idea of juridical equality. Instead, it is simply a part of human well-being. On such an understanding, the interpretive errors of others do not provide a reason for caution as they do on a Lockean understanding.

Raz might object that if one admits that the right to do evil is not a right that must be protected, it is unclear what could ground toleration if not the contribution of freedom to human well-being. Why, if this is the case, should we forgo opportunities to perform actions that might promote well-being? The claim that we must do so out of a "respect for persons" is unpersuasive since, in his view, we show respect for persons precisely by valuing their well-being. I have tried to argue that this objection is not a strong one against the Lockean position. The Lockean legislative point of view does not rule out all perfectionist goals from political life. Rather it merely claims that if we believe in a common set of moral principles that are general and public and addressed to us as fallible moral agents, then our recognition of these ideas should lead us to assess perfectionist ideals from a legislative point of view. The legislative point of view should make us more cautious about imposing perfectionist ideals than we would otherwise be.

Beyond Neutrality and Perfectionism

As the title of this chapter indicates, the Lockean position has the potential to move us beyond the current debates between neutralist and perfectionist liberals in a helpful way. The problem with this debate is its tendency to make neutrality, or its absence, the central theoretical point.

This need not be the case. Locke, because he was writing in an earlier time, did not get entangled in this debate and gives us an alternative model. Liberals should be cautious about the pursuit of perfectionist aims because states might well pursue the wrong goals, and because different people may interpret vague goals very differently. If one insists on defining the debate in terms of neutrality, then the Lockean position is a perfectionist position since the Lockean public good is broader than the enforcement of negative liberties. But in this concluding section I want to illustrate how in reality Locke suggests a way of stepping beyond the current debate.

Consider Joseph Chan's recent defense of perfectionism. He argues that even on contractualist terms the state need not be neutral with respect to the good life. He begins by noting that many of the arguments against perfectionism are good arguments only against an extreme version of perfectionism. Extreme perfectionism holds that goods and ways of life can be ranked in a comprehensive list, that the state should coercively require persons to lead valuable ways of life, that only the good life is of value, and that the state must be the agent responsible for directly promoting the good. None of these further assumptions is necessary, and one can arrive at a progressively more moderate version of perfectionism by endorsing the following alternatives: that local, but not global and comprehensive, judgments about the good are possible, that the state should use noncoercive means to promote valuable ways of life, that nonperfectionist values are also important, and that the state need not be the primary agent. This list of ways perfectionism can become more moderate is not exhaustive. Chan argues that there is no reason to believe, as Rawls claims, that a perfectionism of this more moderate sort could be maintained only by the oppressive use of state power.[47] Raz makes a similar move insofar as many of the instances of the government promoting the public good are only coercive in the sense that they require coercively collected tax dollars. He notes that from the standpoint of autonomy and well-being, coercion of this sort is far less harmful than torture or imprisonment.[48]

There are a variety of reasons, ranging from the metaphysical to the very practical, why one might prefer moderate perfectionism to extreme perfectionism. But as we have already seen, the legislative point of view provides a straightforward explanation. If a comprehensive ranking of ways of life is possible at all, it is extremely controversial and very difficult. Telling governments that they should undertake such

---

[47] Joseph Chan, "Legitimacy, Unanimity, and Perfectionism," *Philosophy and Public Affairs* 29 (2000), pp. 10–20.

[48] See Raz, *The Morality of Freedom*, especially pp.148–157 and 400–429.

a ranking and that they should then compel persons to live the worthiest ways of life would be a prescription for disaster. To paraphrase Locke, not one government in one hundred would get the rankings right. It would be far better, from a legislative point of view, for the government to make only particular judgments (where the probability of error is lower) and to use less draconian means (so that the harm of errors is lower) to pursue the identified goods. We should prefer this position even if the best of all possible worlds was one in which governments required people to live the best possible lives. When selecting principles from the legislative point of view, we do not assume the best of all possible worlds.

Chan then considers another argument in favor of the neutralist position. This position claims that we treat people as means and fail to respect them as ends when we force them to serve an end with which they may reasonably disagree, unless a higher order unanimity obtains. The last clause is intended to avoid the objection that there is reasonable disagreement about essential matters of justice as well, such as national defense. If there is reasonable disagreement about everything, so the objection goes, reasonable disagreement is not a helpful criterion. The "higher-order unanimity exception" responds by providing that in cases where there is unanimous agreement that there must be *some* common policy (such as national defense), the government may adopt a particular policy even if there is reasonable disagreement about whether the particular policy is the best one possible. Chan thinks that the most reasonable interpretation of this higher-order unanimity principle would allow government action despite the existence of reasonable disagreement about a policy if the following conditions are met:

(a) Collective action through the agency of the state is a better means than individual action to promote the desired end.
(b) Policies made by the state do not engage in repression or intolerance of those who have different views. In other words, the polices respect basic individual rights.
(c) The members of the decision-making bodies . . . may change from time to time so that each interest- or opinion-group may have a fair chance to influence the decision-making process.

Chan argues that:

(1) The individual's pursuit of a worthwhile life requires or can better be promoted by collective efforts coordinated or supported by the state.
(2) Moderate perfectionism, as defined above, does not advocate the use of coercion to promote the good life. . . .
(3) The making of perfectionist policies need not be done in a way that

sounds offensive and arrogant, or in a way that generates serious injustice of a kind that cannot be tolerated.[49]

The specific arguments that he makes on behalf of these last three claims need not concern us. Suppose that his claims are correct. Notice how the entire argument could be recast in light of a legislative point of view. When we ask whether an end could better be promoted by collective state action or individual action, we are asking one of the questions characteristic of the legislative point of view as described in chapter 3. The scope of government action should be determined from the perspective of a legislator who compares alternative arrangements in just this way. Perfectionist policies that meet Chan's three criteria are more likely to be acceptable from a legislative point of view.

The legislative point of view also draws our attention to an important issue that tends to be neglected when the debate is cast in terms of neutrality. Thinking of the problem from a legislative point of view allows us to realize that "higher-order thinking" need not imply "higher-order unanimity." Chan frames the question in terms of unanimity because he is arguing against neutralists whose aspiration is toward principles that all can accept. The legislative point of view is a form of higher-order thinking, but it does not require us to think that everyone (or even every reasonable person) wants protections from foreign invasion, only that we think such a position is reasonable from a legislative point of view. And it is here that our earlier discussion of Rawls becomes relevant. There are two separate moral insights that can be distinguished: 1) that we should act only on principles that reasonable people would unanimously accept, and (2) that we should legislate on the basis of principles that seem reasonable from a legislative point of view. The legislative point of view gives us a way to affirm the second without affirming the first while still giving real moral weight to the fact of disagreement and showing respect for others as moral agents.

Once we set aside the goal of proving that there is a radical asymmetry between the right and the good, we notice that many of the goals typically associated with antiperfectionist liberalism are more likely to be affirmed from a legislative point of view. Programs like public health, police, national defense, and so on are more likely to be affirmed from a legislative point of view because, from that point of view, we realize that a collective decision is needed. So long as perfectionism defines itself by showing that there are exceptions to the neutrality requirement, it will not adequately describe which values governments should promote. In a sense neutralists may have made it too easy on perfectionists by making

[49] "Legitimacy, Unanimity, and Perfectionism," p. 28.

the extreme claim that the state may not promote controversial conceptions of the good. A more defensible position might be to raise traditional concerns about how the state may overstep its bounds in pursuing (even with good intentions) perfectionist goals. Such a defense will not try to repudiate all such goals for governments but will instead subject them to close scrutiny.

The legislative point of view thus stands in a complex relationship to both neutrality and perfectionism. There is a minimal interpretation of the legislative point of view in which it functions as a supplement to either of the theories. It asks advocates of both political liberalism and perfectionism to consider the way contested terms are used to justify coercion. I have not tried, in this chapter, to argue definitively for one approach or the other. The legislative point of view has this flexibility because the basic assumptions on which it rests (generality, publicity, moral equality, and moral agency) are sufficiently broad that both neutral and perfectionist versions of liberalism could affirm them. This is a strength of the theory.

There is also a stronger interpretation of the Lockean position in which it functions as an alternate framework rather than as a mere supplement. In this reading, the Lockean position is able to capture the ideal of reciprocity as a constraint on political action without requiring general neutrality and without preventing people from appealing directly to controversial foundational beliefs in political debate. We respect others by considering them in their capacity as agents who will also make moral decisions, rather than in their capacity as persons who may veto actions that affect them. Although it allows people to propose and act for controversial goals and on controversial grounds, including perfectionist ones, persons may not simply decide what they think is best and urge the state to pursue that policy. Instead, they must consider their proposal from a legislative point of view and honestly ask themselves whether their support for the principle is contingent on their preferred interpretation of the good in question prevailing. By acknowledging that there are cases where people may appeal to controversial foundational beliefs, even beliefs about the good, we move beyond the current debate by asking how we should determine *which* controversial principles justify political action. Locke's legislative point of view allows us to do so without assuming a radical asymmetry between disagreement about rights and disagreement about the good. We assume disagreement about both and ask how much disagreement is acceptable from a legislative point of view.

PART II

The Legislative Point of View and Constitutional Roles

CHAPTER 5

Institutional Roles and the Legislative Point of View

To this point we have looked at the application of the legislative point of view to situations where a person must decide whether to use state power to punish a moral wrong or promote the public good. A Lockean legislative point of view provides a moral perspective that the persons who must make these decisions, particularly legislators and the citizens who elect them, should employ. The previous chapters simplified the discussion by assuming that the actors are either legislators or citizens trying to bring about a change in the law. In fact, the realities of political life are considerably more complicated than that. The government is not a monolith with a single undivided will. Government actions result from the decisions and actions of a multitude of people acting in specific roles and contexts. Many persons who hold judicial or executive positions have opportunities to articulate principles that will direct the way government uses its power. We can ask not only what the government as a whole should do, but also what particular people in particular institutional roles should do. In this chapter I argue that many public officials who do not occupy traditional legislative roles should also make use of the legislative point of view, although in a somewhat different way from the previous chapters. To make that case I must move beyond the argument for a legislative point of view, strictly defined. Whether or not the legislative point of view is applicable to a particular role depends in large part on how we define that role. For example, if the proper role of the executive is simply to follow the orders of the legislature, one might conclude that the former need not take on a legislative point of view. Locke's understanding of these constitutional roles makes interpretation of a "higher law" a pervasive feature of all of them and thus makes the legislative point of view applicable to all of them.

One might object to Locke's characterization of executive and judicial roles on several grounds. One might object that because Locke's was a natural law theory that gave a primary place to individual conscience, there is little room for institutional roles. Since natural law is higher than positive law, it seems to follow that one should always act on natural law as one understands it rather than subordinating one's own interpretation because of an institutional role that is a creation of positive law or custom. Arthur Applbaum has made an analogous argument in a contemporary setting. He argues that occupying a certain role generally should *not* restrict the reasons to which an actor can appeal. Although role morality is easy to justify from a consequentialist perspective (if we get better results if each abides by her role, then each should so abide), it is not clear why someone who is not a consequentialist should do so.[1] The objection is analogous in that both claim that occupying a role does not exempt one from following what basic morality seems to dictate in a particular case. Applbaum's concern is with adversarial roles, whereas my concern is with roles in which persons act as a judge, in some sense, rather than as an advocate. For that reason our positions may not be, strictly speaking, incompatible. In fact my argument in chapter 6 will bolster the claim that members of the federal government should not view interbranch competition from an adversarial perspective. Nonetheless, the idea of a legislative point of view provides a rationale for adopting role-specific restrictions on deliberation not simply because it will produce the best consequences, but because one would want others to do the same.

In the next section of this chapter I show how Locke's natural law theory is compatible with a recognition of institutional roles by focusing on the two political roles he discussed in detail, the legislative and the executive. Taking on an executive role implies deference to legislative interpretations of natural law. This discussion of Locke's theory of separation of powers is important because it shows that a theory like Locke's, which gives such an important place to individual conscience, does not require public actors automatically to act on their preferred interpretation of morality. This reduces the anarchic tendencies that a theory like Locke's would otherwise have. The idea of a legislative point of view also gives persons a nonconsequentialist reason to bracket certain moral considerations when acting out a role. I conclude the section by arguing that Locke's legislative point of view not only is compatible with institutional roles but actually provides a nonconsequentialist reason for accepting them.

A second objection finds Locke inapplicable because of his understanding of the judicial role. It is striking to the modern reader that, leaving foreign policy to the side, Locke recognized only two basic governmental powers rather than three. A critic could take this to be a sufficient reason for dismissing Locke's views on institutional roles. According to a modern view, particularly prevalent in the United States, unless the interpretive power is separated from the executive and legislative powers, the rule of law is compromised. According to the critic, Locke mistakes the

[1] Arthur Isak Applbaum, *Ethics for Adversaries: The Morality of Roles in Public and Professional Life* (Princeton: Princeton University Press, 1999), pp. 13–14.

law as it ought to be for the law as it is because his jurisprudence was firmly rooted in the natural law tradition, which denies that unjust law is really law. In doing so he allows judges to act in ways that are appropriate only for legislators. Locke wrote that positive laws "are only so far right, as they are founded on the Law of Nature, by which they are to be regulated and interpreted" (*Treatises*, 2.12). Many modern readers take it for granted that a judge may not have recourse to personal moral beliefs when adjudicating cases, but this seems to be exactly what Locke's theory requires. If we imagine a cohort of Lockean trial judges, would they each go about using their own idiosyncratic interpretations of moral principles so long as *they* were convinced that *their* moral principles would be adopted from a legislative point of view? Such a prospect should be chilling and would raise questions about whether a theory like Locke's that is based on a natural law jurisprudence can account for contemporary understandings of what the judicial role requires. Although I will discuss this problem in terms of natural law, it has implications for persons who think moral principles should guide judicial action, whatever metaphysical standing those moral principle may have. Thus, as in the previous chapters, the arguments developed here apply by analogy to a wider set of moral positions.

It is true that Locke's understanding of governmental powers presupposes a conceptual framework that will strike many modern readers as odd. When we confront a conceptual gap of this kind, the first question must be whether the older conceptual scheme really is inferior to the contemporary one. If there are nonantiquarian reasons for studying the history of political thought, one of them must surely be that not all conceptual changes have been for the best. I argue that Locke's older theory, which describes institutional roles primarily in terms of a distinction between legislative and executive functions, is in many respects superior to one that uses the more familiar legislative, executive, and judicial division.[2] The third section of this chapter will explore this claim by examining the place of courtroom judges within this framework and the implications of Locke's alternative way of conceptualizing the nature of legislative, executive, and judicial roles. Locke helps us to realize that the people we call judges actually exercise legislative powers on a regular basis and that they should, for that reason, take on a modified version of

[2] Although Locke's doctrine of the "separation of powers" has been discussed in light of the general argument of the *Two Treatises*, it has not been discussed in relation to the idea of toleration. This is partly understandable since the *Letter* speaks only of a "magistrate" who combines both legislative and executive powers, and since the *Two Treatises*, does not raise the subject of toleration. Locke's theory of natural law provides a conceptual bridge between the two works.

the legislative point of view. Locke's surprising thought is that there is no distinct judicial function, but rather a continuum between purely legislative and purely executive cases. I argue that this Lockean account actually better describes the proper moral aspirations for legislative, judicial, and executive officials.

This last answer raises another objection. If Locke's position is that there is no distinct judicial role, this would appear have enormous implications for constitutional design. Put another way, it suggests that if judges are often legislating, this calls into question the legitimacy of their actions. The fourth section answers this objection by focusing on the function of courts as institutions within a Lockean constitutional framework. I will argue that Locke's distinction between powers and persons makes clearer the institutional implications of his theory. One of the principle difficulties in understanding Locke's theory is the differences in vocabulary. Locke relies on a distinction between powers and persons that is likely to mislead readers who are not familiar with his technical terminology. For the sake of clarity I will use the term "function" in place of "power," and "institution" in place of "person."[3] A Lockean theory simultaneously rejects the idea of a unique judicial function and recognizes the importance of courts of law as institutions. Because there is not a unique judicial function, when judges are asked to perform legislative functions Lockean arguments addressed to legislators are applicable to them as well. This distinction also lays the conceptual groundwork for chapter 6, where I apply the legislative point of view to situations where the principles that define an agent's institutional role are themselves contested. Since it is possible for a court to be a part of the supreme legislative power, conflicts over the roles of the three branches of the United States government in constitutional interpretation are both disputes over the proper organization of the legislative power *and* disputes between the

---

[3] When Locke used the term "power" in the *Two Treatises*, he used it in a different way from the way he did in the *Essay Concerning Human Understanding*. In the latter, the term was merely descriptive, referring to the ability of one body to bring about some change in another or to be changed by the other body (*Essay*, 2.21.2). In the *Two Treatises* the idea is normative and refers to actions that a person has a moral right to perform. Because "power" is used in so many senses in contemporary works, I will use "function" to draw attention to the relevant aspect of "power." The crucial question is with the functions that the holder of a particular office may legitimately perform. In place of "institution" Locke used the term "person" in a technical sense. Locke in the *Essay* defined a person as an entity capable of responsible agency (*Essay*, 2.27.26). Thus the United States Senate and Supreme Court would be thought of as persons, since we can meaningfully say, "The Supreme Court decided. . . . " Since this seventeenth-century usage is now rare, I will use "institution" with the caveat that a Lockean institution might consist of only one person. There are some similarities between this distinction and the distinction between functions and branches. See Pasquale Pasquino, "Locke on King's Prerogative," *Political Theory* 26 (1998), p. 199.

executive or legislative branches and the judicial branch considered as institutions.

Through the process of answering these objections, a positive picture will emerge of Locke's understanding of the different constitutional roles and of the relationship between powers and institutions. Rather than a rigid distinction among legislative, judicial, and executive powers, Locke suggests something more like a continuum between legislative and executive powers. If Locke's account is correct, most judges and executive officers are in a legislative position to some extent, and, to the extent that they are, the legislative point of view is applicable to them.

Locke on Legislative and Executive Powers

The clearest example in Locke's thought of subordinating one's own interpretation of natural law to that of another because of one's institutional role is Locke's discussion of the executive power. To understand it we must understand the legislative role as well. Sections 2.88–89 of the *Two Treatises* are typical of Locke's usage and at first glance puzzling to the modern reader. Locke referred to the powers individuals had in the state of nature and the corresponding powers that are transferred to civil society. He claimed that the commonwealth acquires the power to determine what punishments will be annexed to which transgressions for the furthering of the public good. The power to punish transgressions is equated with the executive power as we would expect, but the power of "judging offenses" is equated with the legislative, not the judicial, power.[4] The power of judging what the law of nature requires and directing the use of force is the legislative power; actually using one's force to carry out the directive is the executive power. In Locke's theory, the use of force must always be justified through natural law, by showing either

---

[4] "But though every Man who has enter'd into civil Society, and is become a member of any Commonwealth, has thereby quitted his power to punish Offences against the Law of Nature, in prosecution of his own private Judgment; yet with the Judgment of Offences which he has given up to the Legislative in all Cases, where he can Appeal to the Magistrate, he has given a right to the Commonwealth to imploy his force, for the Execution of the Judgments of the Commonwealth. . . . And herein we have the original of the *Legislative* and *Executive Power* of Civil Society, which is to judge by standing Laws how far Offences are to be punished, when committed within the Commonwealth; and also to determin . . . how far Injuries from without are to be vindicated. . . . For hereby [by consenting to join the commonwealth] he authorizes the Society, or which is all one, the Legislative thereof to make Laws for him as the publick good of the Society shall require; to the Execution whereof, his own assistance (as to his own Decrees) is due. And this *puts Men* out of a State of Nature *into* that of a *Commonwealth*, by setting up a Judge on Earth . . . which Judge is the Legislative, or Magistrates appointed by it" (*Treatises*, 2.88–89).

that an individual has violated an enforceable moral rule or that the state is promoting a legitimate conception of the public good (2.135). In both cases, the exercise of the legislative power is essentially a matter of asking what natural law requires. When defining what counts as theft, for example, the legislature is simply "drawing closer" the law of nature and affixing a specific human punishment to it. Even when the state decides whether to lower the interest rate, it does so on the basis of an interpretation of what is required to promote the fundamental law of nature, a strong economy being an intermediate step to the preservation of the members of the community.

Interpretation is not only an essential component of the legislative power, it is also an essential part of the executive power. The legislative power creates a written law on the basis of its interpretation of the unwritten law. The executive carries out the directions of the legislature, but we must also interpret those directions. In interpreting and applying those instructions, the executive may legitimately appeal to natural law in cases where the law is unclear or seems manifestly contrary to natural law.[5] Locke's basic moral picture, which I refer to as juridical equality, holds that all persons are moral agents who must interpret the commands given to them in order to obey. Interpretation and judgment will be required at every step, from the legislature that must interpret moral principles down to the citizen who must interpret a particular judgment by a police officer or trial judge. The executive and legislature do not differ in requiring judgment; they differ in their degree of freedom in interpretation and their legitimate scope of action on the basis of those judgments. The executive is bound by the legislative interpretation of natural law and may only appeal to his own understanding of it when the legislative directions are unclear, provided that the government is legitimate. The particular authority of the executive is the authority actually to use force as sanctioned by law (natural law in the state of nature, positive law in civil society). For Locke, a law is an authoritative rule that authorizes punishment for violation of the rule. Law is incoherent without sanctions.[6] The legislature articulates these rules, the executive applies them to specific cases, but both use judgment and are constrained by moral principles.

The next step is to describe how the legislature and executive relate to one another. Locke makes the supremacy of the legislature in the area

---

[5] The latter involves Locke's doctrine of prerogative and is discussed below.

[6] See Locke's *Essay*, 2.28.6. An account of laws that distinguishes "secondary rules," which are not themselves backed by threats, from "primary rules," which are, is consistent with, though not required by, this account. For this view, see H.L.A. Hart, *The Concept of Law* (Oxford: Oxford University Press, 1961), chap. 5. The important point is that laws affect, directly or indirectly, how force will be used.

of interpretation clear in the unpublished *Critical Notes on Stillingfleet*, which he co-authored with James Tyrrell. "For the power of making laws and of interpreting them to others are so areas of kin that they are always thought to belong to and be inseparable from the legislative according to the known rule *ejus est interpretari cujus est condere* for he rules not who makes laws, but who declares what the laws signify."[7] This position requires only that ultimate interpretive authority rest in the legislative power; the legislature is free to delegate some of its authority to lower courts. It is also possible that the fundamental constitution might delegate a portion of the legislative power to the executive.

Locke is clear that there must be a legislative power and that one of its tasks will be to authoritatively interpret natural law since disagreement about its content is to be expected. There are a number of passages in which Locke assumes that there will be disagreement about rights and specifies the legislature as the place where authoritative decisions are made about what rights we have. Perhaps Locke's clearest endorsement of the position that rational people could disagree on some points of natural law is found in the *Essays on the Law of Nature*.

> Secondly, I answer that, although even the more rational of men do not absolutely agree among themselves as to what the law of nature is and what its true and known precepts are, it does not follow from this that there is no law of nature at all; on the contrary it follows rather that there is such a law, when people contend about it so fiercely. For just as in a commonwealth it is wrong to conclude that there are no laws because various interpretations of laws are to be met with among jurisprudents, so likewise in morality it is improperly inferred that there is no law of nature, because in one place it is pronounced to be this, in another something different.[8]

Given this expectation about disagreement in law and morals, the citizens of a commonwealth will need to come up with some way of deciding on a common answer to difficult questions if they are to live together under

---

[7] MS Locke c.34, p. 21. References to unpublished materials indicate the shelf mark and page number of the originals held in the Locke room at the Bodleian Library, Oxford University. John Marshall argues that Tyrrell was little more than Locke's secretary in composing the *Critical Notes*, in *John Locke*, p. 97, n. 34. The content of the text's arguments, written in 1681, is quite consistent with what Locke wrote elsewhere, taking an intermediate position between Locke's *Essay on Toleration* (1667) and the *Letter Concerning Toleration* (composed c.1685).

[8] *Political Essays*, 86. It is worth noting that this passage comes from Locke's early (and unpublished during his lifetime) *Essays on the Law of Nature* because Locke's earliest writings are the ones most likely to assume universal agreement about natural law. In fact, Locke was in the process of rejecting the view that natural law's content could be established from the universal consent of mankind when he wrote the first essay of that collection, the

law. Locke designated the legislature as the institutional body that would make these determinations.[9]

It is important to remember that natural law includes the positive goal of preservation. A society in which there was no authoritative interpreter would be anarchic and would be unable to fulfill its primary purpose. Admittedly, people can live without an authoritative interpreter; that is part of the point of a doctrine of the state of nature, and it is best exemplified by international relations. The purpose of civil society, however, is to remedy the inconveniences of the state of nature and the absence of an authoritative interpreter is one of the constitutive inconveniences of that state. Contrast two frameworks, one in which the authority to interpret natural law and bind others by that interpretation is given conditionally to some institution and another in which each individual is in every case required to obey his own understanding of natural law. Given the reasonable assumption of disagreement about essential matters of law, the former is better able to fulfill the goals of natural law than the latter.[10] One of Locke's assumptions is that natural law, from God's perspective, is rational. Any interpretation of natural law that makes civil society impossible is an incorrect interpretation.[11]

The delegation of power to the legislature is conditional. This is an important qualification for understanding the sense in which the legislature is authoritative. I noted in chapter 2 that Locke distinguished between two senses of "judge," one where we form moral evaluations and another where we make those evaluations binding on others through force. In a state, the latter power is exercised by the legislature, but the former is never given up. One reason that it is not given up is that citizens must be able to inquire whether the legislature is attempting in good faith

---

essay from which the passage is taken. (Compare *Political Essays*, 81–85 and 106–116.) Thus even the early Locke, who was more inclined to portray natural law as a matter of consensus, assumed disagreement about some matters. This fits well with the suggestion I have advanced elsewhere that Locke thought there was a periphery of natural law that would be the subject of dispute. See Tuckness, "The Coherence of a Mind: John Locke and the Law of Nature," *Journal of the History of Philosophy* 37 (January 1999).

[9] *Treatises*, 2.135–136. On this point, see Jeremy Waldron, *The Dignity of Legislation*, chap. 4. Key texts for Waldron's position include *Treatises*, 2.87–89, 123, 136.

[10] For a contemporary natural law account along similar lines, stressing the need for an institutional authority in any political society, see Philip Soper, "Some Natural Confusions about Natural Law," *Michigan Law Review* 90 (1992), pp. 2417–2422.

[11] This is the natural law reasoning that supports Locke's doctrine of majority rule and argues against a unanimity principle in civil society. Since Locke assumed that disagreement would exist, he thought it obvious that unanimity would be an unworkable decision procedure. On Locke's assumptions about disagreement and unanimity, see Waldron, *The Dignity of Legislation*, pp. 79, 136–141.

to further the goals specified for it by natural law. If the people believe the legislature is maliciously attempting to subvert those goals, the legitimacy of the state collapses. Locke's position thus recognized that there would be disputes and that some earthly judge must be authorized to make binding decisions, that earthly judges would be fallible and potentially evil, and that judges' powers were not absolute.

If we combine these insights with the earlier distinction between legislative and executive functions, we see why a Lockean jurisprudence is not a prescription for anarchy, for a society where each government official independently rules according to his preferred moral conception. The legislature, however constituted, is the supreme interpreter of natural law so long as legitimate government persists. The executive is in a position much like the citizen. The executive may have his own opinions about the proper interpretation of natural law. He may sometimes think that the legislature has wrongly articulated a general principle. In such a situation, he has a choice to make. If he believes that the wrong principle flows from a malicious attempt to subvert morality, then he may appeal to heaven, and both legislator and executive are then bound to act on natural law as they understand it. Often, however, the citizen or executive will believe that the legislature has made an honest mistake. It has sincerely inquired but erred. Since disagreement is to be expected and unanimity is an unworkable decision procedure in such cases, persons must anticipate living with laws they think unjust. In this situation, the citizen has two choices: obedience or willingly accepting punishment for violating a law that is wrong, yet legitimate (*Letter*, 48–49). Locke does not address this topic explicitly, but it follows that the executive similarly faces a choice between carrying out the legislative directive or resigning. In any case we should remember that Locke's main point in the *Two Treatises* is that laws can be sufficiently unjust to merit more drastic action by both citizens and executives.

We can extend Locke's argument and claim that the idea of a legislative point of view helps provide a nonconsequentialist grounding for the acceptance of institutional roles.[12] Applbaum has noted that it is not hard to understand how consequentialists justify role morality; they simply show that the net effect of persons occupying such roles at least breaks even. He thinks it far less clear why nonconsequentialists would

---

[12] While Locke does not make the argument explicitly, he does make the more general argument that unless the legislative power is allowed to judge and interpret natural law, the inconveniences of the state of nature would remain. Locke takes this to be sufficient grounds for his conclusion (*Treatises*, 2.98, 134). His implicit assumption is that the evidence that a framework would be unable to achieve its stated goal is evidence that the framework has been incorrectly described.

think that a role can authorize persons to perform actions that would otherwise be immoral.[13] The Lockean legislative point of view is an example of a nonconsequentialist moral perspective that has no trouble accounting for institutional roles. Unlike consequentialism, it claims that we should adopt the legislative point of view out of respect for others as equal moral agents under a common moral framework. But like rule-consequentialism, it defines the framework from the perspective of someone viewing the entire system rather than one individual's decision within it. Such a legislator might reasonably decide that because of human fallibility the relevant moral goals (which need not be utilitarian) will be better fulfilled by a system in which certain persons act out particular institutional roles.

When the legislative power gives directions to the executive, it should do so on the basis of moral principles that are reasonable from a legislative point of view. Where these directions are clear, they are normally binding on executive officials. In practice, they often will be unclear and will leave significant room for interpretation. As Locke said in a passage quoted earlier in this chapter, positive laws are to be interpreted in the light of natural law. By analogy, the claim is that where executive officials have discretion in carrying out the duties of their offices, they should not feel that they are at liberty to do as they please so long as they stay within the letter of the law. Rather, the law should be executed in light of moral principles. Sometimes there may be explicit constitutionally or legislatively enacted principles to guide discretion. For example, if there have been specific constitutional or legislative pronouncements about the scope of the public good, the executive should make use of those pronouncements. If not, the executive official should select the best moral principles possible from a legislative point of view. In still other cases, the legislative power may specifically delegate a portion of legislative authority to executive officials. In these cases, it becomes even more important for executive officials to make use of the legislative point of view.

The supremacy of the legislative over the executive in matters of interpretation reduces the unpredictability that would result from interpreting positive laws in the light of moral beliefs. The legislative body, however constituted, can bind those officials fulfilling executive functions by using precise language where doing so seems prudent. At the same time, executive officials are not absolved of the responsibility of acting as moral agents and considering their actions in the light of moral principles. In extreme cases they may even have to resign or disobey unjust legislative decisions.

---

[13] *Ethics for Adversaries*, pp. 13–14.

Locke and the Missing Judicial Power

With this understanding of the executive and legislature, it becomes clear why Locke did not recognize a distinct judicial function. In saying that the legislature makes the law, the judiciary interprets it, and the executive enforces it, we actually blur the reality. In fact, courts not only interpret what the law means, they also investigate the facts of particular cases to see if a particular law applies to a particular person. In doing so, their function is part and parcel with the executive function of enforcing the law. When a judge dutifully checks to see that a will has the appropriate number of signatures, is she interpreting the law or enforcing it? Clearly the latter. Insofar as judges can describe their actions as simply applying clear rules to particular cases, it is more accurate to think of their jobs as the exercise of an executive power. There are also instances where courts exercise what Locke would have termed a legislative power. The German Constitutional Court, for example, is authorized by the German Basic Law to strike down laws that violate human dignity. It could decide whether abortion is constitutionally protected based on a judgment about whether abortion is consistent with a respect for human dignity. For Locke, this is the essence of a legislative function, since the court will articulate a principle that will direct the use of force on the basis of its understanding of what the moral law requires, precisely what a legislature does when it "draws closer" the laws of nature. In between are a vast array of cases in which judges interpret laws that contain terms requiring significant judgment.

In place of a three-part distinction among legislative, executive, and judicial functions, it is better to think of a continuum between the pure legislative and the pure executive case. The pure cases of legislative or executive action are rare if they exist at all. When a police officer decides not to issue a ticket or a district attorney decides not to prosecute a case that falls within the letter of the law, their actions cannot be described as purely executive. Because most legislatures are constrained by constitutions, whether written or unwritten, that limit their discretion, their actions are not purely legislative. At different times, the people we call judges occupy different places along this continuum. Locke's unwillingness to recognize a unique judicial function was not a result of his downplaying the interpretation of law as an important part of government. Rather, it was because the interpretation of law is a part of *all* exercises of governmental authority.[14] Since a Lockean theory does not

---

[14] See Laslett's introduction to Locke's *Two Treatises*, pp. 118–121. Laslett writes that the judicial function is simply an attribute of government as a whole; this should be expanded to say that "judicial" behavior is an attribute of every part of government, not only the whole.

assume a simple one-to-one correspondence between functions and institutions, courts can, as institutions, perform both legislative and executive functions at different times. Insofar as they approximate one or the other, the institutional roles of that ideal type will apply to judges.

Even if there is not a distinct judicial function, it might still be the case that there are forms of reasoning, such as analogical reasoning, particularly appropriate to the type of mixed function that judges must often perform. Locke's theory does not provide anything like a full theory of judicial reasoning. It rather provides a general perspective from which we can evaluate different approaches to judicial reasoning. Cass Sunstein, for example, has argued that rather than making appeals to abstract principles, courts should seek "under-theorized" agreements arrived at by analogy to previous decisions.[15] One might adopt that approach to judicial reasoning because, from a legislative point of view, that is the approach one would want other judges to adopt. The very fact that a set of officials often operate in a gray area between the legislative and executive situations may necessitate developing cannons of legal reasoning appropriate to that intermediate state. The fact that different types of reasoning work better at different points along the continuum does not prove that there is no continuum or that there is a distinctive judicial function. The problem of judicial reasoning is taken up in more detail in chapter 6.

The Lockean grounds for describing the legislative/executive distinction as a continuum rather than a dichotomy are found in Locke's doctrine of delegation. Although there will be a legislative power that is ultimately supreme, it may conditionally delegate discretion to lesser officials as seems prudent. Consider the following example. Locke contrasts two different constitutional arrangements in the *Two Treatises*, one where the constitution sets the intervals at which parliament should meet and another where the king is given discretion to call and dissolve parliament (2.154). In the latter case, the rule the king must follow is sufficiently vague that he will have significant recourse to his own understanding of what would best further the purposes of natural law. If the constitution declares the exact dates on which parliament is to convene and adjourn, the king's only task is to punish deviation from the rule, and little interpretation will be required. The executive's institutional role limits his recourse to natural law in cases where the legislative direction is clear. The people must weigh the costs and benefits of discretion when deciding whether to employ clear rules or more vague standards in the constitu-

---

[15] See Sunstein, *Legal Reasoning and Political Conflict* (Oxford: Oxford University Press, 1996), chap. 3.

tion.[16] Insofar as standards are employed, a portion of the legislative power is delegated to the executive who, within the constraints of the standard, will be able to articulate general principles directing the use of force. The people when they design a constitution are in an analogous position to the legislature when it passes laws.

Once we discard the notion of a distinct judicial function, we can better describe the aspiration for legislators and executives. We should not think of legislatures as the forum of will and courts as the forum of judgment. Legislatures should aspire to justify their laws with respect to principle, either a substantive moral prohibition or a conception of the public good. Merely to invoke will is to disregard one of the principle aspects of juridical equality. The point is not so much that judges should act more like legislators, but that those entrusted with legislative power in the Lockean sense should see the discovery and articulation of principle as an essential element of their task. As one moves toward the executive pole of the continuum, discretion does decrease. Yet it is crucial that those executives to whom the legislature has delegated a share of the legislative power exercise that authority in accordance with principle. In extreme cases where the legislature becomes illegitimate, both the executive and the people will judge it in terms of principle. This way of understanding legislative activity is the corollary to the idea of consent developed in chapter 3. If we think of law as emerging from legislative rather than contractual consent, legislative action involves persons rendering judgment about what the relevant moral principles require. The contractual consent model focuses more on the pursuit of interest and thus the imposition of will. Legislative consent describes not only the attitude of citizens, but also those public officials given authority to determine the law. Not only should legislative consent be in accordance with principle, but the principles should be ones that are reasonable from a legislative point of view.

Suppose that in a given constitution the office of judge is seen as essentially executive in function; that is, the judge helps apply the law to particular persons. Since the judge is exercising an executive office, she is bound to abide by the legislature's interpretation of natural law. This will also be the case for all lower court judges on matters of principle: they may provisionally interpret the law in the light of moral principles, but they must abide by the instructions given them by the legislative authority, which is supreme. So long as legitimate government persists, there

---

[16] The distinction between rules and standards is most clear in example. Contrast a law against "excessive speed" with one against "exceeding 65 miles per hour." The former is a standard containing the evaluative and potentially controversial term "excessive," while the latter is a relatively clear rule. See Sunstein's distinction in *Legal Reasoning*, pp. 21–28.

will not be judicial anarchy because the supreme legislative power will have the authority to make its interpretation of moral principles binding on the judges and magistrates who must actually put the law into practice. If the government does become illegitimate, then citizens and judges are no longer morally bound. Of course, in a contest of strength with the government, private citizens will likely lose. But the question is who is in the right, not who will win.[17]

Consider the following example. Suppose that the United States Constitution had been written such that it specifically authorized judicial review but contained the following qualification: in cases where the meaning of the text is in doubt, the court should defer to the legislature unless it believes the legislature's interpretation is wrong beyond a reasonable doubt.[18] This is perfectly consistent with the claim that moral principles should guide interpretation of the vague parts of the text. A judge in such a system would realize that in the normal workings of government the people have specified the legislature as the proper forum for interpreting vague provisions of the Constitution and would have a strong presumption against ruling a law unconstitutional when disagreements arise between court and legislature. A doctrine of natural law still leaves open the question of who will be the interpreter of natural law within the Constitution, and judges do not have to be the final interpreters.[19] If the constitution makes other arrangements, that is acceptable. Natural law is compatible with a variety of different institutional arrangements about who will be its authoritative interpreter.[20]

My emphasis on delegation and discretion in Locke may seem vulnerable to the objection that it does not account for Locke's emphasis on clear standing rules. My first response is to point to Locke's doctrine of prerogative. That doctrine suggests that delegation of authority to an executive who must act without a clear rule is not necessarily arbitrary. Actions are arbitrary in one of two ways: either because a written law does not sanction them or because they cannot be justified with respect to a legitimate moral principle. Prerogative is arbitrary in the first sense

---

[17] "You will say then the Magistrate being the stronger will have his Will, and carry his point. Without doubt. But the Question is not here concerning the doubtfulness of the Event, but the Rule of Right" (*Letter*, 49).

[18] This would be a legal enactment of Thayer's doctrine of clear mistake. See James Bradley Thayer, "The Origin and Scope of the American Doctrine of Constitutional Law," *Harvard Law Review* 7 (1893), pp. 129–156.

[19] Interestingly, Dworkin now concedes a similar point. His views are discussed in chapter 6.

[20] This position is not unique to Locke in the natural law tradition. For of a discussion of natural law and the judicial role from the perspective of Catholic natural law, see Robert P. George, "Natural Law and Positive Law," in *The Autonomy of Law: Essays on Legal Positivism,* ed. Robert George (Oxford: Clarendon Press, 1996), pp. 321–334.

but is acceptable so long as it is not arbitrary in the second sense. The fundamental moral principle legitimating force is the preservation of society, and an act done in accordance with this principle is not a mere act of will.[21] In the case of prerogative, it is only the executive who may exercise it, and then only for the public good.[22] The public good, in a Lockean framework, represents a principled justification of the use of force. Locke believed that it would be foolish for a legislature to try to write the law in such a way that every eventuality is predicted in advance. The modern technique of writing vague laws is simply another method for accomplishing the same end without explicitly recognizing prerogative.

Locke certainly valued clear laws and expressed his impatience with legal wrangling, with attempts to confuse what should ideally be very clear principles.[23] Although the guiding principles should be as clear as possible, there will always be novel cases that produce unexpected conflicts between principles or that challenge existing conceptual categories. It is certainly within the spirit of Locke's argument to note a power in the legislature to delegate decision-making power to other agencies so long as we remember that those who exercise discretion have an obligation to do so in a principled manner. It must also be emphasized that the legislature retains the right to amend the principles articulated by those institutions to which it has delegated power. Locke makes it clear that prerogative may be limited at any time by the people, or by their supreme

[21] For a related discussion see Ruth W. Grant, *John Locke's Liberalism: A Study of Political Theory in Its Intellectual Setting* (Chicago: University of Chicago Press, 1987), pp. 72–77.

[22] This point must be qualified. Grant notes that Locke's doctrine of prerogative could be interpreted as a special case of the general right all persons have to act against the law on the basis of natural law. Anyone may break into a house to save a child from fire, and this is not qualitatively different from the magistrate's right to tear down an innocent person's house to keep a fire from spreading. The executive and the private citizen differ in the power they possess, and thus the former will have more opportunities to act. See ibid., pp. 84–85. In one sense this account is right since a private citizen may be in a situation (as in self-defense) where there is insufficient time to appeal to a constituted authority for protection, and the executive may be in situations where there is no time to convene the legislature in order to receive a ruling on a question of principle. Still, it must be remembered that there is a difference other than quantity of power since a person surrenders the natural executive power to act on the law of nature when entering civil society. It is only when one of the limiting conditions obtain—when the law is illegitimate or when there is no time to appeal to the state—that the citizen may use force directly. Presumably though, a person could break the law believing that the executive would pardon the act if the act is manifestly in the interest of natural law. Even in this case, however, citizens still recognize that so long as legitimate government persists, the constituted state has an authority both to use and to restrict prerogative.

[23] See *Essay*, 3.9.12.

representative.[24] When an executive articulates a principle to justify a particular decision, that principle is only provisional and may be modified by the legislature, which remains supreme in defining the public good, so long as government is legitimate.

Judges as Legislators: Functions versus Institutions

We must be careful not to draw a false inference from the above discussion. Consider the way one might describe the United States constitutional system on the basis of Locke's conceptual framework. The Supreme Court, in Lockean terms, must be understood to be a part of the legislative power.[25] First, much of what the Supreme Court does is define the focal meanings of the moral terms of the Constitution. On Lockean grounds this is a legislative function. Consider, for example, when the Court must decide what speech should receive constitutional protection. This is more like what the German Constitutional Court does than what a probate court does, to return to a previous example. Second, the Supreme Court must be considered part of the legislature because it is institutionally supreme; there is no higher institutional body that can overturn its decisions. This is part of the very definition of the legislative power. Since the Supreme Court has a say in what the law is, and since it has no superior institutional authority, it is part of the legislative power.

Because the legislative is the supreme power, it is tempting to infer from this that a Lockean theory must have little patience with investing nine judges with such a power. That inference is invalid because it ignores Locke's distinction between functions and institutions. The legislative function is to exercise judgment about what natural law requires; the executive executes this judgment domestically, the federative power inter-

---

[24] *Treatise*, 2.163. John Dunn notes in his chapter on prerogative that lurking behind it is the right all citizens retain of acting against the law according to their understanding of natural law. There is no way to construct a political order or set of rules that is guaranteed to work properly; given the fallible and sinful persons who will compose the government, it is always possible that citizens may have to act against the written law in order to uphold the moral law. Because the exercise of prerogative is by its very definition outside of the law, the people must judge directly whether it is legitimate, or at least it cannot be assumed that consent will be mediated by representatives in all cases. That is to say, an act of prerogative does not carry a prima facie authority but is authoritative only insofar as the people recognize it as contributing to the public good. The actual consent of subjects is the ultimate criterion for the legitimacy of prerogative, and they offer that consent based on their understanding of what natural law requires in the situation at hand. See *The Political Thought of John Locke*, pp. 154–155.

[25] Compare Hannah Arendt, *On Revolution* (New York: Penguin, 1963), pp. 219–220.

nationally.[26] We misunderstand Locke's theory, however, if we assume that Locke believed there would be a simple one-to-one correspondence between function and institutions. Locke assumed that the king would perform both the federative and executive functions since both require constant attention and substantial military force (2.148). Just as one person can perform two distinct functions, so also several institutions can collectively perform a single function. Locke assumed that the Crown, the House of Lords, and the House of Commons would share the legislative power in England. Natural law does not, in Locke's mind, mandate a particular form of government, although it does govern the purposes that any government may pursue.

Consider Locke's discussion of the different forms of government (2.132). The majority, upon uniting, has authority either to act directly as legislature (democracy) or to entrust legislative power to one or more persons, creating a monarchy or oligarchy. "And so accordingly of these the Community may make compounded and mixed Forms of Government, as they think good." Neither the Bible nor natural law, according to Locke, specifies a particular form of government, in large part because it is perfectly reasonable to believe that at different stages of human history, different forms of government will be appropriate. Locke noted how monarchy might have been the most natural form of government when people lived primarily in clans (2.107–112). Locke's views on church government provide an instructive parallel.[27] The debate over the proper form of church government was raging in Locke's time and his position on it was forcefully articulated in the *Critical Notes on Stillingfleet*. Locke tried to diffuse much of the controversy by claiming that even if one could show that the early church used a particular form of government, this would not prove that that form is mandatory now. The Scriptures do not contain any express instructions for deciding among congregational, presbyterian, and episcopal government; God would have left this ambiguous only if it was left to our reason and prudence to determine what form would best advance the Gospel in a given circumstance.[28]

The most difficult political question is whether courts should have a part of the supreme legislative power. Should they actually have a veto power concerning what rights people have and what goods the state may pursue? Lockean arguments do not, in the end, provide a decisive answer

[26] The federative is analytically distinct from the executive because the law it interprets is the law of nations, natural law, rather than a positive written law.

[27] It was quite common for discussions of church government and civil government to overlap. An influential example in Locke's time was Richard Hooker, *Of the Laws of Ecclesiastical Polity*, ed. A. S. McGrade (Cambridge: Cambridge University Press, 1975).

[28] Ms Locke c.34, pp. 3–4.

to this question, but they can guide our thinking on the subject. On the one hand Locke clearly thought elected assemblies very important. He allows for the possibility of all legislative authority being given to a single person, but he thought such an action very unwise:

> the People finding their Properties not secure under the Government, as then it was . . . could never be safe nor at rest, *nor think themselves in Civil Society*, till the Legislature was placed in collective Bodies of Men, call them Senate, Parliament, or what you please. By which means every single person became subject, equally with other the meanest Men, to those Laws, which he himself, as part of the Legislative had established. (*Treatises*, 2.94)

Locke clearly thought that any good legislature would include a large representative assembly. Although he makes it clear that the legislature should include such an assembly, he never says that it should consist only of such an assembly.[29] He seems to have been quite happy with the king and House of Lords exercising legislative power. We will explore this question more in chapter 6 when examining the American case; the important point here is that this indeterminacy in the Lockean position is enough to dispose of the objection that Lockean arguments cannot guide judicial interpretation of a written constitution because he would have found such an activity necessarily illegitimate. A Lockean theory has more to say on the issue of constitutional interpretation than that it is for parliaments and not courts. It is open to a variety of institutional structures, and Lockean arguments are guides to legislative power however it is institutionally arranged, even if that arrangement should include nine unelected judges.

However this question is decided, the distinction between functions and institutions allows a Lockean theory to provide an important institutional role for courts even though it rejects the idea that courts do something qualitatively different than legislate and execute the law. Locke made it clear that appointing courts to settle disputes would be a primary task of the legislature. "The Legislative, or Suprem Authority, cannot assume to its self a power to Rule by extemporary Arbitrary Decrees, but *is bound to dispense Justice,* and decide the Rights of the Subject *by promulgated standing Laws, and known Authoris'd Judges*" (2.136). Locke goes on to contrast the state of nature where each person is "Judge, Interpreter, and Executioner" (note the distinction between judging and interpreting) of the law of nature and the disagreement that follows from

---

[29] Although our positions are similar, Waldron does not sufficiently emphasize this last point. See *Law and Disagreement*, pp. 307–309. Locke's main concern was that there be an elected assembly, not that such an assembly have sole legislative power.

this situation. Locke recognized that a court system would be necessary and that the state would need authoritative interpreters of the general laws laid down by Parliament. Insofar as empowering courts is an effective means to securing rights and promoting the public good, a Lockean theory has no objections. An independent judiciary, for example, is important as a way to ensure that the executive impartially administers the law. In many cases, the greatest danger is not mistakes in high-level theory about what morality sanctions but the biased enforcement of those principles that are widely recognized as true. An independent court system capable of overseeing and correcting the executive is extremely important in practice. On the more difficult question of disagreement about what rights we actually have, the courts may again have an important role to play. The appellate process provides a way for individuals who feel their rights are being denied to make their case heard and considered. In mass society, it is very difficult for an individual to make her case heard before an elected assembly that represents millions. Even if an elected assembly is the highest court of appeals, the appellate process still insures that persons will not be put in a situation where their first choice is between submission to injustice or the appeal to heaven.

Implications for Contested Roles

From this discussion, two important conclusions emerge. First, Locke did not talk about the "judicial role" because there is no such thing. There are a variety of judicial roles that correspond to the different functions judges are asked to perform. Some are more legislative and some are more executive. As one moves in either direction, the nature of the role will change. Legislative activity is largely about defining the focal meanings of the key moral and legal terms that will regulate the use of force. Executive activity is largely concerned with applying these legislatively defined terms to particular cases. In practice, many government officials are asked to do some of both. Interpretation is something that all branches do; it is not the special function of a particular branch. We thus see more clearly the normative implications of a Lockean theory for executives and legislators. Locke's theory applies to legislators in the first instance and other officials insofar as they perform legislative functions. Legislators, and those whom they represent, should see the legislative task in moral terms and should ask what moral principle or conception of the public good justifies the coercion they authorize. Applying the argument from chapters 2 and 3, the principles should be ones that respect juridical equality and are reasonable from a legislative point of view. Persons who hold executive offices are asked to respect legislative interpretations of fundamental moral principles because of the need to have some common decision procedure in states characterized by moral disagreement. The legislative point of view is thus applicable to what are not traditionally thought of as legislative situations.

Second, because the "legislative power" need not be confined to an elected assembly, the people have considerable institutional flexibility when adopting a constitution. Locke thought the king and House of Lords were part of the legislative power. In the United States, for example, the offices of Supreme Court justice and president are, in part, legislative offices. This is of great importance for the discussion in the next chapter. In instances where the legislative power is shared by several institutions, it is predictable that there will be disagreement about the relative roles of the different institutions. When disputes break out about the allocation of power between the various parts of the legislature, there is no higher institutional body to which they can appeal to settle the dispute. From a Lockean perspective, disputes between the Supreme Court, Congress, and president over the relative roles of each in interpreting the Constitution are analogous to disputes in the state of nature where there is no higher earthly authority. In the following chapter I explore problems of this sort. I argue that the legislative point of view is not merely consistent with the idea of institutional roles but also of use when those roles are contested. It is possible to draw an analogy between the right of the people to define constitutional roles and the legislative point of view as it applies to moral principles.

CHAPTER 6

Contested Roles, Interpretation, and the Framer's Point of View

Constitutional crises come in all shapes and sizes. The 2000 Florida election crisis raised questions about the proper roles of state and federal courts, state and federal law, and various state officials in administering federal elections. In 1974 a constitutional crisis arose over the extent of the president's "executive privilege." The American Civil War was a constitutional crisis on a far greater scale. These are the sorts of crises that make headlines and history books. But there are also smaller, more mundane "crises" that occur so often we hardly recognize them as such. The pitched battles every time a Supreme Court nominee is confirmed or rejected reflect lingering controversy over what the proper role of the Court is, a controversy that continues with each controversial decision. What all of these crises have in common is that the constitutional rules and principles that are supposed to allocate power and define roles are themselves contested.

This final chapter applies the idea of a legislative point of view to situations where the institutional roles that political actors occupy are themselves contested. I claim that the legislative point of view is useful not only for making particular decisions about the use of force, but also for defining the roles that political actors occupy where these are vague and contested. If "No cruel or unusual punishment" is a contested principle, so is "The judicial Power of the United States, shall be vested in one supreme Court, and in such inferior Courts as the Congress may from time to time ordain and establish."[1] Just as there is disagreement about which punishments are cruel, so also there is disagreement about what the "judicial Power" entails. It is not uncommon for political actors to confront both substantive and jurisdictional contested principles at the same time. Locke is a particularly apt theorist to consider when the meaning of the constitution is itself in question. The political disputes of his own day involved a constitutional crisis about the relative roles of king and Parliament. Locke's political theory called for each person to exercise sober judgment in such situations.

---

[1] From the Eighth Amendment and Article 3, Section 1, of the United States Constitution.

It may already be clear, from the argument of the previous chapters, how a legislative point of view would apply to situations of this kind. Persons who occupy vague and contested roles should imagine themselves in the position of a hypothetical framer or legislator who will specify the guidelines for and the jurisdiction of the disputed role. Such a framer will realize that a variety of fallible persons will occupy the role in question. In the next section this chapter, I argue for this conclusion. I claim that because constitutional jurisdictional disputes are analogous to the state of nature the Lockean insights from the previous chapters apply. Just as persons in a Lockean state of nature must interpret a higher law for themselves with no higher institutional authority to guide them, so also persons who hold a portion of the supreme legislative power must interpret a constitution, and often the constitution's specification of their particular roles, without a higher earthly authority to give them the correct answer. Locke's legislative point of view is of great value in situations like this.

In the remaining sections I apply this insight, taking disputes over the U.S. Constitution as the focal case. In the third section I discuss the case in general terms. I argue that the relative roles of the three branches of government in interpreting the U.S. Constitution are contested. Supreme Court justices therefore face contested principles at two different levels: they must interpret substantive clauses that are contested in meaning, and they must interpret contested principles defining the proper role of the Court itself. I argue that debates over which theory of interpretation Supreme Court justices should use are to an important extent debates about the proper institutional role of the courts. For this reason, a Supreme Court justice should select her theory of constitutional interpretation using a variant of the legislative point of view. The fourth and fifth sections in this chapter show a more specific application of the theory. Building on the claim that debates over how Supreme Court justices should interpret the Constitution are actually proxies for debates about jurisdiction, I present a critique of two prominent schools of American constitutional interpretation from a legislative point of view. The final section examines the application of the legislative point of view to specific cases. Since a discussion of American constitutional interpretation may seem oddly placed in what has been a fairly abstract exercise in political theory, I explain the reasons for its inclusion below.

The most important reason is precisely that the foregoing discussion has been, in many respects, rather abstract. I have been arguing for a general moral perspective that constrains but does not determine the results of deliberation. Presenting the position as a general perspective makes it possible for a wider array of persons to accept it, but it also renders the conclusions indeterminate. My claim is that a theory that merely constrains but does not determine results is nonetheless significant. In this chapter I look at actual theoretical positions in more detail to show how this moral perspective clarifies the criteria we should use in evaluating competing proposals, again without arguing definitively for a particular one. Taking up these specific issues also gives me an opportunity to argue more explicitly in my own voice rather than Locke's. Locke did not himself explicitly apply the legislative point of view to constitutional disputes, but his own arguments may be easily understood to make use of that point of view. One cannot say with confidence that the historical Locke would extend his theory in this way. For rather obvious chronological reasons, the historical Locke could not have an opinion on the American founding or the history of American constitutional practice. Taking a contemporary example thus illustrates the analogical method. Disputes about constitutional interpretation, although admittedly different from Locke's own historical situation, are similar in morally relevant ways.

While these reasons support applying Locke's theory to some particular dispute, they do not justify the choice of constitutional interpretation as a case. Constitutional interpretation is a particularly helpful case for our present purposes because, as we shall see, it shows how when applying the general Lockean legislative point of view one can make use of a number of other insights that we have gleaned from Locke along the way. In particular, this discussion can help fulfill the promise made in chapter 5. There I claimed that Locke's understanding of separation of powers and institutional roles could clarify the moral aspirations of political actors. A discussion of the problem of constitutional interpretation can illustrate the way in which a different conception of the judicial role would make a practical difference in how a Supreme Court justice should perform the duties of his office. Second, since American constitutional interpretation is generally framed around disagreements about how one should interpret a "higher law," it presents a striking analogy to Locke's argument, which was about how to select between conflicting interpretations of natural law. It therefore provides an excellent opportunity to apply the analogical approach. Third, insofar as this book is a contribution to debates about the proper scope of toleration, it makes sense to look at questions of constitutional interpretation since in practice questions about toleration are often decided at the constitutional level. For example, Americans tend to think of religious toleration as primarily an issue for the courts because of the First Amendment, which protects the free exercise of religion and bars the federal government from establishing a religion. The courts take the leading role in determining what the religion clauses actually prevent the government from doing. Since questions of toleration center on the appropriate legitimate scope of government, they are among the most likely to be considered at a constitutional level.

Contested Jurisdiction and the "Framer's Point of View"

In chapter 5 we noted the following relevant facts about Locke's theory of institutional roles. First, his commitment to natural law is consistent with asking persons to give some deference to legislative interpretations of natural law because of the institutional role that they occupy. Second, one of the tasks of the people, when they found a constitution, is to give the legislative power some form of determinate institutional shape. Third, the people have considerable flexibility in selecting among different institutional arrangements. There need not be a one-to-one correspondence between powers and institutions, and the people may, if they wish, place a portion of the legislative power in a person or body that is not elected.

The problem is that in many, perhaps most, countries, the actual reality is considerably messier than that. Regardless of whether the constitution is written or not, it must be interpreted, and where the allocation of power is concerned, disputes will be the norm. The degree of contestation does vary from time to time and from country to country. In the United Kingdom, for example, the House of Commons gradually emerged as the center of legislative authority. Even though there are still lingering disputes about what role the monarch and House of Lords should play in the constitutional structure, these are relatively minor when compared with the disputes in Locke's time about the relative roles of Parliament and Crown. During Locke's time, the situation was very ambiguous and intermittently violent. How should one resolve such disputes over constitutional jurisdiction? Locke's answer was that because both Parliament and Crown were part of the legislative power, there could be no appeal in such cases except to heaven (*Treatises*, 2.168). The argument I develop below would thus be of more relevance to England in the seventeenth century than in the twenty-first. Even so, the United Kingdom faces interesting constitutional jurisdictional questions in its relationship to the European Union; the United Kingdom is also considering the adoption of a judicially enforceable bill of rights. Thus even in cases where the full legislative power seems to be firmly in the hands of a single institutional body, the possibility of jurisdictional disputes remains close at hand. Other nations confront analogous problems.

In theory, a written constitution should ameliorate the problem considerably. The people would adopt precise language either locating supreme power in a particular body or clearly articulating the specific roles that several different branches are supposed to play. In practice, this is often not the case. Those constitutions, like that of the United States, that make use of a doctrine of separation of powers may actually have a more difficult time if the written constitution is vague and imprecise about how constitutional disputes are to be resolved. Federalism presents another layer of complexity. This vagueness should not be regarded as a mere defect in the drafting process. One of the difficulties of adopting a written constitution is precisely that one must get enough votes to ratify it. Adopting vague provisions and postponing difficult questions until a later date are often unavoidable if one wants to insure that *some* document is adopted. Thus it is quite common for there to be significant disagreement about what role different branches of a government should play in defining the scope of their powers and adjudicating constitutional disputes.

There is a striking analogy between jurisdictional disputes of this type and disputes in the state of nature. In both cases there is a recognized source—God in the one case and the people in the other—capable of settling the dispute. The problem is that God has left natural law unwritten and the people have not explicitly answered the relevant question in the constitutional text. Given the fallibility of human beings, there will be disagreement both about how some ideas in natural law are to be interpreted and about which jurisdictional interpretation of the constitution is best. One of the defining features of the state of nature is that there is no institutional authority to whom one could appeal to receive a ruling that would bind both sides of the dispute. In a similar way, where there is dispute about what the constitution says about how to resolve constitutional disputes, there is no institutional authority above the contending parties that can settle the question. In one sense, of course, the people could resolve the question. But because it is rarely possible for one side to force a constitutional convention to settle the question, in practice the situation is similar. This is why Locke thought that disputes about fundamental issues between the king and Parliament involved an appeal to heaven. When what is in dispute is who speaks for the people, the people can only settle the question by siding with the person or group that they think really speaks for them.

These disputes about constitutional jurisdiction will affect the way the government uses its coercive power. The use of coercion involves making oneself "judge over" another and therefore triggers the requirement that a person approach such questions from a framer's point of view. If Parliament says to the king, "We speak for the people, and you do not," they are making themselves "judge over" the king and, in an institutional sense, "judge over" the people as well. Any assertion of legislative power is an assertion of the right to coerce and thus should be made from a legislative point of view. To fail to do so would be to disregard the moral equality of persons, and would fail to respect them as moral agents under a common moral framework.

For this reason, we should ask persons in constitutional disputes to apply a variant of the legislative point of view that I will call a "framer's point of view." This means that an official's job description should be thought of as issued by the people in their capacity as framers of the constitution. As we have seen, in Locke's original theory, interpreting a disputed higher law meant trying as best one could to reason from God's perspective. In this secular analogue, persons think of themselves as proposing a moral framework that will guide both themselves and others rather than thinking that they propose rules only for themselves.[2] In constitutional disputes about jurisdiction, it is the people, acting in their capacity as constitutional framers, who could settle the dispute, and thus proposals must be reasonable from their perspective rather than from the situated perspective of a particular justice, president, or senator.

Whereas in normal legislative situations one tries to take on a legislative point of view, in constitutional debates of this sort one tries to take on a framer's point of view. I use "framer" to make more concrete what is always implicit in the legislative point of view, the claim that the relevant standpoint of evaluation rests with a higher source of authority than oneself. In the legislative case the legislator considers whether she would want other legislators to legislate on the basis of the same moral principles that she does. "Framer's point of view" makes it explicit that one of the things that must be justified is the particular role that a public official claims for himself when that role has not been clearly defined by the people. This is precisely what a framer does when writing a constitution. I also use the change in terminology as a reminder that since natural law contains no direct commands as to the proper constitutional arrangement, we are in the realm of human prudence. Locke's legislative point of view was originally a way of discerning the will of God as legislator. Lockean framers are very much human.

The framer's point of view should not be confused with the doctrine of original intent. A person does not ask what the actual historical framers intended. Rather, one asks whether the proposed allocation of power among branches is one that would be reasonable from the perspective of

---

[2] When they do so, they should try to keep the institutional level constant. That is to say, in a genuine state of nature they would ask what principles others in a genuine state of nature should employ. In a constituted state they might adopt procedural rules that they would not have adopted in the state of nature, but that they would want other constituted states to adopt.

hypothetical framers. I will explain my reasons for rejecting the "original intent" version of the argument later in the chapter. Rather than asking for the original intent of historical framers, the framer's point of view works as follows. Suppose the king of England in Locke's time thinks that he should rule as an absolute monarch. Charles II, for the record, did entertain the thought.[3] What moral criteria should the king use in evaluating such a proposal? He may not reason, "I am a particularly good monarch and would do more good for the people if I did not answer to Parliament." Instead he would have to argue, "If I were one of the people founding a constitution, I would support the establishment an absolute monarchy, fully aware that monarchs are fallible and that they vary greatly in quality." The framer's point of view specifies the type of argument required to overcome the presumption against setting oneself up as judge.

Contested Constitutional Jurisdiction in the United States

Since the previous illustration from Locke's time may seem far removed from our own historical situation, in this section I begin discussing a very real, practical, and important case of contested jurisdiction, disputes over constitutional jurisdiction and interpretation in the United States. The text of the U.S. Constitution does not specifically include the power of judicial review among the powers granted to the Supreme Court. It contains little by way of instruction as to how the document is to be interpreted, whichever branch of government may do the interpreting. Those instructions that it does contain are often more difficult to interpret than the substantive provisions. The Ninth Amendment is an interpretive instruction and is one of the most mysterious clauses in the entire Constitution. It reads, "The enumeration of certain rights in the Constitution shall not be construed to deny or disparage others retained by the people." What are the other rights and, more importantly, *who* identifies them? The same considerations of vagueness that guide the construction of substantive clauses also apply to interpretive clauses. Interpretive instructions also have to be interpreted. This does not mean that a text can be interpreted to mean just anything, but it does mean that we should not expect constitutional interpretation to be a mechanical process.

What the Constitution does say is that "The judicial Power of the United States, shall be vested in one supreme Court, and in such inferior

---

[3] Richard Ashcraft, *Revolutionary Politics and Locke's Two Treatises of Government* (Princeton: Princeton University Press, 1986), pp. 17–19.

Courts as the Congress may from time to time ordain and establish." It also says that the Constitution is the "supreme Law of the Land" and that all government officials, including judges, are bound by it.[4] The problem is that since the scope of the judicial power is not defined, we have all the makings of a contested principle. History has not disappointed us. Throughout American history, both private citizens and politicians have fiercely disputed the proper roles of the Supreme Court, Congress, and president in interpreting the Constitution. Thomas Jefferson never recognized the authority of *Marbury v. Madison*.[5] Andrew Jackson and Franklin D. Roosevelt also spoke out against the Court's dominance of the realm of constitutional interpretation.[6] Most famously, Abraham Lincoln in his first inaugural address rejected the idea of judicial supremacy in the wake of *Dred Scott* and claimed that although the Court could decide individual cases, it did not have the final say on matters of principle. Much more recently, the United States Congress overwhelmingly passed and President Clinton signed the Religious Freedom Restoration Act, an attempt to overturn part of the Supreme Court's interpretation of the free exercise clause by requiring all infringements of religious liberty to meet a much more stringent standard.[7] The Supreme Court has consistently rejected these claims, especially in *Cooper v. Aaron*[8] and most recently in *City of Boerne v. Flores*,[9] where the Supreme Court overturned the Religious Freedom Restoration Act. We will discuss this history of disagreement from a more theoretical perspective in the next section when we address Ronald Dworkin's theory.

Questions of who interprets the Constitution are highly intertwined with the question of how the Constitution should be interpreted. Which theory of interpretation a Supreme Court justice adopts will at least partially determine how she resolves these jurisdictional disputes. A Supreme Court justice who adopted James Bradley Thayer's rule of striking down acts of Congress only if Congress had made a "clear mistake" in interpreting the Constitution would give the elected branches a much larger role in interpreting the Constitution.[10] By contrast, a justice who followed the rule of simply adopting the interpretation that, on the merits, seemed

---

[4] See Article 6.

[5] 5 U.S. 137 (1803).

[6] The relevant excerpts can be found in Walter J. Murphy, James S. Fleming, and Sotirios A. Barber, eds., *American Constitutional Interpretation* (Westbury, NY: Foundation Press, 1995), pp. 307, 313, and 317, respectively.

[7] 42 USCS §§2000bb et seq.

[8] 358 U.S. 1 (1958).

[9] 521 U.S. 507 (1997).

[10] Thayer, "The Origin and Scope of the American Doctrine of Constitutional Law."

best to him would give the elected branches a smaller role in interpreting the Constitution. When a justice must choose between competing theories of interpretation, there is no higher institutional authority specifying the correct answer (the Constitution certainly does not), and which theory he selects will have a significant impact on the way the government uses its coercive force. Because of this, proposals about how the U.S. Constitution should be interpreted must be regarded as contributions to this debate over the proper role of the various branches. Since a constitutional amendment to overturn judicial review is unlikely, to say the least, persons who want the elected branches to play a larger role make their case by proposing more restrictive theories of constitutional interpretation. The fierce debates over interpretation are one sign of the deep division that still remains about the appropriate roles of the three branches. Indeed, Senate confirmation hearings have become a forum where such wars are fought.

In such circumstances, justices should choose interpretive strategies from a legislative point of view. Since any interpretive theory will implicitly or explicitly be a partial proposal for settling the jurisdictional dispute, interpretive theories must also be reasonable from the framer's perspective. When an interpretive theory is proposed, the one proposing must recognize that other persons may interpret the proposal in different ways than he intended. If an interpretive proposal contains vague terms that would give broad discretion to judges, the one proposing cannot endorse it on the condition that his preferred explication of the interpretive paradigm prevails. Here a framer's point of view means imagining a set of instructions that would be given to all present and future justices clarifying how they should interpret the Constitution. It is of course unlikely that the people will adopt any such constitutional amendment. The point is that the framer's point of view functions as a helpful guide to conduct.

A Supreme Court justice will therefore face a rather complicated set of choices when trying to adjudicate a particular case because there are so many layers of contested principles simultaneously present. First, the specific clause of the Constitution will likely contain a contested principle, such as the "due process of law" requirement. Second, the proper role of the justice in interpreting that clause is also contested. Selection of a theory of interpretation to assist in rendering judgment will entail a controversial claim about the proper role of the Court relative to the other branches in interpreting the Constitution. The justice will thus first need to adopt a framer's point of view and ask what role for the courts a good interpretive theory should presuppose and restrict the choice of interpretive theories accordingly. Next, to the extent that the chosen interpretive theory permits the judge to make use of substantive moral principles not explicitly in the text (as many approaches to "due process" do), those principles should be acceptable from a legislative point of view as described in the preceding chapters.

The framer's point of view encourages people to seek principles of interpretation that are more "neutral" and less "contested." It will thus call to mind Herbert Wechsler's famous article "Toward Neutral Principles of Constitutional Law," in which he argued forcefully that judges should find general and neutral principles in the constitutional text rather than simply acting as a third branch of the legislature.[11] His main argument is that the principles should be general in that they reach farther than the case immediately at hand and that judges should neutrally apply those principles to those other cases even when doing so causes their preferred side to lose. The framer's point of view, though different from Wechsler's proposal, captures some of the same aspirations.[12] In particular, both approaches ask us to act on general principles even when we would rather not do so. Insofar as a judge issues a ruling on a ground of principle that reaches beyond the case in question and realizes that her ruling will serve as a precedent that will guide others in the future, she must ask the Lockean question, "Would I want my fellow judges to interpret and apply the principle that justifies my verdict in this case to other cases as well?" The framer's point of view takes this logic one step further by applying it to the justice's self-definition of her role. One interesting fact about constitutional interpretation is that a judge writing an opinion is much more likely than the average person to be in a position where

[11] *Harvard Law Review* 73 (1959), pp. 1–35.

[12] The differences are worth noting briefly. First, Wechsler bases his argument on the assumption that the Constitution does contain a clear delegation to courts that they be the forum of neutral principles. His argument rests primarily on the Supremacy Clause. His argument is not obviously wrong; indeed, if it were then the Constitution would not be as ambiguous as I claim it is. But it is not obviously right either. One could grant the supremacy of the federal government in interpreting the Constitution as law without assuming the judicial branch of the federal government is the primary forum of constitutional principle. I defend this position in more detail below. Second, Weschsler is *implicitly* rejecting contested principles, in the sense I use the term, in his demand for principles that are, in his sense, neutral and general. His most famous example is school desegregation, which he takes to be primarily about the problem of freedom of association. He saw no way to derive, from the principle of freedom of association as such, a principle that favors the freedom of those who want to associate with the other race over the freedom of those who do not. If Wechsler had thought it permissible to include a contested term like "worthwhile" in the original principle, there would not have been a dilemma. He rejected that option because for him neutrality was primarily about following the rule even when it causes your side to lose. Contested principles, in my sense, could (if used liberally) allow judges to appear to follow rules without their preferred side ever losing. A Lockean theory asks the further question of how we proceed in a principled way when there is no neutral position between the two sides.

other persons actually *will* interpret and apply the very same principle. Future judges will actually read the opinion he writes and interpret the justificatory reasons he gives. In practice, judges often do give considerable thought to how other people will interpret their opinions. For this reason, the judge has a practical as well as a moral reason to think in Lockean terms.

Since all of this is still quite abstract, in the next two sections I want to indicate the relevance of this approach by comparing it with two very different alternatives. Although my discussion will not settle once and for all which interpretive strategy justices should use, it will reveal weaknesses in some prominent interpretive proposals. Specifically, it can show that they try to bypass this justificatory requirement and can clarify the grounds on which such theories could be endorsed, if they can be endorsed at all. I will apply this Lockean insight to two very different approaches: that of Ronald Dworkin and that of the originalists, especially Antonin Scalia.

Dworkin and the Legislative Point of View

The most important aspect of Dworkin's theory for our present purposes is his account of the criteria we should use in evaluating different interpretations of the role of the courts in American constitutional practice. For these criteria to make sense, however, I must briefly and roughly describe Dworkin's interpretive approach, drawing primarily on *Law's Empire*.[13] He claims that we must move beyond a simple "plain fact" view of law and recognize that the interpretive process is essential to describing what the law is. Different people will offer different interpretations of a given law, and they are really disagreeing about what the law is, not what they would like it to be. The judge must then ask which of the competing interpretations is best. Dworkin claims that competing interpretations of law should be judged on the basis of fit and justification. The judge must first ask how well the judgment in question can account for past precedents and statutes. The second question is which interpretation of the law is most just. The fact that a numerical majority passes a statute does not make it legitimate; only higher moral principles can do that. Positive law must be interpreted in light of those principles that can render it legitimate.

Behind Dworkin's theory is a desire to account for the actual practice of judges when they interpret the law. One conspicuous feature of legal

---

[13] *Law's Empire* (Cambridge: Belknap Press of Harvard University, 1986).

interpretation is that it places great weight on previous decisions. Dworkin compares three different theories that can account for this concern with "fit": conventionalism, pragmatism, and integrity. Dworkin claims that law as integrity not only better accounts for the way judges actually render decisions but also puts our practice in a better moral light than the competing theories of interpretation. Neither of the competing approaches, according to Dworkin, can adequately account for the role that principles play in actual adjudication. Moreover, an understanding of our legal system as concerned with principle puts that system in the best light.

There is much in this approach that is congenial to a Lockean one. The emphasis on moral principles as criteria for legitimacy and the role of moral principles in interpreting the law is a noted similarity between Dworkinian and natural law approaches. An important difference, however, is in the ways they understand legislation. Dworkin, operating with the sharp distinction between judicial and legislative action that is characteristics of so much American jurisprudence, must develop a rather complex theory to assure us that when judges appeal to principles they are only interpreting, not legislating.[14] The analysis in chapter 5 shows us the problem with this approach. Insofar as a meaningful distinction can be drawn between adjudication and legislation, it will follow the distinction between executive and legislative functions. The former applies principles to specific cases while the latter articulates general principles on the basis of an interpretation of either a higher positive law, morality itself, or both. Judges are not performing a unique function so much as occupying various points along a continuum. When they have more discretion they are more like legislators since a larger portion of their task will be the articulation of a new principle. Dworkin is most concerned with how the abstract provisions of the Constitution will be interpreted. Insofar as the court is determining the focal meaning of key words and phrases, rather than taking terms whose focal meanings are clear and applying them to new cases as they arise, it must be understood to perform a legislative function.

For the primary question under consideration here, this point is a semantic one. In a Lockean theory, part of the very definition of the legislature is that it is the highest institutional forum for settling questions of principle. Dworkin does not refer to judges as legislators, but he does claim that they should be the highest institutional forum for questions of

[14] This may be largely rhetorical. Dworkin, after all, is the champion of the view that the judicial activism/judicial restraint dichotomy is misleading. His argument is really about reshaping our conception of interpretation, not about assuring us that judges are really acting as conventionalists say they do.

principle and realizes that this is no small thing.[15] Despite the difference
in terminology, there is an important similarity. A Lockean theory grants
that the people could invest a portion of the legislative power in a Supreme Court but does not require them to do so. Dworkin, likewise,
grants that a court may be the highest forum of principle but does not
claim that it has to be. He even admits that there are weighty reasons why
a nation might decide not to do so. What he wants to stress is that democracy is compatible with either institutional arrangement. Dworkin admits
that a moral reading of the constitution is compatible with the belief that
the people, rather than the courts, should take the lead in interpreting.[16]

From this similar position, Dworkin makes an inference that is on
Lockean grounds illegitimate. Dworkin grants that when a constitution is
founded, the people may place the final interpretive authority in the
hands they choose, that they can decide whether to include abstract standards in their constitution or limit themselves to readily interpretable
rules.

> The situation is different, however, when we are interpreting an es-
> tablished constitutional practice, not starting a new one. Then au-
> thority is already distributed by history, and details of institutional
> responsibility are matters of interpretation, not of invention from
> nothing. In these circumstances, rejecting the majoritarian premise
> means that we may look for the best interpretation with a more open
> mind: we have no reason of principle to try to force our practices into
> some majoritarian mold. If the most straightforward interpretation
> of American constitutional practice shows that our judges have final
> interpretive authority, and that they largely understand the Bill of
> Rights as a constitution of principle—if that best explains the deci-
> sions judges actually make and the public largely accepts—we have
> no reason to resist that reading and to strain for one that seems more
> congenial to majoritarian philosophy.[17]

Dworkin claims that there is a best theory (or at least better and worse
theories) of interpretation and that *whichever* institution is charged with
interpreting the constitution should make use of that best theory.

> It is perfectly intelligible to insist that our judges should not be
> charged with final and authoritative interpretation of the Constitu-

---

[15] Dworkin does not believe that the courts are the highest forum of principle absolutely. He argues in chapter 8 of *Taking Rights Seriously* that individuals can engage in civil
disobedience as a matter of conscience.

[16] *Freedom's Law: The Moral Reading of the American Constitution* (Cambridge:
Harvard University Press, 1996), p. 12.

[17] Ibid., pp. 34–35.

tion. If you fear too great judicial power, that is what you should say. It is a serious confusion to disguise your dislike of judges having great power, which can be remedied, in theory, by changing their jurisdictional power, as a false theory of legal reasoning.[18]

In our case it is judges who interpret the Constitution, but Dworkin would claim that the jurisdictional question should not prevent them from using the best interpretive theory and that we can assess the interpretive theory without addressing the jurisdictional question.

Rather than taking on the whole of Dworkin's theory, I want to focus on these particular claims from a Lockean perspective. At least in a country like the United States where the original grant of jurisdiction was vague, interpretive questions and jurisdictional questions are much more closely related than Dworkin admits. I want to focus first on the authority of history and "American constitutional practice." Let us suppose that Dworkin is right that judges in fact have final interpretive authority, that they understand the text to be a document of principle, and that the public accepts as legitimate the judgments handed down by the courts. These assumptions do not warrant the conclusion that the institutional questions that might lead us to place interpretive authority in other hands are irrelevant when deciding how judges should interpret the Constitution.

I will briefly sketch the objection to Dworkin before filling it out in more detail. Dworkin, as he must, cites as support for his conclusion popular acceptance of judicial review in the United States. Both he and Locke allow the people to put legislative authority in unelected hands, but the people granting that authority is a necessary condition of its legitimacy. Nine people who appeared from nowhere and claimed a right to strike down legislation based on their interpretation of the Constitution would have no legitimacy. Since the text of the Constitution itself does not give judges this power, Dworkin appeals to the history of American constitutional practice in which judges have, in fact, emerged as the final interpreters of the Constitution and to the popular acceptance of that role. I do not want to base my objection to Dworkin's claim on a distinction between explicit and tacit consent. If over the course of our history an overwhelming consensus had emerged among the people that judges should occupy the role that Dworkin prescribes for them, it would hardly be less authoritative than an explicit provision written hundreds of years ago. The problem with Dworkin's claim is that it ignores a gap that has always existed between the judicial process he describes and the popular justification of judicial review. As a result of this gap, unresolved questions about who should interpret the Constitution manifest themselves as

---

[18] "In Praise of Theory," *Arizona State Law Journal* 29 (1997), p. 360.

disputes over how the Constitution should be interpreted. Since both the text of the Constitution and current public opinion can be construed in very different ways, the legislative power in the United States, in Lockean terms, is partially unsettled. Since only a decisive declaration by the people, for example through a constitutional amendment or constitutional convention, could settle the question, judges must be able to justify their interpretive strategy from the standpoint of the people, from a framer's point of view. This means asking what interpretive theory should be prescribed for all judges, and this will force judges to take into account questions of institutional competence.

The first claim upon which this objection rests is empirical. At the time of the founding and subsequently throughout American constitutional history, the people have never decisively settled the jurisdictional question. The U.S. Constitution does not clearly specify who is to be its authoritative interpreter. The text of the Constitution does not list judicial review as a power of the Supreme Court. It is mostly silent on the question of how the document should be interpreted. The interpretive instructions that it does contain are often more difficult to interpret than the substantive commands.

The seeds of the dispute were thus planted in what the Constitution does not say and sparked a vigorous debate between Federalists and Anti-Federalists. "Brutus," the most theoretically sophisticated of the Anti-Federalists, claimed that the Constitution was imitating the British system correctly in giving judges tenure during good behavior so that they could make politically unpopular rulings and serve as a check on the executive. This system worked well in England in part because judges were *not* the highest court, Parliament was. Brutus was concerned that the Constitution would be construed as giving institutional supremacy to the Supreme Court.[19]

Hamilton's argument in *Federalist* 78 was a response to this fear, and it remains the most popular justification of judicial review, at least outside of academia. The Federalists were sufficiently committed to the idea of a democratic republic that they were unwilling to argue that the justices of the Supreme Court should possess supremacy over the people's elected representatives. Instead, Hamilton claimed that the people are superior to the representatives who act as their agents; the people directly enact a Constitution that is superior to those laws that are not enacted directly by the people but through their legislative agents. The orders of a higher power constrain a lower power; thus legislative acts contrary to the Constitution are void. The Supreme Court, as the highest judicial

---

[19] In *The Anti-Federalist: Writings of Opponents of the Constitution*, ed. Herbert J. Storing (Chicago: University of Chicago Press, 1985), pp. 182–186.

power, is obliged to strike down any law that it believes conflicts with the Constitution. This does not imply the superiority of the judicial branch to the legislative, only the inferiority of both to the people. Hamilton twice quotes Montesquieu, noting that the judicial is the weakest of the powers and that it must be separated from the executive and legislative in order to preserve liberty.

When Montesquieu articulated the separation of powers as judicial, legislative, and executive, we might think that he was rejecting the Lockean division of federative, legislative, and executive. Indeed our tendency is (anachronistically) to read Montesquieu in the light of Hamilton.[20] In fact, the British system that Montesquieu was applauding did not have a court empowered with judicial review. When he spoke of the independence of the judiciary he meant something more modest, but still very important. He meant that judges were not employed at the pleasure of the crown. The primary benefit of independent judges was that they could be a check on the arbitrary application of the law by the king: they could actually force the king to abide by the law of the land as passed by king-in-Parliament and hinder him from manipulating it at the level of application. Judges were seen primarily as a check at the trial level, not at the level of formulating the most fundamental principles that would guide the government itself.

Montesquieu actually began the chapter in question by repeating and accepting Locke's division of powers, not rejecting it. The differences between the two are more semantic than substantive. Montesquieu wrote: "In each state there are three sorts of powers: legislative power, executive power over the things depending on the right of nations, and executive power over the things depending on civil right." By the third power the magistrate "punishes crimes or judges disputes between individuals."[21] This is Montesquieu's "judicial power." He used executive where Locke used federative and used judicial where Locke used executive, but the substance is almost identical. The danger of joining legislative and judicial powers is not that the former gets to be the highest forum of principle, but that it gets to apply its principles directly to particular persons. Throughout, it is assumed that the judges will be applying clear rules, not engaging in deliberation about the ends of the state or the basic rights of the people. "But though [the membership of] tribunals should not be

[20] This is not the place for an in-depth treatment of Montesquieu's thought. There is some disagreement over whether thinkers in the Anglo-American tradition have overemphasized the British influence on Montesquieu. If they have, Hamilton is as guilty as any. In that case, the argument I present here shows that even if one accepts a British-biased interpretation of Montesquieu as correct, Hamilton's interpretation is still unpersuasive.

[21] *The Spirit of the Laws*, trans. and ed. Anne Cohler, Basia Miller, and Harold Stone (Cambridge: Cambridge University Press, 1989), pp. 156–157.

fixed, judgments should be fixed to such a degree that they are never anything but a precise text of the law. If judgments were the individual opinion of a judge, one would live in this society without knowing precisely what engagements one has contracted."[22] "But the judges of the nation are, as we have said, only the mouth that pronounces the words of the law, inanimate beings who can moderate neither its force nor its rigor." Only the legislative power can moderate the letter of the law.[23] Montesquieu also argues that a magistrate who refuses to enforce the law must be tried by the nobles in the House of Lords rather than by judges because he cannot be judged by an inferior power.

Montesquieu and British legal practice argue for Brutus, not Hamilton. The analysis in the previous chapter helps us to see where the confusion enters. Hamilton tried to evade the charge that the Constitution gives supremacy to the Supreme Court by relying on a formalist understanding of what the courts do.[24] So long as the Court is only comparing clear rules that have uncontroversial meanings, this argument works acceptably. The first part of Hamilton's argument, however, fails to differentiate two senses of the charge that the Court is supreme in the Constitution. Locke noted that we could use "supreme" in two senses, contrasting earthly supremacy with institutional supremacy (*Treatises*, 2.149). In the first sense, the people are supreme because they have the ultimate authority to entrust political power in institutions of their own choosing and retain the right to change the constitution. If political actors misuse their trust, power reverts to the people as supreme. Although the people may abuse their power and act illegitimately (for they are still subject to natural law), they have no earthly superior; the only appeal against the people is to heaven. Hamilton is right to say the people are supreme in this sense. In the second sense, the legislature is institutionally supreme since it has the power to bind the other branches of government by its legal pronouncements. It is subject to natural law, but it is supreme in the sense that there is no higher institution to which one can appeal. The Supreme Court really is supreme in this second sense. Since there is no higher body to which the people can appeal, the Court is part of the legislative power. The question is who will be supreme in interpreting the people's will since

---

[22] Ibid., p. 158.

[23] Ibid., p. 163.

[24] Formalism can mean either the view that in some cases particular legal judgments flow deductively from clear rules or the view that in interpreting the law one only applies someone else's value judgments, generally those of legislators or framers. It is formalism in the second sense that is objectionable and that will concern us in this chapter. For a defense of formalism in the first sense, see Neil MacCormick, *Legal Reasoning and Legal Theory,* 2d ed. (Oxford: Clarendon Press, 1994), pp. 19–52. For a discussion of formalism in the second sense, see Cass Sunstein, *The Partial Constitution*, pp. 94–107.

the people cannot be constantly assembled, and Brutus objects to the supremacy of the Supreme Court in *this* sense. Having unelected judges with tenure for life is good for giving them independence to apply popular rules in cases where they generate unpopular results, but their independence also renders them less accountable to the people.

The second part of Hamilton's argument is the assumption that the judicial power would be restricted to clear rules. Judges would simply exercise judgment in noting contradictions between rules and noting which rule takes priority in the particular case. That is to say, his justification of judicial review rests on a formalist description of judicial practice that is at odds with the actual practice that Dworkin describes. It is also important to remember that *Federalist* 78 was written before the Bill of Rights was added. Most of the prohibitions on legislative power in the original document do appear to be relatively clear rules: no bills of attainder, no ex post facto law, no titles of nobility. Most of the disagreements that have plagued the courts have come from the Bill of Rights and the Fourteenth Amendment. Many of these amendments are worded as standards rather than rules. They contain normatively controversial terms that judges have to apply to specific cases. Contrast the rule that the president be thirty-five years old with the prohibition on cruel and unusual punishment. One could imagine a hard case involving the former, but it is not easy.[25] Insofar as the law makes use of standards that are likely to be interpreted by different people in very different ways, the Hamiltonian argument becomes too simplistic. This does not prove that there should not be judicial review, only that there are historical grounds for interpreting the Constitution's delegation of power to the courts as less expansive than the powers Dworkin wants the courts to exercise.

Dworkin of course does not attempt to derive consent from the text itself or from Hamilton. Instead, he traces the court's authority to a source he claims is of equivalent authority. Regardless of the intentions of people two hundred years ago, the courts have assumed a role that popular opinion supports. "History," Dworkin would argue, has made the courts the interpreters of the Constitution, and if we believe the Constitution includes abstract principles then it is the job of whomever interprets it—in our case the courts—to interpret it in the light of moral principles. Of course Dworkin does not mean that "history," as an abstract idea, actually confers legitimacy in this context; historical people do. Although

---

[25] Suppose a constitutional amendment or Supreme Court decision ruled, in the abortion context, that life begins at conception and that a presidential candidate who would be a few months shy of thirty-five years of age at the time of inauguration, counting from his date of birth, claimed that he would have been alive thirty-five years at that time, counting from conception. I am grateful to Kristen Gammon for helping me think of this example.

there may not have been an authoritative founding moment placing the authority for determining the preconditions of democracy in the hands of the Supreme Court, Dworkin would note that it has been our legal practice for a long time and, crucially, that the American people support our legal practice, taken as a whole. There is a certain appeal to this logic. After all, many have thought that the consent of the dead is a poor substitute for the consent of the living. Dworkin's claim is that we have a higher law and courts that must interpret that law; the only real question is which theory of interpretation is best.

This argument glosses over a rather messy set of facts. The beginning of this chapter noted the long history of disputes over the relative roles of the three branches in constitutional interpretation, from Jefferson to the Religious Freedom Restoration Act. Not only have there been persistent disputes about the jurisdiction of the courts, there have been constant disputes about what style of interpretation is correct. Over the years the Supreme Court has used a wide variety of interpretive approaches, and each one of them has been controversial. The general support people have for the Supreme Court might be more a reflection of their general support for the Constitution than for robust judicial review, although there is no way to test this hypothesis empirically.[26] All of this makes it difficult to argue that the people now consent to the Supreme Court as the forum of principle in the sense Dworkin's theory requires. The Court's right to have the final say on general principles is more controversial than its right to have the final say on particular cases. On this point Dworkin cannot really object because he is caught by his own rhetoric. He writes: "The most popular opinion, in Britain and the United States, insists that judges should always, in every decision, follow the law rather than try to improve upon it. They may not like the law they find—it may require them to evict a widow on Christmas eve in a snowstorm—but they must enforce it nevertheless."[27] Dworkin goes on to point out that this popular opinion is based on formalism, or a "plain fact view of law," that cannot account for the reality of legal practice. Even if Dworkin is right about the reality of legal practice, if there is a gap between the popular justification of judicial review and actual judicial practice, and if popular consent is a necessary condition for the legitimacy of that practice, then the institutional question cannot be treated as settled. Because "history" has decisively answered the question of who will interpret the Constitution, objections to vesting such a power in the Court manifest themselves as

[26] One would have to compare the current level of support with the support that would have obtained in a counterfactual history where Congress played the leading role in interpretation.

[27] *Law's Empire*, p. 8. See also pp. 5–6.

theories of interpretation designed to limit the Court's discretion and leave more choice to elected officials.

Since the proper roles of the various branches in interpreting the Constitution are a matter of dispute, the legislative power in the United States, from a Lockean perspective, is unsettled, and Lockean arguments apply to Dworkin. Where the people as framers have left a fundamental question unanswered, any solution must be justifiable from the perspective of the people. Different interpretive strategies employed by the Supreme Court will generate different roles for the three branches in constitutional interpretation. Only the people, acting in their capacity as the supreme earthly judge on institutional questions, are capable of settling the jurisdictional question. Where they have not done so, different settlements will be proposed. Persons should advocate the solution that they believe the people should choose if a constitutional convention were called. Practically, this means asking what theory of interpretation framers should impose on the judges who will interpret the Constitution. Applying the argument to Dworkin, this means that before a Supreme Court justice can ask which interpretation of a given law produces the best fit and justification in a particular case, he must first ask what interpretive paradigm he would prescribe for all judges, even those who disagree with him substantially on the issues of fit and justification. Dworkin believes that although there are strong arguments on both sides concerning which institution should have the final say and how much discretion judges should have, once history places authority in the judges' hands those questions become practically irrelevant; the only task left is for each judge to make each law the best it can be. Instead we should see that, where these questions are left unsettled, residual jurisdictional disputes should constrain the choice of interpretive strategies.

To see the difference between the two ways of approaching the question, compare Dworkin's approach with Cass Sunstein's. Most of Sunstein's reasons for judicial restraint stem from practical concerns about the relative institutional competence of courts. He lists a number of reasons why "any system of constitutional interpretation must be closely attuned to the risks of judicial discretion." Although some of his claims are contestable, he is at least right that these are the sorts of arguments that should influence interpretive debates. Sunstein claims that elected legislatures are a better forum for settling questions of high principle than courts are. He points out that judges are not usually effective in promoting large-scale social reform, that even in *Brown* significant change did not occur until the more political branches were involved. Even when their verdicts are carried out, judges looking only at a specific case are poorly positioned to know how the part fits into the whole. Granting group A a set of rights may, in a world of finite resources, lead to group

B's rights not being protected. Elected assemblies are better positioned to deal with macro questions of this type. Judicial action can often short circuit deliberation and cut off possibilities for compromise. Judges are also drawn from a relatively narrow demographic group and are thus less representative than legislators, who, if not themselves more diverse, are at least answerable to diverse constituencies.[28] Sunstein asks for a theory of interpretation that is part of a larger theory of the role of the courts within American democracy. Where the Constitution leaves such questions vague, democratic and institutional considerations must be incorporated by individual judges as a constraint on their decision.[29]

This argument helps to bring out why it is not a "serious confusion" to think jurisdictional questions and interpretive questions are related. One might select an interpretive theory that is designed to counter the systemic biases of a particular institutional setting. The Supreme Court might be more likely to err in certain ways and Congress in others. The Court might also realize that it is more competent to answer some questions than others and therefore be more reluctant to strike down laws in those areas where its competence is less. But perhaps the most important relationship is specifically Lockean. Locke asks us to think of government officials as trustees, and we can easily imagine persons giving different instructions to trustees whose actions they can and cannot easily supervise. Once we think of the people as constructing a constitutional framework, we need not think that they must issue the same interpretive instructions to each institution because there is a single "best" theory of constitutional interpretation. One can imagine an amendment to the United State Constitution that would instruct the different branches to adopt different theories of interpretation.[30]

Dworkin could make counterarguments to Sunstein's empirical claims, of course. Dworkin would claim that courts are a superior fo-

---

[28] *Legal Reasoning and Political Conflict*, pp. 175–178.

[29] This Lockean framework can also provide a justification for Sunstein's approach. Although Sunstein is right to ask the interpretive question from a higher level of abstraction than the individual judge deciding a particular case, he does not give adequate grounds for why a judge should restrict herself in this way. Sunstein judges competing legal systems based on their compatibility with deliberative democracy. There is still a difference, however, between a judge asking which verdict in a particular case would most promote deliberative democracy and asking which interpretive theory, if employed by all judges, would most promote it. Insofar as deliberative democracy rests on a moral picture that is similar to juridical equality, it has the resources to explain why persons should make their decisions from the higher level of abstraction.

[30] For example, Congress might be instructed to pass a law only if the "preponderance of the evidence" points to its constitutionality, while the Supreme Court might be instructed to strike laws down only when there is "clear and convincing evidence" that the law is unconstitutional.

rum for settling questions of principle and that therefore it would be perfectly rational for the people to delegate broad authority to interpret abstract principles to courts.[31] The point is that the burden of justification has been raised. Dworkin cannot simply point to the fact of judicial review and take institutional questions as a given. Moreover, when debate takes place at this higher level, other Lockean considerations will weigh against Dworkin's position. The first consideration is that Dworkin bases much of his argument for relative institutional competency on a strict distinction between policy and principle.[32] Policy is about bargaining and personal advantage, while principle is about justice. Elected branches are better at policy and worse at principle. From a Lockean perspective, this is a debasement of the nature of legislation since legislation should be understood as a principled activity. In Dworkin's theory the majority can do whatever it likes so long as no rights are violated. In a Lockean theory, that is not enough. Even if no rights are violated, one must still justify coercion with respect to the public good, and any conception of the public good will be a moral one. Dworkin's distinction between policy and principle is misleading because it limits principle to the question of rights when in fact moral principles are implicit in the idea of the public good.

Second, Locke's analysis helps us to differentiate two different functions that courts perform. One function is to make sure that clear, principled pronouncements are applied in cases where they yield unpopular results. Free political speech is a popular principle, but often unpopular in application to specific cases. A second function is to define the focal meanings of key abstract terms, like speech. There is a difference between the power to apply the principle "Political speech should be protected" in cases where an unpopular group is clearly engaging in political speech, and the power to decide what *types* of speech should receive constitutional protection. It is only giving the judiciary power in this second sense that is really in dispute. It is one thing to prevent majorities from acting directly as trial courts, as with prohibitions on bills of attainder, and to force majorities to abide by their own rules. It is quite another thing to make courts the primary forum of principle. All of the majestic provisions of the Constitution were endorsed by majorities, and the superiority of courts in formulating principles of justice is harder to

---

[31] Dworkin, *A Bill of Rights for Britain* (London: Chatto and Windus, 1990).

[32] See *Law's Empire*, pp. 217–224. Dworkin does not claim that legislation is simply amoral bargaining. He thinks that legislators as well as judges have a duty to construct a system of rights that is consistent with the ideal of integrity. The legislature is not, however, under any obligation to be similarly consistent on policy questions where rights are not affected.

defend than the superiority of courts as the forum where principles are applied to specific cases.[33]

Originalism and the Nature of Law and Legislation

Another important interpretive approach, originalism, uses a very different type of justification. Dworkin is perfectly happy to argue about political theory, and the chief Lockean criticism of him was that he does not do so from the standpoint of a hypothetical framer. Originalists, on the other hand, often attempt to circumvent the entire debate by claiming that their approach follows from the very nature of law. For them the problem is relatively simple (or so it seems): the meaning of a law is the meaning it was understood to have at the time of its enactment. Early versions of originalism focused on "original intent," described as the intent of the framers or ratifiers. In a democracy, the ratifiers of the constitution are the authoritative source of political power, and so we should interpret the laws so that they correspond to the intentions of that source as much as possible. A parallel argument would be that in statutory interpretation the intent of the legislature should guide the courts. There are a variety of familiar objections to this position (at least in its constitutional variant), such as the difficulty of knowing ratifier's intentions from poor historical records and of knowing whether they even intended for their expectations to guide future interpreters.[34] A third objection is that the intentions of the past are not normative for us today. I want to leave these objections aside and concentrate instead on a different formulation of originalism. This is the theory that Robert Bork articulates in chapter 7 of *The Tempting of America* and that Antonin Scalia articulates in more detail in *A Matter of Interpretation*. Here the argument does not rest primarily on democratic legitimacy but rather on our notions of what law is. For Bork and Scalia, what is crucial is not the intent or expectations of the ratifiers or anyone else, but rather the actual meaning of the text itself at the time of its enactment. I will argue that the Lockean ideas developed in the previous chapter provide a better account of the roles of judges and legislators and thus law itself. In the Lockean view one cannot derive the originalist position simply from the meaning of law; one could at best try to claim that we should select that theory of interpretation from a hypothetical framer's point of view.

---

[33] Waldron argues for the moral capacity of citizens and against judicial review in *Law and Disagreement*.

[34] See, for example, H. Jefferson Powell, "The Original Understanding of Original Intent," *Harvard Law Review* 98 (March 1985), pp. 885–948.

Bork makes it clear that the subjective intentions of ratifiers are beside the point in interpreting law; what matters are the words actually set down. It does not matter if some members of Congress only meant to prohibit the "use" of assault weapons when the word they enacted in law was "sale."[35] This is crucial to maintaining a belief that the rule of law, rather than the rule of persons, governs us. Scalia insists that in both statutory and constitutional interpretation, judges should be guided not by speculation about what the framers meant to say, but only by what they actually said.[36] Moreover, part of the meaning of a law is that its content does not change just because time has passed; it has a determinate meaning, and judges who claim that a statute says today what it did not say yesterday are likely engaged in judicial usurpation.[37] By insisting on original understanding rather than original intent, the originalists attempt to show that their theory follows from the very concept of law.

I will argue that the focus on original public meaning as opposed to original intent either fails to do much to clarify the meaning of contested amendments like the Fourteenth Amendment or is parasitic on the expectations and intentions of the ratifiers that Scalia admits are beside the point. The use of vague language in the Constitution makes the claim that meanings cannot change with the passage of time misleading. Locke's arguments shed light on why originalists cannot justify their approach by a simple appeal to the meaning of law and the difference between legislative and judicial roles.

I will begin the first part of the objection to originalism with Dworkin's distinction between semantic-originalism and expectation-originalism and then try to improve upon his formulation of the problem.[38] Semantic-originalists ask what the words meant back then; the expectation-originalist asks what the people thought the consequences of the statute or amendment would be in terms of the way the courts would apply it in the future. The charge is that originalists are inconsistent in their application of this distinction to hard cases like the Fourteenth Amendment. Bork has argued that the Fourteenth Amendment, properly interpreted, upholds the Court's decision in *Brown*. He does this from the standpoint of semantic originalism. Although it was not the expectation or intention of the people to outlaw segregated schools through the Four-

---

[35] Robert H. Bork, *The Tempting of America: The Political Seduction of the Law* (New York: Free Press, 1990), p. 144.

[36] Antonin Scalia, *A Matter of Interpretation,* ed. Amy Gutmann (Princeton: Princeton University Press, 1997), p. 138.

[37] Bork, *The Tempting of America,* p. 143.

[38] Ronald Dworkin, "Comment," in Scalia, *A Matter of Interpretation,* pp. 115–127. Dworkin makes this objection more fully in "The Arduous Virtue of Fidelity: Originalism, Scalia, Tribe, and Nerve," *Fordham Law Review* 65 (1997), pp. 1249–1268.

teenth Amendment, it was clear by the 1950s that doing so was the only way to uphold the meaning of the words, even as those words were understood in 1868.[39] Here Bork takes advantage of the possible disjunction between the words the people adopted and the expectations they had about the consequences of those words.

But while in the case of race originalists are unwilling to allow the expectation that the Fourteenth Amendment did not prohibit segregation to prevent them from reaching that conclusion, they are willing to allow the expectation that the Fourteenth Amendment had nothing to do with gender to limit the application of the Fourteenth Amendment to race and ethnicity. I will extend Dworkin's argument by noting that when a law is adopted it can have unintended consequences in at least two different ways. First, it may be that fulfilling the requirement of the law requires the institution or prohibition of a practice (like segregation) that no one originally thought implicated by the law. Second, it may be that a law is drafted too broadly so that it covers individuals who were not intended (as in the Fourteenth Amendment) or too narrowly so that it fails to cover all of the intended cases (as the Supreme Court argued in *Hans v. State of Louisiana* regarding the Eleventh Amendment).[40] If we allow that we are ruled by law and not by intentions, and that laws can have unintended consequences, we must accept both types of errors.

Scalia says that this misunderstands his position. He describes his position as a third alternative between expectation-originalism and semantic-originalism that he terms "import-originalism." He then attempts to show how this understanding of originalism would apply to a difficult case like the Fourteenth Amendment. He writes:

> I certainly do not assert that it [the equal protection clause] permits discrimination on the basis of age, property, sex, "sexual orientation," or for that matter even blue eyes and nose rings. Denial of equal protection on *all* of these grounds is prohibited—but that still leaves open the question of what *constitutes* a denial of equal protection. Is it a denial of equal protection on the basis of sex to have segregated toilets in public buildings, or to exclude women from combat? I have no idea how Professor Dworkin goes about answering such a question. I answer it on the basis of the "time-dated" meaning of equal protection in 1868. Unisex toilets and women assault troops may be ideas whose time has come, and the people are certainly free to require them by legislation; but refusing to do so

[39] Bork, *The Tempting of America*, p. 82.

[40] 134 U.S. 1 (1890). On under- and overinclusive rules, see Frederick Shauer, "Rules and the Rule of Law," *Harvard Journal of Law and Public Policy* 14 (1991), pp. 647–651.

does not violate the Fourteenth Amendment, because that is not what "equal protection of the laws" ever meant.[41]

This response is inadequate because the only way to get to this conclusion from "import-originalism" is to smuggle in some of the subjective intentions that Scalia admits are beside the point. The difference between "semantic" and "import" I take to be the following.[42] The former is only interested in the actual meanings of words, and therefore we would primarily look at old dictionaries to find out whether words have changed in meaning over the last century or two. In most cases this will not resolve much because the problem is that the words were originally vague, not that they have changed in meaning. Import-originalism looks at what "the text would reasonably be understood to mean" at the time of its enactment.[43] One would look in the historical record at speeches, newspaper articles, etc. (in addition to the above-mentioned dictionaries) to get a general sense of what the amendment was understood to mean. But this involves a bad inference. When people wrote newspaper articles and speeches, they did so with the intended consequences of the amendment in mind because the unforeseen consequences were just that, unforeseen. Scalia and other originalists tend to slip between looking at the historical document to get a sense of what the words meant and finding out what the amendment meant to people at the time.

It will generally be impossible to distinguish through the historical record between the expectations of the ratifiers and the public understanding, because the public's understanding of the amendment may be at odds with the words used. We cannot distinguish between what they understood the amendment to mean (aside from the strict dictionary sense) and what they expected and intended the amendment to accomplish because for them they were the same thing. In all probability no one in 1868 thought the Fourteenth Amendment had anything to do with female assault troops, but it probably did not occur to very many that it might be used to outlaw segregated schools. When we commit ourselves to the rule of law, and thus to living with the fact that drafters can make (sometimes beneficial) mistakes, we must admit that the fact that no one thought the Fourteenth Amendment had this implication is not a conclusive reason for believing it does not have that implication.

The second originalist line of argument claims that time-dated meanings are necessary because laws do not change their meaning simply with the passage of time. The core argument is that when judges cause the

---

[41] Scalia, *A Matter of Interpretation*, pp. 148–149.
[42] Scalia admits that these two concepts are difficult to distinguish.
[43] Ibid, p. 144.

content of a law to change, they are usurping democratic authority because laws can only be changed by Congress, and the Constitution can only be changed by amendment. First, it is of course true that there is nothing about the Earth circling the Sun that causes laws to change; it is not the passage of time by itself. Second, even originalists admit that old principles must be applied to new situations, for example, new forms of communication in the case of the First Amendment, or new forms of torture in the case of the Eighth Amendment.[44]

None of this refutes the fact that laws are often drafted with vague terms *in order* to give judges discretion. Legislators must try to find the golden mean between two vices: the one an incredibly prolix law that is so rigid and inflexible that it is harmful, and the other a vague law that is highly unpredictable and allows for judicial tyranny. Somewhere in between is a good law, and the art of legislation is often the trial-and-error process of finding the right balance. When legislators insert words or phrases like "reasonable" or "due care" in a statute, they do so precisely to give judges flexibility in different cases. What it means practically to operate an automobile with "due care" in the year 2000 may be quite different from what it meant in 1904. It is not that the law has changed, rather it is that the law was drafted to be vague and flexible in the first place. Scalia insists that we are considering the Constitution as law here, and so we must grant that a similar possibility exists here: deliberately vague language could be chosen (knowing full well it would create judicial discretion) because that is what the framers wanted.

A second possibility is that vague terms are strategically inserted into a law for ulterior motives. Sometimes a skilled legislator is able to slip language by her colleagues that they would have changed if they had stopped to think about its implications. What are judges to do? If we are committed to the rule of law, we must sadly say that the sneaky legislator won that round; it is the text of the law that counts, not what the legislators would have done if they had thought about it more carefully. A third possibility is that vague language is used to cover up differences between opposing sides in order to secure passage of the statute or amendment. Here we have contested meaning with a vengeance: not only is the law unclear, there is no legislative intent to which we could appeal, even if we so desired, because the authoritative source itself is divided.

In all likelihood the vague provisions of the Constitution are some mixture of all three. The fact that "cruelty" might change in meaning over time does not undermine the notion of law itself because it is perfectly compatible with our understanding of law that it may include provisions

[44] Ibid., p. 145.

granting judges discretion. Moreover, judges are sometimes put in a situation where they are faced with vague laws and little direction. This variability is the price one pays for drafting a vague law. All of this returns us to originalism in its narrow semantic form. Once we set aside the subjective intentions and expectations of the ratifiers, we are generally no closer to having a determinate law than we were before. The problem is not that the words have changed in meaning, it is that they were contestable to begin with. Treating the Constitution as law means acknowledging the possibility of drafting error. Amendments may have consequences that the ratifiers did not intend, both in terms of scope and by implicating practices that they did not intend to implicate.

Locke's insights into the nature of law and legislation provide the foundation for these objections to originalism. Laws that contain evaluative moral terms must be interpreted by those who apply them, and this means there will be potential disagreement and even change over time. There is nothing in the meaning of law itself that restricts the appeal to moral principles only to those who draft legislation. The originalist concept of law relies on too sharp a dichotomy between legislative and judicial functions. Once we recognize that judges do act in a legislative capacity, then we realize there is nothing about the meaning of law itself that precludes granting judges some legislative authority. Those who draft laws may intentionally delegate discretion through the use of vague terms, understanding that those who must apply them will do so on the basis of controversial judgments. Against the claim that positive law must be understood simply as a rule, a Lockean theory notes that a law is itself an interpretation of a moral principle and that any contestable moral terms contained in the law will have to be interpreted by those who apply it.[45] Sunstein has made the point in more contemporary language by noting that the law contains standards as well as rules.[46] The legislative body in any society will have to give meaning to those standards and principles or delegate authority to some other group to do so. There is nothing in the meaning of law itself that refutes the Lockean description of American constitutional practice. The Constitution does contain contestable moral terms, and one approach, perfectly consistent with the idea of law, is for judges to interpret those terms in the light of moral principles. The question of how law should be interpreted is a moral one, and in cases where the people

[45] Although Locke certainly preferred clear rules with determinate meanings in general, he was under no illusions about the possibility of having a standing rule to govern every possible eventuality. His doctrines of prerogative and delegation modify his insistence on clear standing rules.

[46] *Legal Reasoning and Political Conflict*, pp. 28–29.

have not specified a particular approach, the system will be analogous to the state of nature.[47]

If originalism can be justified at all, it must be on different grounds. It cannot be justified on the basis of the meaning of law itself, and it cannot even be justified by proving that the ratifiers meant for us to construe terms as they would have construed them (if such a thing could be proven) since they never bothered to pass a law or amendment to that effect. Although the nature of law does not prove the originalist case, it does not disprove it either. Instead, if originalism is justified at all, it is as a solution to the question, "What interpretive instructions should the people entrench in the Constitution?" In other words, one must make the case for originalism as the interpretive theory one would choose from a legislative point of view. One could make a case for it on these grounds. Formalism remains the most popular justification of judicial review. One attribute of originalism is that it makes the abstract standards of the constitution much more rule-like. Originalists should argue that only a formalist understanding of judicial review is justified; judges should interpret abstract standards in a formalist fashion when they attempt to justify striking down a law as unconstitutional.[48] The formalist aspiration is for such clarity in rules that judges need not make controversial substantive moral judgments, but only enforce the judgments of ratifiers. Originalism would have to compete with other restrictive interpretive approaches, such as Thayer's clear mistake rule, as well as less restrictive ones. My goal is not to resolve the debate, but to clarify the grounds on which the debate must take place.

One interesting point, drawing on John Hart Ely's work, is that different types of clauses may require different interpretive approaches. Ely argues that courts are more competent at interpreting procedural issues than substantive ones.[49] If that is right, then reasonable framers might propose different interpretive instructions for different parts of the Constitution. Originalists would have to show that for all of the types of clauses considered, their approach is the one framers should choose.

---

[47] Put another way, there is nothing about admitting that judges have discretion that, by itself, shows that judges should always defer to the legislature when they have discretion. The fact that the law is vague leaves open the question of whether the vague law was an intentional delegation of power to the judges.

[48] Indeed, this is how Bork argues at times. The argument here is that the democratic/formalist argument must be made in its own right and not disguised as a deduction from the meaning of law itself.

[49] John Hart Ely, *Democracy and Distrust: A Theory of Judicial Review* (Cambridge: Harvard University Press, 1980), p. 102. Of course, as noted in chapter 3, results-driven criteria of this sort will generally invoke a contested conception of competence.

Boerne v. Flores

Since the foregoing discussion is at the level of interpretive theory, it is worth describing more concretely how the legislative point of view would apply in a specific case. We can distinguish two different levels at which it might apply. At the first and least controversial level, justices would examine their own opinions from a legislative point of view. Justices, when issuing an interpretation of a disputed clause, would realize that the proper interpretation of their judicial opinion will also be a matter of dispute. To the extent that key terms or phrases in their interpretation are vague or contested in meaning, the justices should not assume that their preferred understanding of those vague terms will prevail. This claim is relatively noncontroversial because justices generally do this as a matter of course. They may not always do it well, but in principle they would take it as obvious that they should think about how their directives will be interpreted by lower court judges, police officers, juries, and so on. Judges will sometimes intentionally formulate a "bright line rule" in order to reduce the amount of unpredictability in the effects of their decisions.

The arguments of this chapter, however, have been about a different and more controversial way of applying the legislative point of view. Whereas at the first level the justices take their own position for granted and think about how subordinate officers will interpret their directives, at the second level they take on a "framer's point of view" and imagine a perspective that is higher than their own situated position as a justice. They recognize that the judicial role they occupy is itself contested and that it is the people who have the ultimate authority to clarify the nature of that role. They are aware that any general theory of constitutional interpretation will make contestable assumptions about the role the court is to play and that they must give good reasons for the particular conception of the Court's role that they employ. Those reasons should be reasons that are relevant and persuasive from a potential framer's point of view.

Were justices actually to think in this way, it would have significant, but often indirect, effects on the particular judgments they would hand down. As the discussion of Dworkin and originalism above should make clear, thinking about which theory of interpretation to endorse from a legislative point of view highlights a distinct set of moral issues. To the extent that recognizing these reasons leads a justice to adopt a different theory of interpretation, there will be a corresponding change in the way that justice rules in specific cases. This does not mean, however, that justices will explicitly rehearse the idea of a legislative point of view and the reasons that led them to adopt their particular approach to interpretation in every decision. Judges do not do so now, and the argument I have presented is an attempt to change the set of considerations that guide their choice, not the frequency or choice of forum in which they make that choice known.

It will only be in rare, landmark cases that the types of arguments I have expressed will actually appear in judicial opinions. Those rare cases will be those in which judges are unable simply to apply their preferred interpretive approach (hopefully adopted from a framer's point of view) to a particular problem because the case itself forces them to put forward a defense of a particular understanding of the judicial role. When such cases arise, then it will be appropriate for judges to make arguments from a framer's point of view for why their preferred understanding of their own role is the most reasonable. Below I describe such a case and show how the Court's opinion could have been improved with more careful attention to the contested nature of the judicial role.

The case in question is *City of Boerne v. Flores* (1997). A growing Catholic parish in Texas was denied permission to expand its sanctuary because the building had been designated as a historical landmark. The relevant building restrictions were not adopted with the intent of burdening the free exercise of religion, but they had this incidental effect. This raised the question of what burden the state had to meet in such cases. If the state had to show a compelling interest in preventing the church from modifying its building, the state would very likely lose, given the specifics of the case. The building itself was not actually that old, and the proposed renovation plan would have left the front exterior of the building unchanged. If, however, the government did not have to show a compelling interest because there was no intent to burden religion, the state would likely win.

There were two conflicting interpretations of the free exercise clause on which the Court could base its ruling. One was the Court's decision in *Employment Division, Oregon Dept. of Human Resources v. Smith* (1990), where the Court held that laws against smoking peyote were binding against Native Americans who traditionally used peyote as part of religious ceremonies. The Court reasoned that neutral laws that have the incidental effect of burdening the free exercise of religion must be regarded as valid. One's religion does not give one a right to an exemption from generally applicable laws. To claim that they do would invite chaos. Congress and the president advanced a different interpretation. The Religious Freedom Restoration Act (RFRA), mentioned above, made it illegal to burden the free exercise of religion without showing a compelling interest, even in cases where the law was neutral toward religion. RFRA was a conscious attempt by the elected branches to reverse the

Smith decision and return to the stricter standard used in *Sherbert* and *Yoder*.[50]

Boerne thus forced the Court to address the specific question of whether Congress may reinterpret the meaning of constitutional clauses. Since the legislators who drafted RFRA knew a direct challenge to judicial supremacy was a futile strategy, they took a different approach. They first noted that Section 5 of the Fourteenth Amendment gives Congress the authority to enforce the provisions of the amendment through appropriate legislation. Since the Court has held that the Fourteenth Amendment "incorporates" the First Amendment free exercise clause, making it binding on the states, Congress argued that it was within its powers to enact legislation to make sure that the First Amendment rights of citizens were protected. Second, the Court had, in a previous case discussed in more detail below, upheld legislation that went beyond what the Court had previously deemed a violation of constitutional right.[51]

The Court, as expected, ruled that RFRA exceeded congressional authority. What is striking about the opinion, however, is that the Court devotes only a few paragraphs to the truly central question: What are the proper roles of Congress and the Court in interpreting the Constitution? The Court talks at length about how Section 5 is primarily remedial. It points out that an earlier draft of the Fourteenth Amendment, which gave plenary powers to Congress, was rejected. Congress, the Court said, was in effect trying to claim, through Section 5, precisely the kind of plenary powers that the original framers rejected. Interestingly though, most of the critics of the early draft that the Court cites were critics because they thought the amendment would give too much power to the federal government over the states, not because it would give Congress too much power relative to the Supreme Court. The Court claimed that *Boerne* was different from the previous cases in which Congress went beyond remedying a constitutional violation already identified by the Court. In the Voting Rights Act cases there was such a long history of discrimination that preventative action could be thought of as remedial. The Court held that there was not a similar history of discrimination against religious persons via neutral laws. All of these arguments dodge the central question, since the congressional action would have been constitutional if the Court had held that Congress could independently identify classes of First Amendment violation.

In a few paragraphs, the court deals with the main issue head on. Can Congress pass legislation to enforce the Fourteenth Amendment on the

---

[50] *Sherbert v. Vernor*, 374 U.S. 398 (1963), and *Wisconsin v. Yoder*, 406 U.S. 205 (1972).

[51] See the discussion of *Katzenbach v. Morgan* below.

basis of a different reading of the Constitution than the Court's? Since this is the key argument, I will quote Justice Kennedy's argument at length:

> If Congress could define its own powers by altering the Fourteenth Amendment's meaning, no longer would the Constitution be "superior paramount law, unchangeable by ordinary means." It would be "on a level with ordinary legislative acts, and, like other acts, . . . alterable when the legislature shall please to alter it." Under this approach, it is difficult to conceive of a principle that would limit congressional power. Shifting legislative majorities could change the Constitution and effectively circumvent the difficult and detailed amendment process contained in Article V.[52]

> When Congress acts within its sphere of power and responsibilities, it has not just the right but the duty to make its own informed judgment on the meaning and force of the Constitution. This has been clear from the early days of the Republic. . . . Were it otherwise, we would not afford Congress the presumption of validity its enactments now enjoy.

> Our national experience teaches that the Constitution is preserved best when each part of the government respects both the Constitution and the proper actions and determinations of the other branches. When the Court has interpreted the Constitution, it has acted within the province of the Judicial Branch, which embraces the duty to say what the law is. When the political branches of the Government act against the background of a judicial interpretation of the Constitution already issued, it must be understood that in later cases and controversies the Court will treat its precedents with the respect due them under settled principles, including *stare decisis*, and contrary expectations must be disappointed. RFRA was designed to control cases and controversies, such as the one before us; but as the provisions of the federal statute here invoked are beyond congressional authority, it is this Court's precedent, not RFRA, which must control.[53]

The crucial move is the assertion that "When the Court has interpreted the Constitution, it has acted within the province of the Judicial Branch, which embraces the duty to say what the law is." Otherwise, the legislature would be the judge of the limits of its own power, an intolerable conclusion. From a framer's point of view, this is a relevant reason for thinking Congress does not have the power it is claiming for itself.

---

[52] *City of Boerne v. Flores*, 521 U.S. 507 (1997), p. 529 (internal citation omitted).
[53] Ibid., pp. 535–536 (internal citations omitted).

Kennedy's opinion does, therefore, present arguments that would be relevant from a legislative point of view. The problem is that such arguments are made in passing without considering the best arguments in opposition to his preferred reading. Put another way, the entire opinion reads as if the proper role of the judiciary is already settled, rather than recognizing that this is a case of genuinely contested jurisdiction. The fact is that the Constitution does not say that it is the sole responsibility of the judiciary to "say what the law is." When there is a dispute between two branches of government that share in the legislative power, as Congress and the Court do, and where the foundational document is vague and contested, the situation is similar to a dispute in the state of nature. In such a dispute, for the Court to prove the supremacy of its position by appealing to previous decisions of the Court is as question begging as it would be for Congress to prove its case by appealing to previous legislation. The Court notes the problems that go along with allowing Congress to be judge in its own case without recognizing that in a "constitutional state of nature" all members of the legislature (broadly defined to include president and Court) are "judges in their own case." If Congress will not be the judge of its own powers, it is because the Court will be the judge of its own powers.

A more persuasive argument would explain why, from a framer's point of view, it would make more sense to allow the Court to be judge in its own case than to allow Congress to judge the extent of its own powers. In this particular case, the most relevant question is which institution should have the final say on the appropriate balance between states and the federal government. If Congress wants to restrict its own power by interpreting the First Amendment more broadly than the Court requires, there is nothing the Court can do to stop it. Congress would merely refrain from exercising certain powers that the Court would have allowed it to exercise. This case presents a different problem in that Congress, by adopting a more expansive reading of the First Amendment, is restricting the power of the state legislatures as well. The Fourteenth Amendment is arguably the most important precisely because it restricts the power of state legislatures. The question is whether it would be better for the Court or for Congress to have the final say on such questions.

It is also important to note that we need not pose the question quite this coarsely. As noted earlier in the chapter, the contestation of roles in a contemporary context normally takes place not by directly challenging the doctrine of judicial supremacy (as the above paragraph does) but instead by arguing about the proper interpretive method that the Supreme Court should employ. The earlier case of *Katzenbach v. Morgan* provides an example of how the Court could have ruled in *Boerne* had it wanted to permit Congress to expand its role in constitutional interpretation.

That case is, despite the Court's protestations, quite similar to *Boerne*. In both cases the Court had previously ruled that laws of a certain sort did not violate the Constitution. In *Katzenbach* the Court ruled that Congress could bar states from using literacy tests even though the Court had held in *Lassiter* that literacy tests were constitutionally acceptable.[54] On its face Congress seems to be forcing states to abide by a more expansive reading of the equal protection clause via the Voting Rights Act in the same way that RFRA expanded the free exercise clause.

Justice Brennan, speaking for the Court, argued in *Katzenbach* that Section 5 is an affirmative grant of power to Congress.

> A construction of 5 that would require a judicial determination that the enforcement of the state law precluded by Congress violated the Amendment, as a condition of sustaining the congressional enactment, would depreciate both congressional resourcefulness and congressional responsibility for implementing the Amendment. It would confine the legislative power in this context to the insignificant role of abrogating only those state laws that the judicial branch was prepared to adjudge unconstitutional, or of merely informing the judgment of the judiciary by particularizing the "majestic generalities" of 1 of the Amendment.[55]

Brennan claimed that the real question was whether this is a reasonable way for Congress to enforce the equal protection clause. In a footnote Brennan makes it clear that this power is asymmetrical: while Congress may go beyond the Court, it may not dilute the Court's reading of constitutional protections. He then notes that the Court should be deferential to congressional findings as to whether such a law is needed to make the equal protection clause effective. The entire opinion is crafted so that the Court can recognize the validity of congressional interpretation without actually abandoning the doctrine of judicial supremacy. The Court still has the final say, but it exercises restraint in its use of judicial review.

The Court could have made a similar move in *Boerne*. It could have noted that the reading of the First Amendment put forward by Congress expands rather than dilutes the protections of the free exercise clause and made it clear that Congress has no power to do the latter. It could then claim that although, as indicated in previous cases, the stricter standard is not necessary to satisfy the First Amendment, Congress's interpretation is sufficiently reasonable that it is a legitimate extension of its Fourteenth

[54] See *Katzenbach v. Morgan*, 384 U.S. 641 (1966), and *Lassiter v. Northampton* 360 U.S. 45 (1959).

[55] See *Katzenbach v. Morgan*, 384 U.S. 641 (1966), pp. 648–649. (Internal citations omitted.)

Amendment power. Whether the Court should in fact make that move is an open question. Whether it should have done so depends on whether, from a framer's point of view, we believe the congressional role in constitutional interpretation should be further expanded. If so, a case like this provides an opportunity to move in that direction. Those who find such arguments unpersuasive will likely agree with the Court's ruling in *Boerne*. Whichever position one finds more appealing, the case illustrates the way our evaluation of contested roles from a legislative point of view may play itself out in a specific case.

Contested Roles and the State of Nature

Although one of the purposes of government is to provide an institutional framework for settling the inevitable disagreements between persons, there is always the possibility that the persons empowered to settle disputes will disagree with one another. To eliminate this condition without an infinite regress would requires something like an absolute sovereign whose decisions could not be questioned, hardly an attractive solution. Whatever institutional structure we select, including absolute monarchy, at least one person will be put in a situation where he must make controversial judgments about the legitimate use of force with no higher earthly authority to direct him. To put it in Lockean terms, even in a state, traces of the state of nature remain. When individual citizens step into the voting booth, when senators vote on whether to recognize a right, when Supreme Court justices deliberate about the scope of the Supreme Court's powers, they shape principles that will direct the use of force, and they have no higher earthly authority to tell them how they should vote. There is still, of course, a very great difference between traces of the state of nature and the state of nature itself. The traces I have described are constrained by recognized laws. There is no one to tell the citizen how to vote, but there are (sometimes inadequate) rules about how to count the votes and what follows from one side gaining more votes than another. There is nothing to tell the senator how to vote, but there are rules that govern how to settle disagreements within the Senate. The applications of the Lockean framework I have developed are broad precisely because these traces of the state of nature are pervasive. I have tried to show that breadth in this chapter by applying Lockean arguments to disputes about constitutional jurisdiction. I have used debates over the relative roles of the three American branches as an example and have suggested how Lockean arguments could influence the selection of an interpretive approach to the Constitution. If we begin from a moral picture of juridical equality, holding persons to be equal moral agents under a common set of public, moral principles that regulate the use of force among them, a Lockean perspective can guide deliberation about the content of those principles. Those principles should be conceived as a framework and should be rational as a framework, from the perspective of the one who has authority to construct it. The recognition of other persons as equal, fallible, and moral agents requires us to consider the differences in the way they would interpret the framework we propose. When disputes arise between those who are equals with no higher earthly authority to settle the dispute, each participant should propose solutions that would be reasonable as a common framework for all.

Conclusion

Contested principles are pervasive in politics. In the most obvious cases, one side proposes a principle that the other side rejects. In this first case, both sides interpret the principle in the same way and anticipate similar applications of it. In this book we have focused on a second type of contested principle, principles that both sides accept in the abstract but that one side rejects because of the way others will interpret and apply it. Contested principles of this second type are found at all levels of political debate. In chapter 2 we examined simple assertions of moral right and wrong that are contested in this second sense. In chapter 3 we examined contested conceptions of the public good. In chapter 5 we examined the way persons who occupy legislative, executive, and judicial roles confront contested principles. In chapter 6 we looked at constitutional questions where the very rules that determine an agent's institutional role are themselves contested in this second sense.

Citizens, legislators, executive officials, and judges face a difficult moral choice when a situation such as this arises. They must decide whether, in the case at hand, toleration is the appropriate response. When these situations arise there is, by definition, some moral principle that the actor thinks valid or true. As a fact of human psychology, it is hard not to think one's own interpretation of the principle is the best one. After all, if you think someone else's interpretation superior, you should adopt it if you are acting in good faith. We thus face the classic paradox of toleration: If I believe a principle is right, why should I refrain from acting on the best interpretation of it? Part of the answer to this question, I have argued, rests on the fact that we have moral views on means as well as ends. The use of force and violence to achieve our goals and enforce our sense of right and wrong is suspect. That is not to say that it is always wrong, but it is to say that there is a presumption against it. To use force against another person is to make myself judge *over* that person and is in tension with respect for that other person as my moral equal. If a person is to legitimately use force or authorize its use against another, a simple appeal to one's own will or desire is not enough. Only appeal to a higher principle can satisfy the requirement that we show respect for the other person as morally equal.

I have argued that not all true moral principles automatically function as authorizations for force because they are not reasonable from a legislative point of view. My account of the legislative point of view derives from Locke's discussion of how we determine which laws of nature one person can enforce against another. Respect for others as moral agents under a common set of general and public rules implies that those rules are reasonable from the perspective of a legislator deliberating about them. For this reason, where questions of coercion are concerned, we should ask whether we would want our fellow fallible citizens to act on the same principle on which we act, realizing that they, as moral agents, may interpret contested words, phrases, and clauses differently. We may believe that there are right and wrong answers to moral questions and that others are answering them wrongly. Nonetheless, out of respect for both the dignity and fallibility of human beings, we think of the rule we appeal to as one that we would want fallible human beings to interpret and apply.

The Lockean legislative point of view presents a way of thinking about the problem of disagreement that differs from better-known liberal approaches. Unlike act-utilitarianism, it requires us to think about consequences that are merely hypothetical. We must ask what would happen if other persons acted on our principle even in those cases where we have no reason to believe that others will ever know the principle on which we act. Unlike rule-utilitarianism, it gives us a nonconsequentialist reason based on respect for persons to adopt the legislative point of view in those cases where we could produce better consequences by not taking on the legislative point of view. And unlike both, it does not require us to assess outcomes in terms of whether happiness and utility are maximized. Although one could imagine a utilitarian adopting the legislative point of view and inserting the principle of utility as the substantive principle for judging better and worse legislative outcomes, nothing about the theory requires or even recommends such an approach. One could just as easily believe that requiring certain persons to perform wicked acts is so horrible that no amount of increased utility could justify making them do it. The legislative point of view, as I have described it, provides a general moral perspective that is compatible with a wide variety of substantive moral theories. I have presented it at the level of intermediate principles precisely so that persons who hold a wide variety of foundational approaches could endorse it.

The view here is also importantly different from the Kantian legislative point of view. First, as described above, it is a partial theory and thus much less restrictive of the substantive views people will employ when utilizing the legislative point of view. Second, and perhaps more importantly, it provides a different way of understanding the concept of reciprocity. Reciprocity at its simplest means treating others as we would want to be treated. Stated as such, there is an important ambiguity because there are two different perspectives from which we might apply the idea. Persons in the Kantian tradition, and I have used Rawls as an example, apply this to politics by asking whether the principle is one that other persons, from their perspective, could reasonably reject. This variant of contractualism makes use of the moral aspiration toward principles that all persons could reasonably accept and thinks of consent in contractual terms. The great merit of this approach is that it recognizes the problems associated with using force against others. Respecting others as moral equals must mean more than deciding what we think is right and enforcing our views on others as best we can. It must involve a respect for their right to act as moral agents as well. The Lockean view also accounts for these ideas, but in a different way. We respect reciprocity from the perspective of an acting agent rather than that of the person affected by the action. We must take into account the moral views of others and the fact of disagreement before deciding that a moral view we hold authorizes the use of force against others.

The Lockean legislative point of view could be adopted, in principle, by persons who hold a variety of views: rule-utilitarians, Kantians, Rawlsians, and Perfectionists. I have not presented a full refutation of any of these positions. A Kantian could, for example, hold that we use force only on the basis of those principles that we would want other fallible person to interpret and that meet additional Kantian moral requirements, however a particular theorist may specify them. Likewise a perfectionist could adopt the legislative point of view by recognizing that perfectionist ideals are themselves disputed and that she should not assume that her preferred interpretation of those ideals will prevail, even in those cases where the local majority happens to agree with her. In each case, the Lockean view is a supplement, rather than an alternative, to a more comprehensive moral theory.

Even if these other groups accept the Lockean legislative point of view only in its most minimal form, it meaningfully changes the way such actors would think about political disagreement. But there is another benefit to this method of argument that is equally important. The theory I articulate here has a better chance than most of being accepted by groups that are often not thought of as liberal, precisely because of the theological derivation of the argument. It is not that as a matter of logic the original foundations retain a privileged position when the intermediate position is proposed. My method of presentation leaves it an open question which foundational views would best support the intermediate principles. Rather, the point is that the argument may have an important rhetorical advantage in that it can be presented most simply in its original theological form. Although I have presented the theory in a form that secular persons could accept, the theory can also be presented in its theological form to persons who accept the necessary theological beliefs. The fact that many conservative Christian groups, such as Southern Baptists, share the major premises is of some interest. In fact, presenting the argument in its theological form with appeals to Christian theology would be a far less complicated exercise than what we have undertaken here. If nothing else, the theological argument provides a way for persons who do not share Locke's theology to dialogue with those persons who do.

On this last point, Locke's own example is instructive. Locke freely made use of arguments from the Bible to support the case for religious toleration. Moreover, he did not discuss the foundations of natural law in the *Two Treatises* because he did not have to do so for his argument to succeed. The attempt to do so would have caused unnecessary controversies and divisions. Doing so would have forced him to include, among other things, an attack on the doctrine of innate ideas.[1] For practical political purposes, persons on both sides of the innate ideas debate could affirm the substantive natural law propositions Locke needed for his main argument. He therefore, I think wisely, declined to talk about more than he needed to for his main argument to succeed. I have tried to do the same in this book. We thus find a general willingness in Locke to concentrate on those arguments that are most likely to persuade people given their starting point of reflection. I have tried to formulate a Lockean theory in the same way.

Finally, it is my hope that the analogical method I have used in exploring Locke's legislative point of view will help other scholars attempt a similar approach both on other aspects of Locke's thought and on other authors. An analogical reading takes seriously the historical context in which past authors wrote. While the limits of space and the direction of my argument prevent discussing many important aspects of Locke's context, I have tried to do justice to the aspect that seemed most relevant in this particular case, the theological dimension of his theory of natural law. An interpretive approach that simply dismisses central aspects of the original author's thought because they are currently out of vogue risks missing important insights. The analogical approach works best when both the original author and persons today confront a similar problem. In this case the common problem is the legitimacy of contested principles as a justification for force. It also helps if there are alternative grounds from which one might affirm the intermediate principles of the theory. Locke provides, on both counts, one of the best opportunities for applying this method. Moreover, I as attempted to show in chapter 5, not all conceptual changes are for the best. We must remain open to the possibility that some aspects of an earlier thinker's thought that are currently out of fashion may actually be superior to our own.

---

[1] I discuss this point in more detail in "The Coherence of a Mind."

Textual Support for the
Legislative Point of View

Several additional textual arguments are available to confirm that Locke believed the law of nature should be understood from a legislative point of view. First, in the *Second Letter* he explicitly asks, "What if God, foreseeing this force would be in the hands of men as passionate, humoursome, as liable to prejudice and error as the rest of their brethren, did not think it a proper means to bring men into the right way?" (*Works*, 6:84) This is an explicit indication that Locke thought God would take into account the fallibility of human actors.

Second, Locke's other writings use arguments of the form "God is perfect and would not contradict Himself." For example, God's perfection implied that reason and revelation would not contradict one another (*Essay*, 4.18.10). This had important consequences for the interpretation of scripture. Any interpretation of scripture that contradicts reason is ipso facto a bad interpretation of scripture since it falsely impugns God's character. Since reason is the faculty of judgment God has given us, and reason must be used in the interpretation of scripture, the requirement of noncontradiction is an interpretive principle that helps to establish the content of positive revelation. Locke, for example, rejects (at least one interpretation of) the Calvinist doctrine of the Fall because it is inconsistent with reason (*Reasonableness*, 3–4).

Third, Locke makes the argument quoted in chapter 2 above again at a later point in the *Third Letter*.

> [A]ccording to you, the magistrate's commission to use force for the salvation of souls, is from the law of nature. . . . Since the commission of the law of nature to magistrates, being only that general one, of doing good, according to the best of their judgments: if that extends to the use of force in matters of religion, it will abundantly more oppose than promote the true religion; if force in the case has any efficacy at all, and so do more harm than good: which though it shows not what you here demand, that it cannot do any service towards the salvation of men's souls, for that cannot be shown of any thing; yet it shows the disservice it does is so much more than any service [that] can be expected from it, that it can never be proved that

God has given power to magistrates to use it by the commission they have of doing good, from the law of nature. (*Works*, 6:495)

Locke thus makes the point at length on two separate occasions in the *Third Letter*.

Finally, it is worth noting that this argument apparently would have figured very prominently in Locke's *Fourth Letter*, had Locke lived to complete it. The main argument of the opening pages has to do with the fact that Proast should not be able to assume that the correct interpretation of his principle will prevail. Locke wrote: "You say 'every magistrate is by the law of nature under an obligation to use force to bring men to the true religion.' To this I urge, that the magistrate hath nothing else to determine him in the use of force, for promotion of any religion one before another, but only his own belief or persuasion of the truth of it" (*Works*, 6:559). In a subsequent passage Locke wrote:

> And now I desire it may be considered, what advantage this supposition of force, which is supposed put into the magistrate's hands by the law of nature to be used in religion, brings to the true religion, when it arms five hundred magistrates against the true religion, who must unavoidably in the state of things in the world act against it, for one that uses force for it . . . it being demonstration, that the prejudice that will accrue to the true religion from such an use of force is five hundred times more than the advantage that can be expected from it; the natural and unavoidable inference from your own ground of benefit is, that God never gave any such power to the magistrate. (*Works*, 6:566).

It is clear, therefore, that this was a persistent theme in Locke's writings on toleration and that, if anything, it became more important to him as he continued to think about the subject. I have argued elsewhere that if we reread Locke's original *Letter concerning Toleration* with these themes in mind, it is plausible to suggest that Locke was implicitly employing the legislative point of view even in that work.[1]

---

[1] See Tuckness, "Rethinking the Intolerant Locke."

Locke's Theory of Consent and the Ends of Government

In this appendix I develop four lines of argument in support of the interpretation of Locke advanced above. First, the discussion of the ends of government in the *Two Treatises* supports the claim that the ends of government are set by natural law. Second, the actions that Locke believed governments could legitimately perform correspond to this definition of the public good. Third, Locke's discussion of the ends of societies also supports this account. In the *Second* and *Third Letters*, Locke compared familial, political, and economic societies and argued against the claim that any of these could be understood apart from a determinate end. A comparison of conjugal and political society reveals the way in which the ends of each can be inferred from natural law. Finally, I address the question of anachronism and explain why the distinctions I draw pertaining to consent are in the spirit of Locke's argument even though he did not draw these distinctions himself.

The connection between natural law and the ends of government is stated most clearly in a famous passage from the *Second Treatise*.

> Their [the legislature's] Power in the utmost Bounds of it, is *limited to the publick good* of the Society. It is a Power, that hath no other end but preservation, and therefore can never have a right to destroy, enslave, or designedly to impoverish the Subjects. The Obligations of the Law of Nature, cease not in Society, but only in many Cases are drawn closer, and have by Humane Laws known Penalties annexed to them, to inforce their observation. Thus the Law of Nature stands as an Eternal Rule to all Men, *Legislators* as well as others. The *Rules* that they make for other Mens Actions, must, as well as their own and other Mens Actions, be conformable to the Law of Nature, *i.e.* to the Will of God, of which that is a Declaration, and the *fundamental Law of Nature* being *the preservation of Mankind*, no Humane Sanction can be good, or valid against it. (2.135)

This passage is commonly read as emphasizing that natural law does not lapse when civil society begins and that its injunctions provide a standard by which regimes may be judged. A government that violates the negative injunctions of natural law by trying to "destroy, enslave, or designedly to impoverish the subjects" is illegitimate. It is hardly coincidental that Locke's three illegitimate actions correspond to his list of basic rights: life, liberty, and property. What is less often noticed is that the formulation of the law of nature that Locke used in this context was not the negative one but the positive one, the Fundamental Law of Nature. Moreover, it is not merely that governments may not act contrary to the fundamental law, but also that they may not act for any other end than the one specified by that law. The "utmost bound" of the legislative power "is limited to the public good of the Society. It is a power that hath *no other end but preservations.*"[1] Locke is making one broad claim (that the power of the government to pursue the public good is limited to the goals set by the fundamental law of nature) and a narrower one which flows directly from it (that it clearly has no right to violate natural law's negative injunctions).

The fact that the fundamental law of nature governs the whole notion of consent in Locke's theory of private property provides further support for this interpretation. Locke claimed that general consent to individual appropriation of property in the state of nature is unnecessary because that consent would be impossible to obtain. The result of requiring such consent would be unnecessary universal starvation. Not only does natural law regulate the content of consent, it also determines when the doctrine of consent is even applicable (2.29). Locke's claim that there is an obligation to labor and his objection to allowing the product of our labor to spoil can also be understood as restrictions on our freedom of consent in the service of upholding the fundamental law of nature (*Treatises,* 2.31, 36).

Finally, this interpretation makes sense of the way Locke goes about explaining the ends of government. If the ends of government were determined by whatever the consenting parties happen to have agreed to, then the only way to determine the legitimate functions of government would be to engage in historical research to find out what the actual terms of the contract were. Those theories that present the contract situation as hypothetical can avoid this problem, but Locke does not present the contract in this way. Nonetheless, he did not believe that it was problematic to know the ends of government even though the origins of government predate written history. The following passage is typical of Locke's approach.

> Men being, as has been said, by Nature, all free, equal and independent, no one can be put out of this Estate, and subjected to the

---

[1] My italics.

Political Power of another, without his own *Consent*. The only way whereby any one devests himself of his Natural Liberty, and *puts on the bonds of Civil Society* is by agreeing with other Men to joyn and unite into a Community, for their comfortable, safe, and peaceable living one amongst another, in a secure Enjoyment of their Properties, and a greater Security against any that are not of it.[2]

Notice that Locke does not say that they join and unite for whatever purposes they desire so long as those purposes do not violate the negative injunctions of natural law. Instead, consent is pictured as the mechanism by which people become obliged to obey the laws of a particular state; the ends are presented as given, not as the outcome of consent.

We can now turn to passages where Locke discusses the public good both to confirm the proposed interpretation and to avoid a possible misunderstanding. The possible misunderstanding is the familiar libertarian interpretation of Locke. In that view, the public good consists only in the protection of persons from rights violations (injuries to life, liberty, and property). The state may maintain a military and a police force, and a minimal staff to keep track of property records and to insure fair bargaining in the negotiation of contracts, but that is all.[3] It is true that not every good is a legitimate end of government; Locke's argument for toleration admits that true religion is a good, but it denies that it is an end of civil government. Yet it is important to the position articulated here that it is the positive, not the negative, formulation of natural law that sets the bounds of civil society. The fundamental law allows governments a wider sphere of activity than a libertarian theory would.

We can begin by looking at a passage from the *Third Letter* that seems to support the libertarian interpretation strongly.

The end of a commonwealth constituted can be supposed no other than what men in the constitution of, and entering into it, proposed;

[2] *Treatises*, 2.95. When Locke says that the fundamental law of nature is the preservation of mankind, this is shorthand for the "comfortable" preservation of mankind. Just as Locke believed that it was incompatible with our understanding of God to believe that he would want his creation to perish, so he thought it wrong to believe God would want his creation utterly miserable. To be sure, Locke believed that comfortable preservation was compatible with rather long hours of hard labor, and it can be argued that his own scheme of poor relief fails to meet his own standard; nonetheless, that was his position. Thus, as we will see, it is within the realm of the government's power to help individuals obtain a comfortable existence.

[3] See Robert Nozick, *Anarchy, State, and Utopia* (New York: Basic Books, 1974), pp. 3–25, and Richard Epstein, *Takings: Private Property and the Power of Eminent Domain* (Cambridge: Harvard University Press, 1985), pp. 3–18.

and that could be nothing but protection from such injuries from other men, which they desiring to avoid, nothing but force could prevent or remedy; all things but this being as well attainable by men living in neighborhood without the bounds of a commonwealth, they could propose to themselves no other thing but this in quitting their natural liberty, and putting themselves under the umpirage of a civil sovereign, who therefore had the force of all the members of the commonwealth put into his hands to make his decrees to this end be obeyed. (*Works,* 6:212)

Locke goes on to claim that since worshipping God cannot, in itself, injure another person, the government can have no right to intervene in matters of religion. The libertarian points out that one must show an actual injury to some person, not merely a possible good that might be obtained, to justify state force. This interpretation, however, fails to do justice to the range of options that Locke believed fell within the scope of "protection from such injuries." This included not only restraining individuals within the society from attacking one another, but also measures to keep the state safe from foreign invasion. Locke believed that a large population, a strong economy, wealthy inhabitants, and a strong military were all instrumental goals that served the end of promoting the preservation of the members of society,

> the pravity of Mankind . . . obliges Men to enter into Society with one another; that by mutual Assistance, and joint Force, they may secure unto each other their Properties in the things that contribute to the Comfort and Happiness of this Life; . . . But forasmuch as Men thus entring into Societies, . . . may nevertheless be deprived of them [goods], either by the Rapine and Fraud of their Fellow-Citizens, or by the hostile Violence of Forreigners; the remedy of this Evil consists in Arms, Riches, and Multitude of Citizens; the Remedy of the other in Laws. (*Letter,* 47–48)

The *active* pursuit of "arms, riches, and multitude of citizens" is a legitimate function of government. Locke was hardly an advocate of the libertarian state.

Locke was quite willing to allow governments to restrict individual economic freedom in the interest of these goals. Locke's curious notes on a proposed constitution for Atlantis (*Political Essays,* 252–259) contain numerous restrictions on freedom of bequest and inheritance in the interest of encouraging population growth. This is consistent with his position in the *Two Treatises* where he notes that the father exercises his freedom of bequest "according to the Law and Custom of each Country" (2.72). More notoriously, Locke's scheme for the poor required an active government effort to insure both "opportunities" for labor and minimal compensation for those who might be inclined to idleness. The most important text against the libertarian position is the claim in the *First Treatise* that those in dire need have a claim on the property of the rich, though the rich may of course require labor in return. This is not an incidental remark but part of Locke's theory of natural law.[4] The question whether force is a necessary means is equivalent to the question whether there is an alternate means that would be as effective in promoting the preservation of the community. Locke believed that one must show "injury" to justify state action, but he defined injury more broadly than libertarians do. Anything detrimental to the preservation of the community can be considered an injury to that community.

Locke not only approved of regulation of property, he also claimed that the state could actively support the development of virtue. John Marshall has noted that Locke seemed much more willing to support state enforcement of morals in the later letters on toleration than in his earlier writings.[5] There is at least a tension between saying, on the one hand, that it does me no injury if my neighbor squanders his wealth and acknowledging, on the other, that your neighbor's wealth might be needed to defend the community from an attack. If squandering wealth is not injury in this more indirect sense, then many of the proposals Locke actually advocated would run afoul of his general principle. Given how often Locke advocates policies that do require construing injury more broadly and the prevalence of explicit endorsements of morals legislation, the best explanation is that the claims in the *Letter* are primarily about motives for policies, not policies themselves. If the government is to keep a man from squandering his wealth, its motive must be the general security of the nation and not the individual man's own well-being. Marshall is likely right that Locke also became increasingly convinced as he got older that the law was needed to insure sufficient virtue for the preservation of the community.[6]

All of this, however, could open up an objection from the opposite direction. Perhaps the description of the public good given here is too

---

[4] *Treatises*, 1. 42. This passage also provides a decisive objections against the interpretation in C.B. Macpherson, *The Political Theory of Possessive Individualism: Hobbes to Locke* (Oxford: Clarendon Press, 1962). The most important objection to Macpherson is James Tully, *A Discourse on Property, John Locke and His Adversaries* (Cambridge: Cambridge University Press, 1980). See especially pp. 131–132, where Tully discusses the relevant passage from the *First Treatise*. A more persuasive version of Tully's main argument is found in Gopal Sreenivasan, *The Limits of Lockean Rights in Property* (Oxford: Oxford University Press, 1995).

[5] John Marshall, *John Locke*, pp. 376–383.

[6] Ibid., pp. 378–379, 381–383.

narrow to really have been Locke's. Natural law leaves a large number of acts indifferent, and surely the power of government extends to indifferent acts. To collapse the content of "public good" into the ends of natural law, so the objection goes, is to remove this sphere of indifferent actions from the control of the government, surely a misinterpretation of his theory. The confusion here stems from the fact that when Locke talks about actions that are "indifferent," he is referring to acts that are not absolutely required by natural law. Natural law always requires us to refrain from murder, theft, and assault, but it also contains imperfect obligations, like the duty to preserve others. The former class of actions is never indifferent, while the latter is indifferent in a qualified sense. We are not at liberty as to whether we will pursue the end—the end is given—but we do have some flexibility in deciding which actions to perform in order to fulfill that duty. This is exactly the case in terms of the most common use of "indifferent actions" in Locke's thought, religious worship. To say that religious worship is in large measure indifferent does not imply at all that we are free with respect to the ends of religious worship. In the *Essays on the Law of Nature* (*Political Essays*, 123), Locke claimed the obligation to worship God was binding on all persons through natural law, not just obligatory for adherents to a revealed religion. He believed that through reason alone we should be able to discover that we owe gratitude to a supreme being. There are, however, many things that both reason and revelation do not specify regarding the *manner* in which worship is conducted. Shall we stand or sit while we pray? That is indifferent; whether we shall pray is not. Questions like these are the focal cases of indifferent actions.

Locke did not want to say that the public good extended to all indifferent action, since clearly the power of the state does not include regulation of the time, place, and manner of religious ceremonies in order to make those ceremonies more pleasing to God (much less all "innocent delights," that is, actions that are neither commanded nor condemned by any valid moral principle). It is perfectly compatible with Locke's position that many actions of government concern "indifferent matters" to say that the ends of that government are set by a moral principle. The ends of both religious worship and political rule are set by moral principles, yet both admit a significant sphere of indifferent actions. The state can fulfill its function and still leave quite a lot of room for citizens both in their deliberation as citizens and in their private lives.

It is well known that much of the discussion of the *Two Treatises* is framed in terms of "societies." Locke compares familial, conjugal, economic, and political societies in the *Two Treatises*. In his writings on toleration, he was forced to ask more sharply how one determines the proper ends of a given society. Locke's most explicit account of this takes place in the *Third Letter*. There he notes that the power of any society can be taken in two senses. In one sense it is simply the "natural force of all the members of any society" (*Works*, 6:217). That is, it is whatever the members of that society could accomplish by acting together. In another sense, the power of a society consists in "the authority and direction given to those that have the management of the force or natural power of the society, how and to what ends to use it, by which commission the ends of societies are known and distinguished" (6:217–218). In the first sense the powers of societies differ only in magnitude, not end. When we ask what is legitimate for a society, rather than what is possible, it is the second sense that is relevant. It is part of the very definition of a society that it exists for the sake of some specifiable end. Proast would have the end of civil society be the production of all of the good that force can procure. Locke replied that this would be to use the first, rather than the second, understanding of the power of societies; if one continued that logic, one would come to the conclusion that all societies exist for all of the good that they can produce. The state, the family, and the East India Company, to use Locke's example, become interchangeable.[7]

Both conjugal and political societies are power conferring. In each society, individuals take on new obligations in common pursuit of some end. In conjugal society, parents obtain authority over their children, but they also have an obligation to provide for the education and mainte-nance of their children. The partners will have new obligations to each other and to the child which restrict their previous freedom. In political society, individuals likewise take on an obligation to obey the laws of the society that direct their combined efforts in the pursuit of their comfort-able preservation. Consent plays an important role in the formation of both societies. It is by consent that individuals enter into conjugal union and by consent that they enter into political society. Locke does not, how-ever, treat the basic ends of either society as completely open ended. Con-sent does, however, specify many of the details of how that society will work. In the case of conjugal society, men and women may specify be-forehand the possible terms of divorce, the disposition of children, and

---

[7] Consider, for example, the utilitarian position that says that all persons and socie-ties should maximize the good. In this sense all societies can be said to have the same end, and differentiation occurs only because it so happens that families are better at raising chil-dren and states are better at punishing criminals. If a society saw an opportunity to produce happiness by acting outside its normal sphere, there would be no objection in principle.

perhaps the distribution of roles and duties within the marriage.[8] They may enter into a permanent relationship, or they may agree to separate once the children are grown.

There are two important themes to notice in Locke's discussion. The first is that although individuals are not required to procreate by natural law, if they do then they are required by natural law to enter into a society of a particular sort. The purpose of that society is mutual support in the raising of children. The duty of parents to provide for the preservation of their children flows quite easily for Locke from the fundamental law of nature, for God declares through that law his desire for the preservation of the species. Indeed, it is presented as a natural law in the strong sense that it applies to animals as well as persons (2.79). Thus the ends of the society are in large part determined by natural law. Second, Locke made it clear that any power the husband might acquire over his wife existed only insofar as it was necessary to the purpose of the marriage itself. He gained no additional power over her life, liberty, or her property.

The ends of conjugal society are not set by whatever goals the persons entering into that society happen to choose.[9] Rather, from the decision to procreate they follow deductively from the content of natural law. Conjugal society is defined in terms of a characteristic action, procreation, and its ends follow from a reflection on the relationship between that action and natural law. A similar story can be told in the case of political society. The characteristic action of government is punishment, the use of force. The ends of that society flow from reflection on the relationship between that means and the ends of natural law. Consent is the means by which we enter into civil society, but the ends of that society are not subject to our preferences.

Finally, someone might object that it distorts Locke's thought to sharply distinguish contractual consent from legislative consent and the problem of political obligation from the problem of determining the legitimate ends of state government. It is true that I draw distinctions that Locke did not draw, but I think that given proper context the distinctions help to clarify his thought. There are two main reasons Locke did not need to draw the distinctions himself. The first is that he believed contractual

[8] See especially *Treatises*, 2.77–83. The state may pass laws regulating marriage, divorce, and child custody that restrict the freedom of the married couple. Locke also believed that revelation placed additional restrictions on legitimate family arrangements for Christians.

[9] Locke's point is not that procreation is the only reason for sexual union, though he thinks it the main one. Locke's point is that the rights and responsibilities peculiar to conjugal society arise only from relationships that have procreation as the goal.

consent *was* the solution to the problem of political obligation. The second is that he believed there would be substantial agreement about the core of natural law, and in particular about the fundamental law of nature. Although Locke talks about the legislature as the place where persons will "draw closer" the law of nature, he certainly gives the impression that they will not be starting from scratch. I have argued elsewhere that Locke distinguished between a core of natural law that he thought would be apparent to all rational beings to whom it was proposed and a periphery that would only be known by those with the time and talent to inquire properly.[10] If one assumes that persons form political societies by voluntary agreement and that there is already substantial agreement about the fundamental law of nature that defines the scope of the public good, then legislative and contractual consent will overlap quite substantially. It will only be natural that people think of the ends of government as specified by the fundamental law of nature that they all recognized when they contracted to form a political society.

It is only if one is less convinced than Locke was that the obligation to obey a government comes from an act of conscious consent, less convinced that there will be significant agreement about the fundamental law of nature, that it becomes crucial to draw these distinctions. The distinctions in a sense disaggregate two different moments in the act of consent. Locke combines agreement to common political society and approval of the fundamental law of nature as specifying the ends of government into a single act. My analysis separates these two moments to draw attention to the complex relations between them. These distinctions help us to see new ways in which Locke's thought is applicable to contemporary theory. But they also bring out an important element in Locke's thought insofar as they help us to see the sense in which the ends of government are set by consent and determined by the fundamental law of nature. It is not enough to say that we cannot contract to do something contrary to natural law; Locke claimed that the state can only act in pursuit of the goals of natural law. In those cases where the interpretation of natural law is in dispute (whether this is the exception or the rule), Lockean consent is better understood as an act of legislative approval than contractual negotiation and agreement.

[10] Tuckness, "The Coherence of a Mind," pp. 78–82.

BIBLIOGRAPHY

Applbaum, Arthur. *Ethics for Adversaries: The Morality of Roles in Public and Professional Life*. Princeton: Princeton University Press, 1999.

Aquinas, Thomas. *Summa Theologica*. In *The Basic Writings of Thomas Aquinas*. Edited by Anton C. Pegis. 2 vols. New York: Random House, 1945.

Arendt, Hannah. *On Revolution*. New York: Penguin, 1963.

Ashcraft, Richard. *Locke's Two Treatises of Government*. London: Allen and Unwin, 1987.

————. *Revolutionary Politics and Locke's Two Treatises of Government*. Princeton: Princeton University Press, 1986.

Augustine, St. Bishop of Hippo. *City of God*. Translated by Henry Bettenson and edited by John O'Meara. New York: Penguin Books, 1984.

Baldwin, Thomas. "Toleration and the Right to Freedom." In *Aspects of Toleration: Philosophical Studies*. Edited by John Horton and Susan Mendus. London: Methuen, 1985.

Barry, Brian. *Justice as Impartiality*. Volume 2 of *A Treatise on Social Justice*. Oxford: Clarendon Press, 1995.

————. *Political Argument*. Berkeley and Los Angeles: University of California Press, 1990.

Bentham, Jeremy. *An Introduction to the Principles of Morals and Legislation*. Edited by J. H. Burns and H.L.A. Hart. London: Althone Press, 1970.

Berman, David. *A History of Atheism in Britain: From Hobbes to Russell*. London: Croom Helm, 1988.

Bork, Robert H. *The Tempting of America: The Political Seduction of the Law*. New York: Free Press, 1990.

Budziszewski, J. *True Tolerance: Liberalism and the Necessity of Judgment*. New Brunswick: Transaction Publishers, 1992.

Chan, Joseph. "Legitimacy, Unanimity, and Perfectionism." *Philosophy and Public Affairs* 29 (Winter 2000): 5–43.

Chen, Selina. "Liberal Toleration in the Thought of John Locke and John Rawls." Ph.D. dissertation. Oxford University, 1996.

Cohen, Joshua. "Freedom of Expression." In *Toleration: An Elusive Virtue*. Edited by David Heyd. Princeton: Princeton University Press, 1996.

Colman, John. *John Locke's Moral Philosophy*. Edinburgh: Edinburgh University Press, 1983.

Cranston, Maurice. "John Locke and Toleration." In *On Toleration*. Edited by Susan Mendus and David Edwards. Oxford: Clarendon Press, 1987.

Damico, Alfonso J. "Reason's Reach: Liberal Tolerance and Political Discourse." *Poznan Studies in the Philosophy of the Sciences and the Humanities* 46 (1996): 25–44.

Dunn, John. "Freedom of Conscience." In *From Persecution to Toleration: The*

Glorious Revolution and Religion in England. Edited by Ole Peter Grell, Jonathan Israel, and Nicholas Tyacke. Oxford: Clarendon Press, 1991.

———. *The Political Thought of John Locke*. Cambridge: Cambridge University Press, 1969.

———. "What Is Living and What Is Dead in the Political Theory of John Locke?" In *Interpreting Political Responsibility*. Princeton: Princeton University Press, 1990.

Dworkin, Gerald. "Non-neutral Principles." *Journal of Philosophy* 71 (1974): 491–506.

Dworkin, Ronald. "The Arduous Virtue of Fidelity: Originalism, Scalia, Tribe, and Nerve." *Fordham Law Review* 65 (1997): 1249–1268.

———. *A Bill of Rights for Britain*. London: Chatto and Windus, 1990.

———. *Freedom's Law: The Moral Reading of the American Constitution*. Cambridge: Harvard University Press, 1996.

———. *Law's Empire*. Cambridge: Belknap Press of Harvard University, 1986.

———. "In Praise of Theory." *Arizona State Law Journal* 29 (1997): 353–376.

———. *Taking Rights Seriously*. Cambridge: Harvard University Press, 1978.

Ely, John Hart. *Democracy and Distrust: A Theory of Judicial Review*. Cambridge: Harvard University Press, 1980.

Epstein, Richard. *Takings: Private Property and the Power of Eminent Domain*. Cambridge: Harvard University Press, 1985.

Filmer, Robert. *Patriarcha and Other Writings*. Edited by Johann P. Sommerville. Cambridge: Cambridge University Press, 1991.

Finnis, John. *Natural Law and Natural Rights*. Oxford: Oxford University Press, 1980.

Fried, Charles. *Right and Wrong*. Cambridge: Harvard University Press, 1978.

Fuller, Lon L. *The Morality of Law*. 2d edition. New Haven: Yale University Press, 1964.

Gallie, W. B. "Essentially Contested Concepts." *Proceedings of the Aristotelian Society* 56 (1956): 167–198.

Gauss, Gerald F. *Justificatory Liberalism*. Oxford: Oxford University Press, 1996.

Galston, William A. "Civic Education and the Liberal State." In *Liberalism and the Moral Life*. Edited by Nancy Rosenblum. Cambridge: Harvard University Press, 1989.

———. *Liberal Purposes: Goods, Virtues, and Diversity in the Liberal State*. Cambridge: Cambridge University Press, 1991.

George, Robert P. *Making Men Moral: Civil Liberties and Public Morality*. Oxford: Clarendon Press, 1993.

———. "Natural Law and Positive Law." In *The Autonomy of Law: Essays on Legal Positivism*. Edited by Robert George. Oxford: Oxford University Press, 1996.

———. ed. *The Autonomy of Law: Essays on Legal Positivism*. Oxford: Clarendon Press, 1996.

———. ed. *Natural Law Theory: Contemporary Essays*. Oxford: Oxford University Press, 1992.

Goodin, Robert E. *Utilitarianism as a Public Philosophy*. Cambridge: Cambridge University Press, 1995.

Graham, Gordon. "Tolerance, Pluralism, and Relativism." In *Toleration: An Elusive Virtue*. Edited by David Heyd. Princeton: Princeton University Press, 1996.

Grant, Ruth W. *John Locke's Liberalism: A Study of Political Theory in Its Intellectual Setting*. Chicago: University of Chicago Press, 1987.

Gutmann, Amy, *Democratic Education*. Princeton: Princeton University Press, 1987.

———. "Undemocratic Education." In *Liberalism and the Moral Life*. Edited by Nancy Rosenblum. Cambridge: Harvard University Press, 1989.

Gutmann, Amy, and Dennis Thompson. *Democracy and Disagreement*. Cambridge: Belknap Press of Harvard University. 1996.

Halbertal, Moshe. "Autonomy, Toleration, and Group Rights." In *Toleration: An Elusive Virtue*. Edited by David Heyd. Princeton: Princeton University Press, 1996.

Hamilton, Alexander, James Madison, and John Jay. *The Federalist Papers*. Edited by Clinton Rossiter. New York: New American Library, 1961.

Hart, H.L.A. *The Concept of Law*. Oxford: Oxford University Press, 1961.

———. "Review of Fuller: *The Morality of Law*." *Harvard Law Review* 78 (1965): 1281–1296.

Harris, Ian. *The Mind of John Locke*. Cambridge: Cambridge University Press, 1994.

Hick, John. *A John Hick Reader*. Edited by Paul Badham. London: Macmillan Press, 1990.

Hill, Thomas E., Jr. *Autonomy and Self Respect*. Cambridge: Cambridge University Press, 1991.

———. *Dignity and Practical Reason in Kant's Moral Theory*. Ithaca: Cornell University Press, 1992.

Hobbes, Thomas. *Leviathan*. Edited by Richard Tuck. Cambridge: Cambridge University Press, 1991.

Hooker, Richard. *Of the Laws of Ecclesiastical Polity*. Edited by A. S. McGrade. Cambridge: Cambridge University Press, 1989.

Horton, John. "Three (Apparent) Paradoxes of Toleration." *Synthesis Philosophica* 9 (1994): 7–20.

———. "Toleration, Morality, and Harm." In *Aspects of Toleration: Philosophical Studies*. Edited by John Horton and Susan Mendus. London: Methuen, 1985.

Horton, John, and Susan Mendus, eds. *John Locke: A Letter Concerning Toleration in Focus*. New York: Routledge, 1991.

Kant, Immanuel. *Groundwork of the Metaphysics of Morals*. Translated by Mary Gregor. Cambridge: Cambridge University Press, 1997.

———. *The Metaphysics of Morals*. Translated by Mary Gregor. Cambridge: Cambridge University Press, 1996.

King, Martin Luther, Jr. "Letter from the Birmingham City Jail." In *American*

Political Thought. 2d ed. Edited by Kenneth M. Dolbeare. Chatham, NJ: Chatham House Publishers, 1989.

King, Preston. *Toleration.* London: George Allen and Unwin, 1976.

Kordig, Carl. R. "Concepts of Toleration." *Journal of Value Inquiry* 16 (1982): 59–66.

Locke, John. *Correspondence.* Edited by E. DeBeer. 8 vols. Oxford: Clarendon Press, 1976–1982.

———. "Critical Notes on Stillingfleet." Unpublished. See shelfmark MS Locke c.34 at the Bodleian Library, Oxford University.

———. *Epistola de Tolerantia: A Letter on Toleration.* Edited by Raymond Klibansky and J. W. Gough. Oxford: Clarendon Press, 1968.

———. *An Essay Concerning Human Understanding.* Edited by P. Nidditch. Oxford: Clarendon Press, 1975.

———. *Essays on the Law of Nature.* Translated by Wolfgang von Leyden. In *Political Essays.* Edited by Mark Goldie. Cambridge: Cambridge University Press, 1997.

———. *A Letter Concerning Toleration.* Edited by James Tully. Indianapolis: Hackett Publishing Company, 1983.

———. *A Paraphrase and Notes on the Epistles of St. Paul to the Galatians, 1 and 2 Corinthians, Romans, and Ephesians.* Edited by A. Wainwright. 2 vols. Oxford: Clarendon Press, 1987.

———. *Political Essays.* Edited by Mark Goldie. Cambridge: Cambridge University Press, 1997.

———. *Political Writings.* Edited by David Wootton. London: Penguin, 1993.

———. *The Reasonableness of Christianity as Delivered in the Scriptures.* Edited by George W. Ewing. Washington, D.C.: Regnery Gateway, 1965.

———. *Some Thoughts Concerning Education and on the Conduct of the Understanding.* Edited by Ruth Grant and Nathan Tarcov. Indianapolis: Hackett, 1996.

———. *Two Tracts on Government.* Edited by P. Abrams. Cambridge: Cambridge University Press, 1967.

———. *Two Treatises of Government.* Edited by P. Laslett. Cambridge: Cambridge University Press, 1988.

———. *Works.* 10 vols. London, 1823. Reprinted. Germany: Scientia Verlag Aalen, 1963.

McCabe, David. "Joseph Raz and the Contextual Argument for Liberal Perfectionism." *Ethics* 111 (April 2001): 493–552.

MacCormick, Neil. *Legal Reasoning and Legal Theory.* 2d ed. Oxford: Clarendon Press, 1994.

Macedo, Stephen. *Liberal Virtues: Citizenship, Virtue, and Community in Liberal Constitutionalism.* Oxford: Clarendon Press, 1990.

Macpherson, C. B. *The Political Theory of Possessive Individualism: Hobbes to Locke.* Oxford: Clarendon Press, 1962.

Marshall, John. *John Locke: Resistance, Religion, and Responsibility.* Cambridge: Cambridge University Press, 1994.

Mendus, Susan. "Locke: Toleration, Morality and Rationality." In *John Locke:*

A Letter Concerning Toleration in Focus. Edited by John Horton and Susan Mendus. New York: Routledge, 1991.

———. *Toleration and the Limits of Liberalism*. London: Macmillan Education, 1989.

———. ed. *Justifying Toleration: Conceptual and Historical Perspectives*. Cambridge: Cambridge University Press, 1988.

Mendus, Susan, and David Edwards, eds. *On Toleration*. Oxford: Clarendon Press, 1987.

Mill, John Stuart. *On Liberty*. Edited by Alburey Castell. Arlington Heights, IL: Harlan Davidson, 1947.

Montesquieu, Charles Louis de Secondat, Baron de. *The Spirit of the Laws*. Edited by Anne Cohler, Basia Miller, and Harold Stone. Cambridge: Cambridge University Press, 1989.

Moore, J. T. "Locke on Assent and Toleration." *The Journal of Religion* 58 (1978): 30–36.

Murphy, Andrew R. "The Uneasy Relationship between Social Contract Theory and Religious Toleration." *Journal of Politics* 59 (1997): 368–392.

Murphy, Jeffrie G. *Kant: The Philosophy of Right*. London: Macmillan, 1970.

Murphy, Walter J., James S. Fleming, and Sotirios A. Barber, eds. *American Constitutional Interpretation*. Westbury, NY: Foundation Press, 1995.

Nagel, Thomas. "Moral Conflict and Political Legitimacy." *Philosophy and Public Affairs* 16 (1987): 215–240.

Newey, Glen. *Virtue, Reason, and Toleration: The Place of Toleration in Ethical and Political Philosophy*. Edinburgh: Edinburgh University Press, 1999.

Nicholson, Peter P. "Toleration as a Moral Ideal." In *Aspects of Toleration: Philosophical Studies*. Edited by John Horton and Susan Mendus. London: Methuen, 1985.

Nozick, Robert. *Anarchy, State, and Utopia*. New York: Basic Books, 1974.

Parfit, Derek. *Reasons and Persons*. Reprint with corrections. Oxford: Oxford University Press, 1987.

Pasquino, Pasquale. "Locke on King's Prerogative." *Political Theory* 26 (1998): 198–208.

Pitkin, Hanna. "Obligation and Consent I." *American Political Science Review* 59 (1965): 991–999.

———. "Obligation and Consent II." *American Political Science Review* 60 (1966): 39–52.

Powell, H. Jefferson. "The Original Understanding of Original Intent." *Harvard Law Review* 98 (March 1985): 885–948.

Primorac, Igor. "On Tolerance in Morals." *Philosophical Studies* 31 (1986–1987): 69–83.

Proast, Jonas. *The Argument of the Letter concerning Toleration Briefly Consider'd and Answered*. Oxford, 1690.

———. *A Second Letter to the Author of the Three Letters for Toleration*. Oxford, 1704.

———. *A Third Letter Concerning Toleration*. Oxford, 1691.

Rawls, John. "The Idea of Public Reason Revisited." *University of Chicago Law Review* 64 (Summer 1997): 765–807.

———. *Political Liberalism*. Revised paperback edition. New York: Columbia University Press, 1995.

———. *A Theory of Justice*. Cambridge: Harvard University Press, 1971.

———. "Two Concepts of Rules." *Philosophical Review* 64 (1955): 3–32.

Raz, Joseph. "Autonomy, Toleration, and the Harm Principle." In *Justifying Toleration: Conceptual and Historical Perspectives*. Edited by Susan Mendus. Cambridge: Cambridge University Press, 1988.

———. "Facing Up: A Reply." In *Symposium: The Works Of Joseph Raz. Southern California Law Review* 62 (1989): 1153–1235.

———. *The Morality of Freedom*. Oxford: Clarendon Press, 1986.

Rogers, G.A.J. "Locke and the Sceptical Challenge." In *The Philosophical Canon in the 17th and 18th Centuries: Essays in Honour of John W. Yolton*. Edited by G.A.J. Rogers and Sylvana Tomaselli. Rochester: University of Rochester Press, 1996.

Rorty, Richard. *Objectivity, Relativism, and Truth*. Cambridge: Cambridge University Press, 1991.

Sandel, Michael J. "Book Review: Political Liberalism." *Harvard Law Review* 107 (1994): 1765–1794.

———. *Democracy's Discontent*. Cambridge: Belknap Press of Harvard University, 1996.

Scalia, Antonin. *A Matter of Interpretation*. Edited by Amy Gutmann. Princeton: Princeton University Press, 1997.

Scanlon, Thomas. "Contractualism and Utilitarianism." In *Utilitarianism and Beyond*. Edited by Amartya Sen and Bernard Williams. Cambridge: Cambridge University Press, 1982.

Schauer, Frederick. *Free Speech: A Philosophical Inquiry*. Cambridge: Cambridge University Press, 1982.

———. "Rules and the Rule of Law." *Harvard Journal of Law and Public Policy* 14 (1991): 647–651.

Schauer, Frederick, and R. Zechouser. "Cheap Tolerance." *Synthesis Philosophica* 9 (1994): 439–454.

Schochet, Gordon. "Toleration, Revolution, and Judgment." *Political Science* 40/1 (1988): 84–96.

Sher, George. *Beyond Neutrality: Perfectionism and Politics*. Cambridge: Cambridge University Press, 1997.

Simmons, A. John. *The Lockean Theory of Rights*. Princeton: Princeton University Press, 1992.

———. *On the Edge of Anarchy: Locke, Consent, and the Limits of Society*. Princeton: Princeton University Press, 1993.

Smith, Rogers M. *Liberalism and American Constitutional Law*. Cambridge: Harvard University Press, 1985.

Soper, Philip. "Some Natural Confusions about Natural Law." *Michigan Law Review* 90 (1992): 2393–2423.

Sreenivasan, Gopal. *The Limits of Lockean Rights in Property*. Oxford: Oxford University Press, 1995.

Storing, Herbert J., ed. *The Anti-Federalist: Writings of Opponents of the Constitution*. Chicago: University of Chicago Press, 1985.

Sunstein, Cass R. *Democracy and the Problem of Free Speech*. New York: The Free Press, 1993.

———. *Legal Reasoning and Political Conflict*. Oxford: Oxford University Press, 1996.

———. *The Partial Constitution*. Cambridge: Harvard University Press, 1993.

Tarcov, Nathan. *Locke's Education for Liberty*. Chicago: University of Chicago Press, 1984.

Thayer, James Bradley. "The Origin and Scope of the American Doctrine of Constitutional Law." *Harvard Law Review* 7 (1893): 129–156.

Tuck, Richard. "Scepticism, Toleration, and the Seventeenth Century." In *Justifying Toleration: Conceptual and Historical Perspectives*. Edited by Susan Mendus. Cambridge: Cambridge University Press, 1988.

Tuckness, Alex. "The Coherence of a Mind: John Locke and the Law of Nature." *Journal of the History of Philosophy* 37 (January 1999): 73–90.

———. "Legislation and Non-neutral Principles: A Lockean Approach." *Journal of Political Philosophy* 8 (September 2000): 363–378.

———. "Rethinking the Intolerant Locke." *American Journal of Political Science* 46 (April 2002): 288–298.

Tully, James. *An Approach to Political Philosophy: Locke in Contexts*. Cambridge: Cambridge University Press, 1993.

———. *A Discourse on Property, John Locke and His Adversaries*. Cambridge: Cambridge University Press, 1980.

Vernon, Richard. *The Career of Toleration: John Locke, Jonas Proast, and After*. Montreal and Kingston: McGill-Queen's University Press, 1997.

Waldron, Jeremy. *The Dignity of Legislation*. Cambridge: Cambridge University Press, 1999.

———. "Judicial Review and the Conditions of Democracy." In *Journal of Political Philosophy* 6 (1998): 335–355.

———. *Law and Disagreement*. Oxford: Clarendon Press, 1999.

———. "Locke, Toleration, and the Rationality of Persecution." In *Liberal Rights: Collected Papers 1981–1991*. Cambridge: Cambridge University Press, 1993.

———. "A Right-Based Critique of Constitutional Rights." In *Oxford Journal of Legal Studies* 13 (1993): 18–51.

———. "Autonomy and Perfectionism in Raz's Morality of Freedom." In "Symposium: The Works of Joseph Raz." *Southern California Law Review* 62 (1989): 1097–1152.

Walker, William. "Force, Metaphor, and Persuasion in Locke's *A Letter Concerning Toleration*." In *Difference and Dissent: Theories of Toleration in Medieval and Early Modern Europe*. Edited by Cary J. Nederman and John C. Laursen. Lanham, MD: Rowman & Littlefield, 1996.

Wall, Steven. *Liberalism, Perfectionism, and Restraint*. Cambridge: Cambridge University Press, 1998.

Walzer, Michael. *Interpretation and Social Criticism*. Cambridge: Harvard University Press, 1987.

Walzer, Michael. *On Toleration*. New Haven: Yale University Press, 1997.
———. *Spheres of Justice*. New York: Basic Books, 1983.
Warnock, Mary. "The Limits of Toleration." In *On Toleration*. Edited by Susan Mendus and David Edwards. Oxford: Clarendon Press, 1987.
Wechsler, Herbert. "Toward Neutral Principles of Constitutional Law." *Harvard Law Review* 73 (1959): 1–35.
Williams, Bernard. *Problems of the Self*. Cambridge: Cambridge University Press, 1973.
———. "Toleration: An Impossible Virtue?" In *Toleration: An Elusive Virtue*. Edited by David Heyd. Princeton: Princeton University Press, 1996.
Windstrup, George. "Freedom and Authority: The Ancient Faith of Locke's Letter on Toleration." *Review of Politics* 44 (1982): 242–265.
Wolterstorff, Nicholas. *John Locke and the Ethics of Belief*. Cambridge: Cambridge University Press, 1996.

COURT CASES CITED

City of Boerne v. Flores, 521 U.S. 507 (1997).
Cooper v. Aaron, 358 U.S. 1 (1958).
Hans v. State of Louisiana, 134 U.S. 1 (1890).
Katzenbach v. Morgan 384 U.S. 641 (1966).
Lassiter v. Northampton 360 U.S. 45 (1959).
Marbury v. Madison, 5 U.S. 137 (1803).
New York Times v. Sullivan, 376 U.S. 254 (1964).
R.A.V. v. St. Paul, 505 U.S. 377 (1992).
Rosenberger v. University of Virginia, 515 U.S. 819 (1995).
Sherbert v. Vernor, 374 U.S. 398 (1963).
Wisconsin v. Yoder 406 U.S. 205 (1972).

INDEX

abortion, debates over, 17
act-utilitarianism, 2n.2, 3, 175; and view of violence, 22
agency. *See* moral agency
agreement, 1
American Founding, 151–154
anarchy, 125
Anti-Federalists, 151. *See also* Brutus
Applbaum, Arthur, 118, 125
Aquinas, Thomas, 85
Aristotle, 106
Augustine, 85
autonomy. *See* liberty

Baldwin, Thomas, 105n.40
Barry, Brian, 87
Bentham, Jeremy, 3
Bork, Robert, 159, 160–161
"bracketing," 17, 102, 118
Brennan, Justice, 171
Brown v. Board of Education, 156
Brutus, 151, 153
Buber, Martin, 85
Budziszewski, J., 18n.6

Career of Toleration (Vernon), 6n.8
censorship, 37–38
Chan, Joseph, 111–113
Charles II, 143
City of Boerne v. Flores, 144, 167–172
civil disobedience, 10, 54–56, 85
Civil War, as constitutional crisis, 137
Clinton, Bill, 144
coercion, 22–23, 53, 60, 67, 141–142
collective consequentialism, 54n.30
common standpoint theories, 86, 87, 88, 103. *See also* utilitarianism
communitarianism, 1
consent, 10, 62–63; constraints on, 76n.24; contractual, 62–63, 66–74, 75–76, 89; hypothetical, 89; legislative, 62–63, 74–84, 89
consequences, actual and hypothetical, 44–45
consequentialism, 125–126

constitutions: adoption of, 136, 141; interpretation of, 138, 139, 144–147; written, 140–141. *See also* U.S. Constitution; Dworkin, Ronald; originalism
contested jurisdiction, and the "framer's point of view," 140–143, 146
contested principles, 35, 78, 174; continuum of more and less, 45n.20; and the legislative point of view, 25–31; and Locke, 39–46; and major/minor premises, 26, 27–30, 33; and Proast, 39–46; and rule-utilitarianism, 36–39
contested roles, and the state of nature, 172–173
convergence theories, 86, 87, 88. *See also* Hobbes, Thomas
Cooper v. Aaron, 144
creationists, 82–83
Critical Notes on Stillingfleet (Locke and Tyrrell), 123; on form of church government, 133

Dignity of Legislation, The (Waldron), 78n.25
disagreement, 1, 25n.22, 49–50
Discourse on Property, John Locke and His Adversaries, A (Tully), 184n.4
Douglas, Stephen, 17
Dred Scott, 144
Dunn, John, 132n.24
Dworkin, Gerald, 34, 36–38, 37n.3, 42n.14, 45n.19
Dworkin, Ronald, 23, 24n.20, 158n.32; and the legislative point of view, 147–150; objection to, 150–159

Ely, John Hart, 165
Employment Division, Oregon Dept. of Human Resources v. Smith (1990), 167–168
England: and constitutional jurisdiction, 140, 143; legislative power in, 133; and the European Union, 140
Epistola de Tolerantia (Locke), Popple translation of, 5n.5